Provocation in Popular Culture

What role can provocation play in the process of renewal, both for individuals and for societies? *Provocation in Popular Culture* is an investigation into the practice of specific provocative performers and the wider nature of cultural provocation, examining the work of provocateurs such as:

- Banksy
- Sacha Baron Cohen
- Leo Bassi
- Pussy Riot
- Philippe Petit
- Archaos.

Drawing on Bim Mason's own twenty-five year career as performer, teacher and creative director, this book explores the power negotiations involved in the relationship between a provocateur and those who are provoked, and the implications of maintaining a position on an edge. Using neuroscience as a bridge, it proposes a similarity between complexity theories and cultural theories of play and risk. Three inter-related analogies for the 'edge' on which these performers operate – the fulcrum, the blade and the border – reveal the shifts between structure and fluidity and the ambivalent combinations of these that can occur in a single moment.

Bim Mason is the Artistic Director and co-founder of Circomedia. Since 1978 he has worked in street theatre, masks, *bouffon*, clown and circus as performer, designer, teacher and award-winning director. Published works include chapters on Lecoq, circus, popular theatre and *Street Theatre and Other Outdoor Performance* (Routledge, 1992).

D1292657

Provocation in Popular Culture

Bim Mason

Routledge
Taylor & Francis Group

LONDON AND NEW YORK

First published 2016
by Routledge
2 Park Square, Milton Park, Abingdon, Oxon OX14 4RN

and by Routledge
711 Third Avenue, New York, NY 10017

Routledge is an imprint of the Taylor & Francis Group, an informa business

British Library Cataloguing in Publication Data
A catalogue record for this book is available from the British Library

Library of Congress Cataloging in Publication Data
Mason, Bim, 1953–
Provocation in popular culture / Bim Mason.
pages cm
1. Performing arts--Social aspects. 2. Performing arts--Political aspects.
3. Theater and society. 4. Performing arts--Philosophy. I. Title.
PN1590.S6M37 2015
306.4'84--dc23
2015005221

ISBN: 978-1-138-85249-5 (hbk)
ISBN: 978-1-138-85250-1 (pbk)
ISBN: 978-1-315-72344-0 (ebk)

Typeset in Bembo
by Taylor & Francis Books

Printed and bound in Great Britain by
TJ International Ltd, Padstow, Cornwall

In memory of Robin Grant.

Dedicated to all the nameless individuals who have been prepared to suffer the consequences of challenging injustice and privilege on behalf of the communities they identify with.

Contents

List of illustrations

Figures

Plates

Table

Foreword: On meeting on an edge

Baz Kershaw

Two weeks. The first doing drama workshops for geriatric dementia patients in a psychiatric hospital. Followed by reminiscence theatre shows in local authority residential homes for the elderly infirm. This might not seem a likely source for especially high-spirited celebration. Yet that was how I first encountered the extreme degree of Bim Mason's talents in early 1980s Devonshire. We were in the upstairs room of a small bistro by the sea the night after Theatre Exchange – also known as Kaboodle Theatre – triumphantly completed the residency I'd organised as part of my first higher education teaching job. There were five artists from the company and three staff from drama at our small college, including me. A long table littered with the detritus of a cheap but nicely choice fusion meal, punctuated by too many wine bottle church spires and candlestick street lights like an old Mediterranean resort, as Flamenco music suddenly turned up loud and Bim was on top with his head just inches from the ceiling beams swirling and shashaying up and down its length with a teetering sweep of wildly eccentric dancing. Ridiculously risky, but every step, shimmy and shake was perfectly placed to leave the flickering-wick capital utterly intact even when he launched a twist jump that landed him back in his seat as the whole room roared with amazement.

Now, something of the ethos of such dangerously unaccountable shenanigans more or less haunts every page of this lively and challenging book. Its many examples of especially excessive but never entirely outlandish performance are truly astonishing. Yet in at least one respect they are not particularly unusual. Because how many of us have ever *not* felt deeply on edge, often even in situations that were hardly out of the ordinary? A rattle toy dropped in a subdued surgery, a plane shuddering heavily on take-off, a wrong-number ringer late at night. Fearfully quotidian crevasses of a routinely random world, paradoxical black holes opening in our everyday personal universes. This is the strange stuff at the exhilarating heart of *Provocation in Popular Culture*, the kind of fatal attraction we might most want to avoid on a planet of imminent global tipping points. Yet the book's many artist–provocateurs deliberately set out to make us all embrace such events as a wholesale Earthly bonus. Every day, in many ways, dancing between endgame death wish and total rebirth as if we humans really could create a hopeful tomorrow.

So this jauntily pitched tome serves up some profoundly affecting ambitions. For example, daring to prompt unfettered trains of reflection by tripping extra-lightly among a few heavy-duty ways of thinking about performance. Maybe a little like learning to waltz in a hall of rotating mirrors. Which also might well reflect what its apparently fearless artists seek to achieve for their audiences. But by plainly performing an extraordinary poise that should be absolutely impossible against the odds they are facing. Yet which pans out to be a piece of cake that everyone can share, an un-expectable treat because in turning the world on its head they show how some very wrong matters might be put to rights. Witness wizard–clown Leo Bassi in 2011 standing by a lake of oil dumped deep in the Spanish countryside with a coachload of spectators perched high on a retaining wall as he floats an election poster of the conservative political party Partido Popular, allegedly linked to this pollution scandal, face down in the black, black poison. The metaphor is an illegal act that puts the *Bassibus* tour party literally on a narrowing edge of multiple criminalities: a playfully surreal dip swirling with atmospheric threats. Observe TV/film star Sacha Baron Cohen as Borat bang centre of a 2006 Texas rodeo ring in full swing. Wearing an American-flag shirt, Stetson, denim and jingly boots, he has the crowd roaring approval at a pro-USA rap that turns to extreme militaristic ranting – kill off all Iraqi men, women and children! – then a cod Kazakhstan national anthem sung to the *Stars and Stripes* tune which claims 'all other countries are little girls'. The crowd bays for *his* blood and the MC warns against any return, yet it's a triple edged provo-gig that greatly boosts Baron Cohen's all round popularity. Peer for invisible graffiti-artist Banksy among the 2011 rioters attacking a downtown Bristol Tesco store for undermining the success of local shops. His out-in-the-open clandestine coups include a poster-print advertising Tesco-bottled petrol-bombs complete with paper wick already well and truly alight, and actually on sale to raise funding for local community arts groups as well as to set against legal costs for protest arrestees. The presence-in-absence of a renegade famous artist spawns edges sharpened by playful menace and a populist anarchism that fires up everyday rights for this street-wise quasi republic.

The all-too-real multiple performance edges of these provocateurs risk raising ambivalent stakes as they court unpredictable extremes in public. But as the centres of 'official' power always threaten to shut down or incorporate acute dissent, creative excess becomes *de rigueur* in making any workable bid for an actually popular democratic polis. So such ethically principled generosity *in practice* makes this book convincing *because* it shows how the extra-over-the-top practitioners can bring on gasps of disbelief *and* relief as they achieve much more complex yet accessible affects than what, apparently, they set out to produce. Achieved through an utterly thoroughgoing engagement with the trickiest niches of their chosen environments.

The same can be said of Bim Mason's radically catholic critical reach. Because, besides his main multi-arts trio, his book explores a stunning panoply of globally distributed provocative acts. From feminist protesting Pussy Riot to chainsaw circus Archaos through to fabulous funambulist Philippe Petit and some weirdly wonderful performers of the contemporary Neo-Burlesque. He also very modestly provides just a few select examples of his own sharply edgy inventions, including key creative training exercises and the uniquely amazing Big Heads. This unassuming tactic of displaying the richness of popular radical performance provocations internationally through a frame of personally initiated experimentation becomes a classic demonstration of less becoming more. Not surprising, perhaps, as the art of all bound-breaking edges must surely rely on especially high degrees of carefully honed discrimination.

I now realise these critical qualities also were fundamental to the personal backstories in the genesis and evolution of Bim Mason's unlikely practitioner–scholarly endeavour, which eventually led him to all the impressive stuff in *Provocation in Popular Culture*. They had, in fact, thoroughly imbued a chance meeting with Bim in the book department of stationery chain store W. H. Smith, when I held the Foundation Chair of Drama at Bristol University. The odd downmarket coincidence somehow prompted him to ask if I thought he'd be 'good enough' to write a PhD thesis. Obviously I said yes, and agreed to be his advisor. But what I didn't know, or simply couldn't recall, was that he had dropped out of the first year in drama at Bristol to join a rural commune in the borderlands of Wales. Given that, the whole idea of a doctoral project and its early history were chronically edgy. So it speaks volumes for the generosity of spirit, exemplary rigour and great good faith of my then colleagues that they interviewed him and offered a second chance at a greatly elevated rating. Also, of course, to Bim Mason's severally expanded manifest talents.

Now here we are at last, like teetering tightrope walkers unexpectedly meeting full on in the middle of a very thin wire: an Emeritus Professor lacking any A-levels and an artist Doctor without a first degree. Three decades and-a-half on, and still grinning at audacities. Who says that edges are defined by leading nowhere fast?

Baz Kershaw
Professor Emeritus of Performance
University of Warwick

Preface

This book is the outcome of a long process, lasting over ten years, in which time I completed a doctoral research on the subject. As well as drawing on thirty-five years of professional practical experience as performer, director and teacher, I used a combination of my ongoing creative and pedagogical research, field research and research into relevant theories. As for formative field research, I was fortunate enough, to interview leading international theatre directors as a rapporteur for the Circelation series of workshops in 2005, which were around the theme of risk. These workshops were run over a period of two weeks and were aimed at developing the practice of emerging circus and theatre practitioners in the UK. The directors included Rose English, John Wright, Liam Steele (Stan Won't Dance, DV8), Terry O'Connor (Forced Entertainment), Pascualito (Archaos), Deborah Batten (Legs on the Wall) and Steven Tiplady (Improbable Theatre, Indefinite Articles). Although useful to understand how those artists use risk in their own creative and performance practice I have chosen not to give special focus to their work because, however provocative it may be, with the exception of Archaos, it mostly occurs within the context of conventional theatre spaces. Interviews with Pascale Larderet (Cacahouete), Adrian Evans (UK producer for Archaos) and Leo Bassi have provided useful international perspectives and a depth of understanding derived purely from practice. As well as these, I have conducted formal interviews of colleagues with whom I have shared many rewarding provocations; these include members of the Natural Theatre Company, Desperate Men, Stickleback Plasticus, the Bigheads and Jonathon Kay. These artists work using walkabout performance and, although they could all easily recognise what might be meant by the concept of a play/risk 'edge', I have not foregrounded their work because their impact has been more localised and less involved with power negotiations.

Knowledge that has been acquired from practice is built up over a long time with different methods and strategies being trialled and reviewed over very many repetitions in different contexts. This leads to an awareness of most effective or efficient best practice, which can be identified through, for example, nuances of body language. These are most simply described in terms of impressions, but this may seem subjective. There are at least two outcomes of this practice-based process in relation to producing a book. Firstly, it is difficult to identify one single moment that seems adequately significant to draw more general conclusions from. Secondly, if detail of practice in many different contexts is the starting point of analysis, there is a necessity for a considerable amount of description, especially as the unusual nature of the events and the relative lack of other writing on the subject will make them unfamiliar to many readers. Therefore, in early versions of the writing I tended to include extensive description. At a later stage, I took the opposite approach by using single moments of practice as a springboard to speculate on their theoretical significance in a manner that was in danger of becoming detached from the practice. I hope that the current version balances these two approaches even though there are different emphases in each section.

Acknowledgements

My main thanks go to my PhD supervisor, Baz Kershaw, not only for his support during the decade of writing the thesis, but also for his continuing faith and professional advice over the previous two. I am especially grateful to those who have given their time for interviews, in particular Leo Bassi for his inspiration and generous time. Other interviewees include Adrian Evans, Pascal Larderet of Turbo Cacahouete, Ralph Oswick and Brian Popay of the Natural Theatre Company, Richard Headon and Jon Beedell of Desperate Men, PeeWee Murray and Emma Lloyd of Stickleback Plasticus, Jonathon Kay, Rose English, John Wright, Liam Steele, Debra Batton, Terry O'Connor, Pascualito, Steven Tiplady, David Micklem, Michel Dallaire, Gregoire Carel, Alex Hofgartner, Darryl Carrington and Bigheads performers: Charlotte Mooney, Alex Harvey, Tom Wainwright.

As well as the interviewees, I would like to thank John Marshall, Chenine Bhathena, Jan Winter, Seth Honnor, Simon Jones and Jeremy Shine for their advice. I'm very appreciative of the support of Circomedia staff and students, particularly those who provided written contributions: Maia Ayling, Mike Bell, Emily Redsell, Katie Alexander, Caroline Barner, Matt Mulligan.

Finally, I could not have succeeded in completing this long project without the generosity and active support of Bronwen and Gusto.

1 Background

This book is about cultural provocation, its purposes, its methods and its wider significance. Cultural provocation is the art of using cultural artefacts or events to stimulate processes of transformation in individuals, organisations or social groupings. Because of my background, I use performance as a means to approach this substantial area. Specifically I am choosing to focus on an area that combines a political agenda with populist entertainment, but which is neither political performance with aspects of popular entertainment, in the tradition of agit-prop, say, nor entertainment that simply aims to shock. I am interested in this area because it is more than a set of practices designed to have a transformative effect in specific contexts; it also provides a perspective on wider questions of cultural and social transformation. I approach the subject through an exploration of the relationship between play and risk, and their role in transformative processes. This relationship can be examined through the work of a selection of artists who work with high levels of risk and extreme forms of play. Play is a key topic not only because all art can be considered as forms of play, but also because it offers a useful perspective to consider aesthetic structure, mood, reception and function. Risk is included because it is a major component of some forms of play and provides insight into the experience of provocation. As well as being a study of provocative practice the book also draws on chaos/complexity theories to examine how they might offer comparators to wider processes within social/cultural groupings. I aim to indicate the potential of provocation to help maintain the cultural health of a society. That is to say, to engender a facility in individuals and organisations to communicate easily, and adapt imaginatively, to shifts in the internal or external environment. In a fractured post-modernist world of multiple ideologies, in which values are relative, it is not always clear how artists can apply morality within a progressive agenda. In part, the subject provides a model for artistic practice that addresses this question.

The book is an amplification and development of the brief descriptions of provocative street performance that I wrote in the early 1990s.[1] It has become part of a longer process of developing a deeper understanding of the bouffon style that I was introduced to at the Ecole Jacques Lecoq. Because Lecoq's method of discovering knowledge was through practice, there was very little theoretical or historical explanation provided of the roots of this style and so

I remained curious about how it could be applied. This interest was developed through exploring Mummer's plays with my circus-theatre company Mummer & Dada (1985–91), jesters and clowns in a wide variety of solo work (1978–1994) and Mediaeval carnival practices with my indoor and outdoor theatre companies, The Joy Society and The Bigheads (1999–2007). My teaching work at Fool Time and Circomedia (1986–present) has also provided hundreds of opportunities to experiment with different approaches to group dynamics and practices in the style of Grotesque. In addition, my involvement with artform development and cultural strategy, both locally and nationally, has provided insight into the development of cultural groupings on a wider scale. The different roles in my work: as performer, as director, as writer, as teacher and as strategist, have provided me with a useful variety of perspectives. This is further helped by the distance in time from some of the events that I have been involved with. However, I have chosen to focus most of this book on other practitioners rather than my own work, not only because it enables greater objectivity, but also because the distance from my practice to another facilitates a greater understanding of the relative positions of the practitioners to each other.

Context

The work that I cover emerged in a very specific historical and geographical context: the fifteen years of relative economic prosperity that led up to the financial crisis of 2007–8. In this context the three key artists I discuss all reacted to the hedonistic consumerism and seemingly impervious self-confidence of Western democratic capitalism. All three cite the apathy, passivity or complacency of the general population as a motivation for their provocative work. In this context, provocative acts can be seen as a necessary wake-up call to bring the public into a receptive state before it can be activated to question underlying assumptions. However, they do not follow up the initial actions with any kind of systematic programme. All the artists I discuss are European; the Eurocentric emphasis may seem counter-intuitive in the search for principles of provocation that might be more widely relevant, but the liberal, plural democracies of the West may be more useful in the examination than more conservative or monolithic states. As I discuss in relation to Pussy Riot, in more oppressive conditions, where the opposition(s) are united by resistance to the state, cultural provocation may take on a more distinctly political dimension with a narrower focus. Although censorship and other forms of oppression often engender an intense creative ingenuity in terms of strategies of opposition, it is more fruitful to examine cultural provocation in conditions in which the dominant cultural and political norms are expressed less overtly. In these conditions, censorship is applied more subtly through a gradual paring down of the authentic voice by means of commercial pressures as well as through normative inclinations, such as marginalisation. In liberal democracies, the subtleties of control and the complexity of cultural forces mean that targets for provocation tend to be less obvious and more diverse than in repressive states. The more sophisticated the means of dealing with provocation, the more sophisticated the strategies of the provocateurs need to be. It is to deal with this level of sophistication that I focus on the contemporary rather than the historical. Finally, it must be acknowledged that I devote more space to provocative artists who are male. The reason that there is a predominance of men working in this area will be discussed within this chapter but for the moment it may be sufficient to say that, in the present time, acts of bravado and games of power, inherent in provocateur work, are more commonly associated with men than with women.

There are three other related and relevant areas of practice that, for the sake of focus, I have chosen not to include within the scope of this book. These are direct (political) action, 'avant garde' performance, and some aspects of popular entertainment. These distinctions are only a matter of degree because all the artists to be discussed could be associated, to a certain extent, with at least two of these areas. Firstly, the kind of cultural provocation to be discussed is not direct action because generally it does not seek specific objectives. The artists themselves may well have very defined moral/ethical positions but they are suspicious of any self-righteousness and uncomfortable at assuming a position of superior knowledge. They certainly oppose the imposition of top-down orthodoxy, preferring to stimulate debate rather than offering answers. In this sense they are post-modernist relativists rather than the kind of progressive radicals featured in Jan Cohen-Cruz's *Radical Street Performance* (1998),[2] for example. Although engaged in various forms of power play, they avoid alignment and thus incorporation into formal political organisations. Therefore, even though some of Leo Bassi's work verges on protest, it has a greater emphasis on entertainment as compared with the persuasions of Michael Moore,[3] the activism of Larry Bogad[4] and the stunts of The Yes Men.[5] Other comparable figures in this area are Beppe Grillo,[6] Augusto Boal,[7] the Clandestine Insurgent Clown Rebel Army[8] and the playful activists of UK Uncut.[9] Similarly, although I have included a section on Pussy Riot, I have not given a major focus to their work because their use of aggressive punk rock music is an explicit rejection of Russian popular culture, rather than being used as means of infiltrating it.

Secondly, this area of work is distinct from Live Art, contemporary theatre and contemporary visual art, because it prioritises popular appeal. Breadth of cultural impact is its primary concern rather than expression of personal interests or a specialist exploration of new forms. That said, there are certain Neo-Burlesque/Boylesque artists that operate in an artistic zone in between Live Art and populist 'glamour' shows. I will discuss these because, although they do not challenge institutions, they certainly challenge audiences within popular culture. Thirdly, this area of practice is not a simple form of mass entertainment; it does not easily fit the description of a cultural commodity.[10] Although broadly populist, provocateurs deny the right of widely popular norms to proscribe their activities. That said, the work is designed to be entertaining, to have broad appeal, and the recent history of this area is one of constant negotiation over the limits of what the dominant powers consider acceptable at any one time. Examples of this negotiation are the debates over political correctness in stand-up comedy, the dilution of provocation to the level of cheekiness or 'pranks' (comic innuendo, the hoaxes and pranks of *Jackass*) and the culture industry's oscillations between incorporating or marginalising work that it finds difficult (e.g. attitudes to Banksy's work). There are many other artists and entertainers who touch on this area of practice, including many stand-up comedians such as Joan Rivers, Bill Hicks, Stewart Lee, Jo Brand, Mark Thomas and Tony Allen. In film and TV there is Chris Morris, *Spitting Image* and Trey Parker (*Team America* and *South Park*). In modern street theatre there is Philippe Petit, Turbo Cacahouete, Men in Black, Desperate Men, Chris Lynham and the early work of Natural Theatre. Within feminist alternative theatre there is a tradition of provocation with companies such as Split Britches, Cunning Stunts and the Guerrilla Girls. In modern circus there is Pierre Bidon's Archaos and the early Pickle Family Circus.

This chapter is in two parts. The first provides the background in terms of practical experience and leads into the physiological consequences of those experiences. The second part provides the background in terms of ideas, terms and the conceptual model I have arrived at.

The background of practice

Solo street shows

I will begin by returning to the subject of my previous book on street theatre, using a simple model to approach highly complex relationships and looking back at the experience of performing solo street shows from a more distant perspective. These powerful experiences raised many questions for me and provided a model which has formed my thinking as I examined a wider range of practices and processes. The purpose of this revisit is to flag up some of the key concepts to be used in the body of the book and indicate where they came from. Street performers are useful as an approach to provocation because they start from a marginal position. They work outside the established conventions associated with physical centres of culture and they work outside the conventions of a capitalist economy: setting their own work hours but, more significantly, by taking the risk to receive payment after the product has been delivered. Because of this outsider position they may be able to perceive centres of power more critically.

When working with different materials, visual artists often have to 'discover' and perfect different methods of handling. The myriad number of possibilities of different products and combinations, together with factors like temperature, humidity, time and light means that they must develop a facility to observe well, adapt and develop techniques rather than relying on established formulas. Human beings are far more complex, individual and unpredictable than artists' materials, so it is not possible to predict how they will react to different combinations of other individuals, mood and context. So, rather than describing precise exercises or methods of provocation, I have endeavoured to convey attitudes and principles of practice when describing provocation in this book.

Although descriptions of performance training exercises may be interesting, they may be unhelpful in fostering an attitude of discovery and responsiveness to the chemistry in the people involved. The joy of the early years of modern street theatre was that styles, forms and techniques were being discovered in many variations through practice. As they became classified in order to simplify explanation to those entering the practice, they became standardised; expectations and criteria were created where none had existed before. This shift was partly the result of documentation, such as my book on the subject,[11] and partly because it became a commercial industry. Selling work to promoters requires creating exciting expectations that must be fulfilled, usually by repeating key features or referring to existing models. A prime characteristic of most of the artists described in this book is that they have *discovered* their practice through repeated practical experimentation rather than through attempting to fulfil expectations and criteria set by predecessors.

The street (by which I mean any urban space that has a concentration of pedestrians) is an important space for artists of many sorts because it is a contested space. Theoretically it is a public space but in practice it is controlled by local authorities, and often dominated by advertising images. Despite this, it allows artists access to a random mix of the general public (which obviously varies according to time, place, weather, etc.) and enables them to gauge responses to their work quickly and efficiently. Of course, some performance, such as musical 'busking' may be so common and predictable that it is hardly noticed. Other performance may make a bolder, less predictable statement, imposing itself on the public space in order to draw attention and potentially generate more income. As such, there is an element of risk and if the endeavour has some success, the quality of performance will improve in the long term as well as the short term. So street shows (or to be more precise 'circle shows') are extremely useful as formative experiences because the performer is on an ever-present edge between acceptance and rejection, rising and descending, between popular appeal and challenge.

This kind of street performer begins as an outsider to the situation and is thus vulnerable. They differentiate themselves as outsiders through costume in order to draw attention to themselves. I used to wear workers' overalls over a foolish superman/fairground costume in order to minimise the amount of changing that needed to be done. It seems risky enough to make this transformation in public but it is even harder if it involves removing trousers, out of character, in a lunchtime shopping street. However, once the costume and character have been assumed, the dangers of misinterpretation have been surmounted and the performer enters a second stage of vulnerability. By declaring themselves so visibly as a performer it would be humiliating to fail to attract any interest. I have described elsewhere the various tactics used to attract an audience,[12] but, if the context is unsuitable, none of these may work. The key to all of these tactics is establishing relationships with passing individuals, and then between those individuals, so that a network of relationships builds into a community, perhaps by means of sharing observations of others not in the community. By nurturing a sense of 'us and them' the performer begins to function as a host, the centre of an emerging entity that may grow to include hundreds of spectators. The border between 'us' and 'them' is one of the kinds of edge that I will refer to in this book.

What assists the rapid learning of a street performer (and why it is such a useful learning tool for all types of performer) is the visibility of feedback. A stand-up comedian has the advantage of immediate vocal response but, in their normal context, they cannot see facial expressions or other body language. Away from a designated performance space, street spectators are not seated (initially) so attitudes of interest/disinterest can instantly be read and performance qualities adjusted accordingly. The number of spectators who are attracted is one kind of feedback. The other kind is through the amount of money collected at the end of the show. Even though they allow for variables within the context, the performer cannot escape some equation between the 'size of the hat' (money received) and their 'worth', especially because there is no fixed size of audience and no fixed amount. The public freely 'gives' back some equivalence to what they feel they have received. I will refer to the significance of this feedback loop below, but it aids the performer in striking a balance between sticking to the routine (structure) and improvising (fluidity). This is another kind of edge. In this type of performance there will be an established sequence of actions (and probably words) in order to maximise potential earnings or applause. However, experienced performers keep the structure simple and loose because the pleasure for all concerned is in the unique, unrepeatable occurrences. Opportunities for unpredictability, such as the use of volunteers are built into the sequence. Through these opportunities street performers try to achieve a 'lift off' from the established material. Indeed, interventions from hecklers or authority figures, far from being a problem, may breathe new life into a performance because they switch perception of the performance from pre-planned 'ploy' to a living negotiation, from 'pretended' emotions to 'real' reactions. Because the performer will have established themselves as the centre of their 'world' these interventions can be considered as provocations from outsiders. In effect any interruption – dogs, drunks or weather – can be seen as a provocation to the stability of the set sequence. Power negotiations with authority figures quickly take on a political dimension as the temporary, liminal world of the performance is reminded of its marginal place within the municipal centre. Spectators observing this power-play take sides, usually against the authorities if they are attempting to stop the performance.[13] (In Manchester (1986) we refused to end the performance, so the policeman had to occupy the performing area to prevent us continuing. We sat with the audience applauding his 'performance' until he felt too uncomfortable to remain and we were able to reclaim the space.)

Similarly spectators take sides when volunteers are invited onstage, they identify with those selected who, in effect, become their representatives. How these volunteers are treated thus affects the whole crowd. Although the declared purpose of the volunteering is for practical assistance, the undeclared aim is to elicit expressions of real emotions from them: wonder, confusion, frustration as well as laughter. To this end surprises and obstacles are placed in the way of practical tasks. This may include requests for acting or 'doing it with style'. Inexperienced performers may tend to make themselves look good at the expense of the volunteer. This 'superior laugh' at those who are vulnerable and trusting may empower the audience in the sense of oppressing those who are weak. However, an experienced performer will ensure the volunteer will come out of it with their status raised, thus empowering spectators in a more positive way. To make a success of both empowering spectators through their improvised 'acting' and discomforting them with surprises requires sophistication in play strategies. Volunteers must feel safe in order to be able to 'play' but need to be provoked in order to display real responses. Different volunteers will have different insecurities exacerbated by different contexts and different stimuli. They need to be taken to the edge of their comfort zone but not so far that they begin to tense up. If levels of difficulty and relaxing play are sufficiently finely modulated, qualities of the volunteers will be released or revealed which may have a powerful effect on the 'community' of spectators. This stimulation of release or revelation is a third form of edge.

In the challenge to the volunteer there are three parties involved: the provocateur–performer, the provoked volunteer and the observers of the interaction. As will be seen in the main examples discussed in the book, how the provocation is perceived is critical to its 'success' and therefore provocateurs are always concerned with public relations of various kinds. There are many kinds of provocation within culture but if they are only witnessed by a few people their effectiveness beyond that circle is clearly limited, even though within that circle it may have a powerful effect of strengthening a sense of community. Generating popularity enables more people to engage with the provocation, and the greater the number who identify with the provocateur the more strength they have in power negotiations with those they provoke. As well as these relationships that are internal to the 'world' that the street performer has created around them, there are the relationships with other worlds that surround the performance. The context may vary from safe, regular spaces where locals or tourists expect shows or, conversely, may be in an undesignated space in a foreign country, where laws and cultural norms are unknown and there may even be no shared language. In Dubrovnik (1980) I performed a dictatorial oration in a gibberish that sounded rather Slavic. As the harangue became more heated I ignited a smoke pellet in my suit so that I almost disappeared in a flurry of fumes and agitated gestures before an assistant arrived and threw a bucket of water on me. I gathered later that the amazed reaction of spectators was not simply because of the slapstick elements but because I happened to have a beard that resembled Lenin's and the performance in this Communist country was taken to be a satire of him. The expected 'rules' of spectators or performers may not be observed. In Southern India my conjuring tricks were perceived (correctly) as an attempt to deceive and so child spectators crowded around, prising open my fingers to see what was concealed. By contrast, in East Africa the 'magic' was taken at face value. In Sri Lanka performers of a sacred fire dance were horrified when I demonstrated fire-eating without the accompanying rituals.

A more typical West European context may simply be the public space with its uninterested passers-by and the intruding noise of emergency sirens and aeroplanes. Although it may be typical, a context is never neutral – different times of day have different moods and the performer will be aware of adapting to this atmosphere (many performers favour dusk because the shared experience of transition from light to dark creates a cohesive and 'magical' ambience). So the performer, the centre of their world, needs to be aware of the surrounding context. There may be other shows in the vicinity at the same time and their presence may be either controlled, as in the situation of an organised festival, or uncontrolled in a more competitive 'free-market'. If the latter is the case, one show risks being dominated by another. I experienced an example of this when performing with my company on The Mound during the Edinburgh Festival in the mid-1980s. With up to four shows occurring simultaneously in such close proximity that one audience backed right into another, there was a risk of losing one's audience either to a show that appeared 'better' because of laughter and applause from a swelling crowd (which felt tough but fair) or drowned out by drumming (which felt oppressive). In these situations there may develop an 'arms race' of whipped-up cheering, musical instruments or amplification and hotly contested agreements over time, space and noise. In many touristic city centres, such as Bath, UK, official and unofficial rules, covering distance and audibility are necessary to avoid forceful clashes between those who have become adept at vehemently holding their ground.

Seen from above (as one is able to do from the Pompidou Centre in Paris), there is an evolutionary quality to the formation of crowds as individuals swarm between and around attractors. With the denouement of one show several other performers compete to catch members of the dispersing spectators with variable amounts of success. From this image I have conceived the notion of 'centres' which I will develop below (p. 23). By creating a space for 'their' world, the performer makes a temporary encroachment onto the public space, they claim territory and dominate it. The drive to do so is one that is clearly fundamental to humans and other animals. It is, of course, a major dynamic in world politics and tends to be associated, rightly or wrongly, with the male gender. The 'tagging' (writing one's name) by street/graffiti artists is another form of this claiming of territory.

Most of the artists described in this book have begun their careers with some kind of street performance. The vulnerable position they placed themselves in sharpened their practice and gave them confidence to begin to enlarge their personal freedoms. The powerful experience that they are likely to have had of an internal battle to transgress norms set up a dynamic to take higher risks of transgression. This book combines two approaches to the subject of provocation. One is a very individualistic approach through the psychology of provocateurs – why and how they do their work. The other examines the context and process of shifting relationships with the provoked person(s) and the way these are perceived by the wider population. I will begin by examining an individual because the narrower focus provides an easier entry point into the wider subject. Because provocation is concerned with power negotiations I have selected an example that emerges from the street theatre context and which illustrates the effect of power on an individual.

Philippe Petit

From the non-specific model of circle shows that I have outlined, I will examine a specific example as a way to consider provocation in terms of the processes of interaction between risk and empowerment. Philippe Petit's tightwire walk between the twin towers of the World Trade Center (07/08/1974) provides a good example because the factors implicit in the circle show model were taken to an extreme that it is hard to imagine could be surpassed. Petit had become accomplished at wire-walking and other equilibristic skills while working as a street performer in Paris. His practice was both typical of street performers of this time and exceptional in the degree to which he took it. As described in his book, *To Reach the Clouds*,[14] and, as seen in the documentary film, *Man on Wire*,[15] Petit succeeded in smuggling equipment to the top of the towers, just before construction was finished, and rigged a wire between them that he walked along several times before being arrested.

The historical context of the action reinforced certain aspects of the circle show model. The 1972 oil crisis appeared to demonstrate the weakness of Western capitalism and gave some credibility to those who began to experiment with lifestyles that were independent of normal modes of existence. The cash income gained directly from spectators provided a means to avoid regular employment and payment of tax. The street performers' sense of themselves as an independent centre was enhanced by the confrontations with police that were frequent at this time when the emerging form was not legally recognised (in the UK it was treated as begging throughout the 1970s). In common with other street performers at this time, Petit will have become adept at playing on the edge of legality, using evasions and playing with the power provided by the audience. As the risks of failure, rejection and physical injury were expanded to include taking risks with authorities, the practice of street performers began to take on an ideological dimension that fitted with the cultural shift towards enlarging personal freedoms that was current at the time. It can be imagined that taking risks with authorities and succeeding would have augmented a sense of personal power.

In Petit's case, his life-long refusal to be constrained by rules and laws may be related to problems with his 'strict' parents and various schools. By inference he appeared to be challenging other forms of personal limitations: his own fears. At his first sight of the twin towers and the realisation of the immensity of his project he repeated the word 'Impossible!' with a sense of excitement rather than despondency: 'that's what attracts me: doing something that is supposed to be impossible'.[16] In the event, he absolutely refused to use a safety line[17] even though this would not have been seen from below, presumably because this would have diminished his sense of personal achievement. James Marsh, director of *Man on Wire*, who worked intensively with Petit to collaborate on the making of the film, believes that the towers were 'a monster he had to conquer'. Petit states that from early on in the development of the project he wanted to become 'king of the American sky'.[18] So the towers were both a physical challenge and a psychological testing ground. Marsh suggests in the notes to the DVD: 'It is the hero going on a journey, or a quest, to test himself and achieve a seemingly impossible objective'.[19] In this sense his exploit can be compared with those of mythic heroes such as Hercules, Jason, Sir Gawain and Saint George. Petit, himself, frequently uses epic quasi-religious terminology: 'the Gods'.[20] 'They are masterful, they rule. I am insignificant. Mid-air battle'.[21] His first major illegal stunt, walking between the towers of Notre Dame cathedral, Paris (1971) was described by his partner of the time, Annie Allix, in terms of its symbolic relationship with the institution as much as a physical challenge: 'He was like an angel' rising above it.[22] Marsh does not consider him to be religious: 'if anything he is a pagan'. However, 'he doesn't really live in the same world that I live in ... the fire burns a bit brighter in him'.[23] Petit describes his exploit in poetic terms: 'My life is a fairy tale ... I began to dream of not conquering the universe but as a poet of conquering beautiful stages'. He acknowledges the Very Reverend James Park Morton of the Cathedral Church of St John the Divine, New York, as his 'spiritual father'. Petit frequently refers to his aerial arena as 'the heavens' and he selected the date of the action as the day after 'Transfiguration' in the Christian calendar.[24] The expression of his work in these terms is significant because it contrasts with the hard reality of his practice – not only the extreme danger but also the extensive, obsessive attention to details of equipment, timings and covert strategies.[25] He is accused by his collaborators of being more concerned with the romantic cloak-and-dagger aspects of the operation than the safety aspects (he liked to watch cops-and-robbers movies to relax). After the action, he was dismissive of those who asked why he had done it. 'I did something magnificent and mysterious and I get a practical: "Why?". And the beauty of it is: there is no "Why?" ... If you don't see the virtue of something wonderful and dreamlike and beautiful then I can't help you really'.[26]

The paradoxical combination of purposelessness and the extremity of danger must have been apparent to the office workers who gazed upwards at Petit's action during the early morning rush hour. In the twenty-first century, extreme leisure activities, such as base jumping, have become more well-known but, in the context of New York in 1974, commentators assumed that the purpose was practical: for publicity or to gain a work permit. As indicated above, there was clearly a purpose but this was personal and artistic rather than for functional advantages that would fit within capitalist values. This distinction is the difference between what James Carse calls 'finite play' – playing within clear rules and targets – and 'infinite play' which is open-ended in terms of outcomes.[27] In this example there was a victory of ludic qualities over logic: it did not make 'sense'. There was also an underlying negotiation of power relations between the maverick artist and the business of downtown New York. The twin towers were not only physical summits that he felt he must conquer but also the

World Trade Center, a hub of capitalism that, at this time, was embarking on the processes of globalisation. (The symbolic conflation of dominant height and hegemony was, of course, recognised years later by Al-Qaeda.) The iconic towers become props (literally) for his performance, diminishing their status, as objects to be used for supporting a single human rather than as giant monuments to capitalism. As such, the image could be perceived as a victory of a 'lowly' individual over a system, of humanity over commerce. By physically dominating the Center, the populist street performer, a representative of those on the legal margins, provided an empowering image to those who were literally at the bottom. Through the action he acquired a super-human status that relates to figures from American popular culture such as Superman but also to King Kong's ascent of the Empire State Building: resistant and subversive. Petit does not articulate a political dimension in words but clearly his ludic play with the authorities, exemplified by balancing a policeman's hat on his nose while under arrest (as seen in *Man on Wire*), proposed a visual expression of ideological opposition consistent with that of the 1970's expansion of personal freedoms. His use of the term 'coup' to describe the action may derive as much from the political sense of 'coup d'état' as it does from the phrases 'coup de maître' (master stroke) and 'coup de théâtre' (a surprising and powerful moment within a stage play).

So, despite his being arrested, the action was perceived as a victory for Petit. He was treated as a threat because he outfoxed the security system. However, this was a 'soft' provocation: his friend Jean-Francois Heckel agreed to participate because it was illegal but not 'wicked or mean'. So, although this was not a provocation about injustice or other moral considerations, there were ethical decisions made. Subsequently Petit took pleasure in explaining to those in charge of security how he had pulled off the coup. In this sense he 'revealed' a hidden aspect of the system which, as will be seen, is an important function of other provocateurs. As well as being empowering in terms of its relations with a centre of power, it was also empowering in the sense of enlarging the scope of human capabilities – not only overcoming the terror of the accomplishment but being able to do so with a sense of play, of 'dancing' in the air. He placed himself in extreme danger but did not die and the action was therefore positive and life-affirming, unlike the destructive life-denial provocation of Al-Qaeda. As such, Petit's action was carnivalesque. One of the characteristics of the carnivalesque is described by Bakhtin in these terms:

> Its most common aspect is the simple act of replacing a negation by an affirmation ... In this play with negation, the opposition to the official world and all its prohibitions and limitations is obviously revealed. It also expresses the recreative, festive suspension of these restrictions. It is a carnival game of negation, and this may also serve utopian tendencies.[28]

However a kind of death did occur. Afterwards 'he was starting something else, a new life'.[29] 'It ceases to be like a fairy tale ... real life is not like a fairy tale, relationships do change and fracture ... Real lives don't neatly resolve themselves like stories do'.[30] So what had occurred? As well as practical and technical preparations for the event he also needed to shift his psychological attitude from his initial 'Impossible!' reaction. He did this, for example, by looking down on the towers from a helicopter as 'a way to trick his mind'.[31] Preparations also included evading and deceiving the security, including masquerading as a reporter in order to take detailed photos of fixing points. This research reduced the unpredictability of the practical aspects but also provided a staged approach to building confidence in bluffing others and familiarising himself with the height. However, in the event, it was adrenalin that enabled him to overcome incredible hardship and fatigue. The hardship was shared by his collaborator, Jean-Louis Blondeau, who had to save the mission by hauling up tons of cable ceaselessly for many hours. The stresses of the final preparations were added to by the awareness that time was running out before they would be discovered so that, when he embarked on the walk, with only minutes to spare, 'his face became an ageless mask of concentration, like a sphinx'.[32] Describing shifting his weight onto the wire he is poetic again: 'On one side the mass of a mountain, a life I know, on the other, the universe of the clouds, so full of unknown that it seems empty to us'.[33] So, at this moment, he had been able to reduce the possibility of being crippled by doubt, both through different forms of preparation but also through the action of hormones. He describes reducing the field of his consciousness to the balance of the pole in his hands and the contact between the soles of his feet and the cable. By narrowing his focus he could exclude extraneous anxieties and fears. His written description shifts from practical details to an ecstatic account of physical sensations and the awareness of the circling of a bird. His sense of time altered from the busy-ness of the pre-walk phase ('without consulting me, time accelerates') to a reduced awareness: 'It was magical. It was profound. My friends told me [afterwards] I was forty-five minutes out there. [They said:] "You know you did eight crossings"'. His face is said to have relaxed and he appeared to enjoy himself. He lay down with his back on the wire, he looked down, and he playfully teased the police who later described him as 'dancing'. This surprising effect is as a result of a state that Csikszentmihalyi identifies in other risk takers which he terms 'flow', which I will outline below.

The other notable feature of this example is the shift in relationship with his team. Although this was partly as a result of his subsequent fame, it was not unrelated to the effect of extreme risk. It is clear from the various accounts that 'it was a collective effort to get him up there'.[34] Arguably, Blondeau, his best friend, saved his life by forcing him, over several months, to consider every potential problem, despite straining their relationship to breaking point, and also saved the operation by his heroic effort to haul up the cable. However 'the friendship didn't survive this caper; nor did Annie's'.[35] Annie Allix had been invited to New York to provide emotional support when Petit had become depressed after a previous attempt had fallen through. Yet, immediately after release from police custody, he did not reunite with her and the rest of the team and refused to cooperate in dealing with the media frenzy. Instead he indulged himself in a sexual encounter with a complete stranger. At the end of the film he states: 'For me it is really so simple that life should be lived on the edge of life. You have to exercise rebellion: to refuse to taper yourself to rules'. There is a suggestion that his enhanced sense of himself at that moment allowed him to ignore the 'rules' of social relationships; that, not only the public prestige, but also his sense of having had such an exceptional experience had removed him from his immediate community. He was psychologically no longer the person he had been. The deep emotional wound of this rejection is apparent in the film as Blondeau breaks down in tears recalling the outcome of thirty years before. The film also makes clear that the director and producer found Petit difficult to work with: it was 'an intense relationship that you had to bear'. [36] Petit tried to maintain some control over the direction of the film, keen to emphasise the technical nuts-and-bolts details of his operation, aided by his partner Kathy O'Donnell who is described as 'extremely demanding' and 'fastidious'. It appears that the camaraderie and cooperative practice evident in the film prior to the coup had been replaced by a strident autonomy derived from a sense of personal power. This transformation from team player to controller can be observed in other risk-taking provocateurs, including those studied in this book. I shall relate this process to complexity and other theories but, before entering into an outline of these, I will relate this extreme example to research into neurochemistry.

The 'Winner Effect'

The example of Philippe Petit and his extraordinary exploit raises two questions. Firstly, how did he accomplish it? By this I do not mean in the sense of the technical aspects and clandestine strategies but how did he overcome the terror that most people would experience? The question could be asked of many extreme sportspeople but the documentation of Petit's action provides insight into the processes involved. Secondly, why did he do it the way he did? He is dismissive of those who look for a simple 'functional' motive. The coup appears to be an end in itself not a means to an end but I am interested in why it came about: what are the factors that determined its nature? How can the particular features of the event be best explained: the separation from his team, the impulsive sexual encounter, the determination and monomania and the conflict with those who were trying to help him? Why for example did he refuse to use a safety line even though nobody would be able to see it at such a distance? Answering these questions will enable some general conclusions to be made about the 'pathology' of provocateurs and thus to approach a wider understanding of the nature of provocation. Because Petit's feat is so extreme it brings to light features of provocation that might be overlooked in more subtle actions.

One way to approach these questions is by means of the effects of hormones on the functioning of the brain. Professor Ian Robertson brought together his own research with those of others in his book, *The Winner Effect* (2012).[37] He outlines the effect of increased testosterone and other hormones in terms of acquisition of power and its relationship with risk. This link between power and risk is key to my analysis of provocateurs. He refers to neuroscientific research that demonstrates how winning increases testosterone, which then improves performance in subsequent challenges. Success in these challenges generates a sense of power. In turn, this increases the likelihood of taking more risks in future. In Petit's case 'winning' can be seen as his previous successful wire-walks at Notre Dame and the Sydney Harbour Bridge as well as overcoming increasingly difficult obstacles during his preparation for the coup. Testosterone has the effect of making the individual less anxious and more aggressive. It also raises the pain threshold, and this may explain how Petit was able to sit on a girder for hours and cope with stress and fatigue, and how Blondeau was able to pull up tons of cable over many hours. Robertson indicates that the effects are not only temporary but also have a longer lasting effect by developing the receptors of testosterone.[38] As well as increasing testosterone, 'winning' also reduces the level of cortisol which is part of the emergency response system the body uses to deal with danger or threat.[39] This may partly explain Petit's ability to place himself in such extreme danger.

Robertson suggests that testosterone reduces a general awareness; there is a '"screening out" of distractors ... power ... puts blinkers on us'.[40] This may explain Petit's lack of awareness of how many times he crossed the wire and his ability to block out all concerns about the technical uncertainties, the imminent discovery and the mortal consequences the moment that he transferred his weight onto the cable. This 'screening out' may be a major factor in the state of 'flow' as described by Csikszentmihalyi.

> When the actor's attention is highly focussed in a limited resource field which provides non-contradictory demands for action appropriate to the actor's resources, with clear and immediate feedback in the form of control feelings, a state may be reached in which the ego has, so to speak, nothing to do and awareness of it fades.[41]

However, Robertson makes it clear that, after the event is over, 'success' will enhance a sense of ego and reduce empathy: 'power makes us more egocentric, disinclining us to take on other points of view'.[42] Citing the example of CEOs from the world of business and finance prior to the 2008 financial crash, he observes: 'they were morally disapproving of what others did, but much more lax with themselves when it came to their own personal moral behaviour. Power, in other words, created hypocrisy'.[43]

Robertson also suggests that the increase in testosterone and the decrease in cortisol can be stimulated by simply thinking about past or future successes. From Petit's first glimpse of the towers and his repetition of the word 'Impossible!', he is clearly thrilled by the prospect, flooding his brain with testosterone. All the practical and theoretical preparations over several months also served the purpose of altering his brain processes, increasing his abilities, so that by the time that he was on the way to execute the coup the changes in brain chemistry were visible in his eyes: 'There was real madness in his eyes, a real fury'.[44] Robertson suggests that if there is a successful outcome the hormone dopamine is released creating a sense of well-being and power. However, dopamine boosts 'the appetite for thrill'[45] and this may become 'literally addictive'.[46]

> Like the mountaineer seeking the fix of the next and more dangerous peak ... he yearns for that chemical high that winning triggers in him. Unfortunately, like all such highs, the next stimulus has to be stronger to get the same effect.[47]

The augmentation of scale and risk with each of Petit's exploits from Notre Dame to the twin towers can be seen in this light. This progression can also be seen in terms of expansion. Overcoming obstacles creates a sense of achievement and dominance and thereby an increased desire to expand the scale of subsequent challenges. In Petit's case this is literally in terms of height as well in terms of difficulty and complexity. However, as Robertson indicates, 'There is only so much dopamine that the human reward system can take. Overload it, and you are likely to get the [same] sort of problem ... as compulsive gambling'.[48] Not only is there a drive towards augmenting levels of risk but the assessment of threats becomes impaired. Individuals display a self-conviction that may not be justified: '"certainty" is a symptom of a brain filled up with dopamine, focused on action, and with a reduced capacity for self-scrutiny or caution',[49] 'when our brains are primed by even small amounts of remembered power, this changes us psychologically: power makes us more egocentric, disinclining us to take on other points of view'.[50] This may explain the tension between Petit and Blondeau in the run up to the coup.

Robertson also indicates connections between dopamine derived from 'winning' and dopamine derived from other power-inducing experiences: 'Sex, power, money, cocaine all use the common currency of dopamine and each can rack up the need for the other'.[51] This factor, combined with that of reduced empathy, may explain the sexual encounter and separation from his team immediately after the coup when his brain will have been flooded with dopamine. Having done so, 'cognitive dissonance'[52] may have come to bear to justify his actions to himself, creating 'a sense of exceptionalism and entitlement'.[53]

> arousing feelings of power makes people poorer at decoding other people's emotional expressions ... power also makes people care less about what others think, making them selfish and lacking empathy ... One consequence of lack of empathy and ego centricity is that it induces us to see people as a means to our ends – more as *instruments* of our own goals.[54]

Accompanying the personal challenge there is the concern for having an increased impact with each challenge. The risk-taker needs evidence of their achievement to be seen and acknowledged to get the full dopamine benefit.

Some provocateurs, such as Banksy, enlarge their territory by imposing visual alteration. Sacha Baron Cohen enlarges his territory by entering that of dominant institutions and *being seen* to outwit and dominate their representatives. As Robertson says: '"Impact" also refers to having an effect on people – persuading them or changing their emotions by, for instance, surprising them or shocking them'.[55] However, because of this need to be seen to be taking risks, provocateurs are dependent on members of their team to witness their feats as well as help to achieve them. They need to be 'out there' on their own but they are not simply eccentrics who are content to be different. The continual tension between solitary autonomy and teamwork is symptomatic of their relationship with wider society: they are both part of it but retain independence from it: they straddle an edge.

If successful, risk-takers gain greater freedom of action and become perceived differently. In most cases they feel themselves to represent an interest group or sub-culture but they refuse to limit their personal freedom by conforming to the conventions of that group. As outlined above, there are circumstances in which the 'world' that has been created by a street performer is threatened by adjacent performers who audibly impinge, potentially causing uncommitted spectators to drift towards another show. By this means these autonomous centres of power can become aware of themselves as being 'a sort of node in a network – as a me which exists in a context, not independently of it'.[56] The shifting of emphasis between being a centre and being an outsider can provide insight into the, often complicated, relationship between a provocateur and their team. They are reliant on their teams to mount larger or more complex operations to increase impact but, at the same time, it must be they who take the main risk; otherwise they will not achieve a dopamine 'pay-off'. This may explain why Petit refused to use a safety line. It concerned his self-esteem, his prowess.

The kind of street shows described above can be seen as power-enhancing exercises in territorial domination and therefore it is perhaps unsurprising that many provocateurs such as Petit, Leo Bassi and even Sacha Baron Cohen enjoyed formative experiences as street performers. Differences in testosterone production and reception between genders may account, in part, for the fact that this area of work is performed primarily by men. Of course, the other major factor is the greater culturally inherited confidence to confront others in power but, as in extreme sports, physical bravado, prowess and territory domination appear to be qualities that are currently more attractive to men than women. The spatial arrangement of the street show, with the performer at the centre of a 'world' that they have created, and that they control, is a model that can be up-scaled in terms of wider culture. By inference, provocateurs' challenges to bigger institutions, enlarging or insisting on their own freedom of action can be seen as a refusal to be dominated within a larger centre, just in the way that a heckler refuses to play by the 'rules' of the spectator–performer relationship. For both street performers and stand-up comedians, dealing successfully with hecklers is critical to keeping or 'losing' an audience. Hecklers can be seen as a form of feedback and, although this can be unnerving to performers, the ability to listen openly and respond creatively, rather than blocking or denying its existence, is key to how this contest is perceived by observers. As I shall outline below, this three-way relationship can be scaled up to include challenges to national institutions. However, as a link into this up-scaling I will outline theories of play, risk and complexity, as well as explaining some of the key terms that I use.

The background of ideas

Play

I have begun by outlining the connections between this kind of work and personal or political power; however, it is also about play. Play can be thought of in different ways. Johan Huizinga thought of it in terms of two basic concepts: as a contest for something or a representation *of* something.[57] He viewed contest as operating within rules, and with an attitude of seriousness that could include business, politics and even war. For James Carse, playing within rules was only one form of play – 'finite play'. The other was open, 'infinite play': 'the rules of an infinite game are changed to prevent anyone from winning the game and to bring as many persons as possible into the play'.[58]

> Infinite players do not rise to meet arms with arms instead they make use of laughter, vision and surprise to engage the state and put its boundaries back into play. What will undo any boundary is the awareness that it is our vision, and not what we are viewing that is limited.[59]

In contrast to finite-playing political activists or the serious avant-garde, this kind of provocative artist turns their mockery onto themselves; for them any seriousness or self-righteousness offers itself as a target, regardless of its particular perspective or provenance. Because it is hard to pin down the motives of these game-changers, any 'serious' statements from them may be of only temporary value.

For Gregory Bateson the polarities of play were not so much infinite and finite but real and 'not-real'.[60] Philippe Petit's tightrope walk between the twin towers was signalled as 'play', but was treated by the participants as a bank robbery and initially by the authorities as a major crime. Despite his playfulness, the subsequent court proceedings were not treated as a game, they did not stand in for reality; his friends were deported. Leo Bassi usually has his own lawyers present at his actions in order to be fore-armed against possible litigation. Legal battles may be seen as play within the terms defined by Carse and Huizinga, but they are not pretence or signalled as play. In provocateur work, however much the game is signalled as play, the meta-communication may be that this is not just a game. On this level, laws, politics and commercial interests may prescribe the limits to the 'game' with fixed rules and defined objectives. An outwardly playful action may also present a direct and serious challenge and must be overcome by authorities in order to avoid their public loss of status. Similarly 'official' or normative statements may conceal assumptions and conventions that need to be challenged by provocateurs (sometimes, like Bassi, working with investigative journalists). Clearly, in a world of political spin and advertising, the general public can be very sophisticated in questioning the veracity of public statements. However, provocateurs can not only widen the scope from the usual suspects (such as police, law, religion, etc.), but also, for example, expose the depth and breadth of public prejudice.

Play may also be seen as exploration. Exploration, in this context, is concerned with testing the limits of acceptability, both for the explorer and the world they are making contact with. For example, a child might deliberately knock something over in order to explore parental responses. Similarly a provocateur might test the limits of acceptability within a given cultural context. Pascal Larderet, director of the French street theatre company Turbo Cacahouete, makes comparisons between different cities over the time it takes for the police to halt the performance.[61] Explorers may have limited control because they are dealing with the unknown; by expanding knowledge of the unknown they bring it closer under their control. Experimentation, on the other hand, is more concerned with known elements: the arrangement of parts, function and causation. Among other methods, this will involve deconstruction and re-assemblage. The parts can become more deeply known and their relationships more under control, so that they can be arranged to suit a desired end. Cultural provocations, whether these are mere stunts or calculated to have more profound repercussions, can be seen as open-ended experimentation: 'Let's see what happens if I do this?' The initiating action is like a stone thrown into calm waters; there may be just a satisfying splash but, if the boundaries are unstable, the ripples may cause an edge to collapse resulting in a cascade, an effect out of all proportion to the instigation.

Risk

Csikszentmihalyi's study of chess players, gamblers, dancers, surgeons and mountain climbers[62] documents the continuum of risk in activities ranging from light recreational play to life-threatening seriousness. Risk expands the notion of contest to the idea of a contest with the self. It also unlocks the relationship between play and challenge. Why should risk be a major source of pleasure when it involves activities which are potentially threatening to the individual, particularly when taken to life-threatening extremes? As is widely known, extreme sports enthusiasts, bomb disposers and other risk-takers report the pleasure associated with high levels of challenge. They 'live for it' but it is also the case that sometimes they die for it; the attraction of high levels of adrenalin may override the fundamental human need for self-preservation. Serious consequences do not appear to necessarily diminish the pleasures of risk.

The two contributing factors that Csikszentmihalyi identifies as creating risk are the level of unpredictability and the height of the stakes. As the stakes are raised and the level of predictability falls, increasing levels of stress are experienced. The resulting anxiety may have a negative impact on the person and, therefore, lead to avoidance of challenge, a refusal to engage with unpredictability and consequently a reduced aptitude for development. Conversely, the avoidance of risk is a risk in itself; lack of adaptability can result in inappropriate reactions to any alteration in circumstance. Widening the frame, it is evident that some cultures are less flexible, less prepared for the doubt that comes with open-ended processes. Insecurity leads them to seek certainty in fundamentalism, becoming rigid, blinkered, censorial and closed-off to external change and vulnerable to internal collapse. By contrast, it is evident that living with uncertainty, although making decision-making more complex, is a more appropriate way to respond to the fluctuations of modern life.

Willingness to take risks emerges from play but gives power. If a player has a sense of injustice they may use this power to challenge various forms of dominant power. In addition, having experienced the empowering benefits, these player–provocateurs become advocates of risk-taking so that, by leading others into risk, they may destabilise them out of old patterns of perception and activate them into a search for new systems of thinking. Provocateurs also want themselves to remain in risk so they tend to avoid established patterns and structures. This shift of emphasis between structure and destabilisation is analogous to the operation of a fulcrum. The combination of play and risk means that they propose an opposition that is unstructured, ambiguous in it methods, and ambiguous as to whether it is play or is serious.

Fools and bouffons

Risk-taking provides an experience of a tangible, concrete edge: 'I dare to do this but not that'. As well as physical risks there are cultural ones, such as daring to speak about particular subjects or behaving in abnormal ways. This introduces ideas of a temporary 'liminal' state (from Victor Turner[63]) or a more permanent state of marginality. This liminal perspective on society can be associated historically with fools and the carnivalesque. In her study of Mediaeval and Renaissance entertainers Enid Welsford identifies many different types.[64] These included those who were physically or mentally imperfect as well as those who pretended to be fools or simpletons. Some were highly intelligent, well-educated raconteurs who parodied established literary forms such as eulogy. The ambivalent nature of these different kinds of foolishness was portrayed in Shakespeare's scene in *King Lear* (Act 3, Scene 6) which includes a person pretending to be mad, a jester/fool who uses 'nonsense' rhymes to make acute observations and a 'foolish' king who is beginning to have a nervous breakdown while they enact a parody of a legal trial. The term 'fool' is derived from 'fol' and is associated with *folie*, meaning madness, and madness was associated with second sight and clairvoyance. The notion of imperfect bodies or minds being associated with wisdom, clairvoyance or spiritual powers is an ancient one that has been well documented.[65] 'Fools' may be outsiders because they cannot understand assumptions behind conventions, or through physical/mental suffering, or simply being foreign to the context they are in. Bakhtin refers to *folie* not as an illness or defect but as a profound carnivalesque perspective that provided a counterpoint to feudal power and seriousness.

> Folly is, of course, deeply ambivalent. It has the negative element of debasement and destruction ... and the positive element of renewal and truth. Folly is the opposite of wisdom − inverted wisdom, inverted truth ... Folly is a form of gay, festive wisdom, free from all laws and restrictions, as well as from preoccupations and seriousness ... gay folly was opposed to piousness and fear of God ... It permitted the people to see the world with foolish eyes.[66]

The notion of the 'Wise Fool', the person who can see through conventions and hypocrisy because they are an 'outsider', is highly relevant to this study. Simon Critchley, writing more generally about comedy, puts it succinctly: 'We are asked to look at ourselves as if we were visitors from an alien environment ... When we do this, then we begin to look like outlandish animals, and reasonableness crumbles into irrationality'.[67] The paradox inherent in the term 'wise fool' is a hint of one of the many kinds of ambivalence that is demonstrated by the artists in this book.

The other kind of fool is that of the jester or 'trickster', an archetypal figure well documented in cultures all over the world (e.g. by Joseph Campbell[68]) and used by Jung. Rather than being mad or stupid, this figure uses intelligent craft to make fun, play tricks and/or reveal truths. In European theatre history the character of Harlequin is a representative of this ancient figure. Dario Fo linked the patchwork costume and black mask of Harlequino to the pagan spirit of the woods.[69] Welsford refers to 'Hellequin', who was 'an aerial spectre or demon, leading that ghostly nocturnal cortege known as the Wild Hunt'.[70] Bakhtin suggests a link to the diableries of Mediaeval Christian dramas and the conglomeration of pre-Christian folk culture and the Roman Saturnalia that was manifested in Mediaeval carnival practices.[71] A more recent historical representative was Grimaldi, who, despite establishing the character of Clown, was working in an early grotesque form of the Harlequinade. He was noted by contemporary observers as having a quality of 'spirit possession'.[72] He was 'an expert at death and resurrection tricks'; at his hands 'Harlequin was frequently murdered, his body chopped up and boiled ... before being brought back to life by the nailing of the separated bits to a wall'.[73] The background of the Commedia del Arte provided a link to violence, exploitation, greed and what Bakhtin terms 'the lower body-stratum', including eating, drinking and sex. In addition, Grimaldi parodied military dress and tastes in fashion, making fun of traits of those facing him in the theatre. In parody, unlike in clowning, it is not the comic who suffers the status drop but the established or privileged. By effecting this descent, the comic raises themselves in relationship to the parodied and thus an inversion occurs. The comic actively provides a different perspective which supplies the foundation for potential social change.

From the wearing of clothes turned inside out and trousers slipped over the head to the election of mock kings and popes the same topographical logic is put to work: shifting from top to bottom, casting the high and the old, the finished and completed into the material lower stratum for death and rebirth ... The element of relativity and of becoming was emphasized, in opposition to the immovable and extra-temporal stability of the medieval hierarchy.[74]

Bakhtin emphasises that the descent of the established and privileged is, not simply to empower the parodist and their observers, but to cause a renewal of the target of parody.

The essence of the grotesque is precisely to present a contradictory and double-faced fullness of life. Negation and destruction (death of the old) are included as an essential phase, inseparable from affirmation, from the birth of something new and better.[75]

The term 'making fun' is apt because it suggests not only the critical aspect of the process but its lightness; it is performed in a spirit of play and positivity. The artists in question may laugh off dominant power rather than engage in resistance although, of course, ridiculing is a form of resistance in itself. Abercrombie and Longhurst identified two forms of resistance: firstly, 'oppositional readings that might be developed by audiences are *relatively* codified and almost politicised accounts directed at a uniform form of power that can be identified by audience members' and secondly opposition that 'is rather more evasion, a kind of determined unseriousness, a form of play that refuses to take power seriously and is thus undermining'.[76]

This quality of making fun of privilege from a position of ex-centric, outside the central norms, is at the core of the *bouffon* style. In contemporary theatre practice this style emerged in the late 1960s, coinciding with the West European publication of Bakhtin's analysis of carnivalesque practices.[77] It was developed in different ways by Jacques Lecoq and Philippe Gaulier. The latter taught Sacha Baron Cohen and he is concerned with the perspective of those who are in a more permanent marginal position. I will expand on this aspect in Chapter Three. Because of the challenge to established forms, extreme *bouffon* work is less popular and therefore less seen. Nevertheless, lower levels of illogic and ugliness are validated throughout popular culture, from Halloween costuming through to Monty Python and zombie movies. Bassi, Baron Cohen and Banksy manage to bridge the gap between popularity and discomforting *bouffon* work. The fracturing of form and diversity of perspectives sits well within Post-Modernism and seems an appropriate 'fit' with complexity theories.

Chaos/complexity theories

The edge between levels of challenge and acceptability is different to edges described in chaos/complexity theories; these concern different states of activity.

The selection of complexity theories as a foundation for the analysis may seem odd given that they emerged from non-cultural studies in mathematics, weather patterns, economics, topology and biology, rather than cultural studies. However, for the 'organic' nature of the processes in question, Complexity seems more appropriate than viewing the subject in terms of a consciously designed linearity of progressive development that leads to increasing specialisation and refinement. Dis-ordering and breakdown of systems is as much a part of the subject as formation and ordering. However, some notions from performance studies and anthropology are useful in order to make connections between complexity theories and processes in the human world. This weaving together carries the danger of conflating notions from different contexts, for example, by suggesting that molecules or cells operate within the same patterns as conscious humans. However, I use Complexity simply as a useful framework to analyse provocation and leave open the question as to whether there is a connection rather than just a similarity.

As summarised by James Gleick[78] there are six aspects of chaos theory.

1   Order–disorder: disorder will naturally evolve from order (as in the process of entropy) and order will naturally evolve from disorder (as in evolutionary natural selection).

2   Scale: there are similarities of pattern on different scales of the same system (fractals). Understanding large patterns can help understand the micro-scale and vice-versa. Self-similarity at different scales can stabilise a system.

3   Adaptability: in order to adapt to different internal and external relationships it is important for a system to be able to 'range over different frequencies'.

4   Butterfly effect and avalanches: tiny changes in certain features can eventually lead to remarkable changes in overall behaviour. Sometimes these changes are very rapid.

5   Transition: different systems have similarities of transition processes – if there are internal imbalances in an even, linear system this can lead to a 'laminar phase' with different levels of order and turbulence layered on top of each other and then to 'bifurcations' – where one kind of activity splits off from another. There may be oscillations between the two types of activity. This divergence may lead to a disintegration of the system.

6   Feedback: internal feedback is important to stabilise a system. Too much feedback can become overwhelming.

Summarising complexity theory, Roger Lewin[79] states that the two extremes of stasis and chaos carry dangers for the entity, in that they allow for too little or too much change to occur. The optimum performance can be found at the edge of chaos where strategies for adaptation are invented and tested. Furthermore, entities may take themselves to the edge of chaos. 'Part of the lure of the edge of chaos is an optimisation of computational ability, whether the system is a cellular automaton or a biological species evolving with others as part of a complex ecological community. At the edge of chaos bigger brains are built'.[80] This has parallels with Csikszentmihalyi's observation that risk-taking humans are attracted to their activities because it makes them feel more alive. At a 'sweet point' between anxiety and boredom they experience the positive state of, what he terms, 'flow'.

> When a person is bombarded with demands which he or she feels unable to meet, a state of anxiety ensues. When the demands for action are fewer, but still more than what the person feels capable of handling, the state of experience is one of worry. Flow is experienced when people perceive opportunities for action as being evenly matched by their capabilities.[81]

He quotes the comments of a rock climber: 'The uncertainty factor is the flow factor. Uncertainty is the existence of a flow whereas certainty is static, is dead, is not flowing ... You can't have certain flow any more than an uncertain static-ness. They cancel each other out.'[82] It is plausible that the visceral thrill of extreme sports and fairground rides is the emotional and physical manifestation of the attraction of this edge of chaos. As well as the thrills of physical danger, there is also the excitement of facing what is unpredictable because, as Csikszentmihalyi states: 'discovery and exploration imply transcendence, a going beyond the known, a stretching of one's self toward new dimensions of skills and experience'.[83] In this book I refer to Gleick's 'boundary between one kind of behaviour and another'[84] in terms of a border and Lewin's 'edge of chaos'[85] in terms of a fulcrum. Cultural provocateurs can be seen as part of society's feedback loop, drawing it to the edge of chaos, testing to see if ideas and perspectives are outworn as the context transforms. If this is the case, these provocateurs may fulfil an essential function for the development of societies. The selected artists are in a unique position because they have both the experience of pushing their own boundaries, through considerable personal risk, as well as being engaged in pushing wider cultural boundaries.

'Centres' and 'communitas'

Throughout the book I use the term 'centres'. This denotes 'systems' or 'complex objects' as used in complexity theories. The system is in a constant developing relationship with its environment, 'What is called "progress" or "adaption" is only the necessary result of the inevitable interplay between the system and its surroundings'.[86] The 'interplay' is similar to the notion of 'feedback loops' and to Robertson's awareness of being 'a node in a network', cited above. As it is a system, a 'centre' has internal organisation and order, however simple, that is engendered, in part, by self-similarity at different scales (fractals). The stabilising effect of this 'mirroring' of itself can be observed in improvisation work and the practice of Sacha Baron Cohen.

I have found Victor Turner's notion of 'communitas' useful to analyse the nature and formation of these centres. He identifies three forms of communitas:

(1) existential or *spontaneous* communitas – approximately what the hippies today would call 'a happening,' and William Blake might have called 'the winged moment as it flies' or, later, 'mutual forgiveness of each vice': (2) *normative* communitas, where, under the influence of time, the need to mobilize and organise resources and the necessity for social control among the members of the group in pursuance of these goals, the existential communitas is organized into a perduring social system; and (3) *ideological* communitas, which is a label one can apply to a variety of utopian models of societies based on existential communitas.[87]

The first might be experienced by supporters of the same team at a football match or by fans of the same music at a live performance or in 'special' moments between friends or lovers. This feeling of togetherness, most commonly experienced when others are physically present, appears to have increasing appeal at a time when 'individualism' is promoted to maximise consumer spending, as capitalism promotes competition between individuals and social life is atomised by sophisticated personal technology. Structurally, spontaneous communitas is fluid and volatile, dependent upon the specific conditions of each gathering and thus is constantly changeable and different in each instance. The experience of connection engenders feelings of renewal or rediscovery and these generate an uplift in energy. But, as Walter Benjamin has pointed out, the desire to repeat powerful spontaneous experiences leads to the formation of habits:

> every profound experience longs to be insatiable, longs for return and repetition until the end of time, and for the reinstatement of an original condition from which it sprung … This is not only the way to master frightening fundamental experiences – by deadening one's own response, by arbitrarily conjuring up experience, or through parody; it also means enjoying one's victories and triumphs over and over again … Not a doing 'as if' but a 'doing the same thing over and over again', the transformation of a shattering experience into habit – that is the essence of play.[88]

Thus the first form of communitas can lead to the second, a communitas of norms. Indeed as Turner says: 'it is the fate of all spontaneous communitas in history to undergo what most people see as a "decline and fall" into structure and law'.[89] The communitas of norms replaces the ephemerality of spontaneous communitas by establishing shared practices that can be repeated using a form of structure. The structure reinforces and stabilises the sense of community if it is under threat. The systems are implicit, assumed by its members as shared rather than explicitly articulated via overt public expression of one kind or another. The third form of communitas, a shared system of values or aspirations expressed through language or culture, recovers a 'memory' of spontaneous communitas, for example by describing some form of utopia. It may provide one of the conditions for spontaneous communitas or even be generated by it.

'Popular'

The term 'popular' can have many different interpretations. I distinguish between two different senses of the popular. The first is 'popular' in the sense of the commercial mainstream with its hegemonic influences, promoting norms that are specific to a particular time and culture. The second is more universal and less time-specific, concerning the human condition. I propose that there are three main sources of attraction that make this kind of popularity. Firstly, there is the experience of communitas: the (re-)affirming of togetherness can take many forms and scales, from national displays of patriotism through to a surreptitious shared joke. As Critchley says, 'Shared jokes are signals of cultural connection'.[90] He goes on to outline three theories of humour, one of which is 'the superior laugh': people enjoy sharing a joke at the expense of others, emphasising the differences between 'them' and 'us', be they clowns, politicians or those from other cultures. In provocative practice this experience often takes the form of a community of conspiracy.

The second aspect of the popular is that of risk, chance or danger which, as stated, can be highly pleasurable as long as the level of unpredictability is not so high as to cause anxiety. The third aspect of the popular is that of empowerment. If the other two aspects are associated with reinforcing or destabilising structure, empowerment is concerned with changes within the existing structure by, for example, altering power relationships. Typically this might be identifying with a person who has attained power by becoming famous. The more the person is like 'one of us' the greater the sense of identification. However empowerment may also be gained by witnessing the descent of the high, and this may be achieved through ridicule. The elevation–demotion cycle of celebrities has evident popular appeal. Empowerment may also be derived from seeming to gain the upper hand over commercial institutions, for example, by securing a purchase at a bargain rate. Of more relevance is the sense of enhanced power that may be gained from speaking or behaving in ways that are disapproved of, releasing from internalised hegemony.

The provocation process

Since the purpose of provocation is to cause change, whether individual or societal, what is the process by which this is done? I have found it useful to cross-reference three models. Firstly, in Naomi Klein's, *The Shock Doctrine*[91] connections are drawn between *forced* transformations in different fields. By administering a shock an entity is jolted out of its habitual mode, becomes disorientated, bewildered and, therefore, cannot function as normal. In this state it is much more malleable into other modes of behaviour. The approach was used in mental health in the form of ECT, in warfare in the form of blitzkriegs, such as the 'Shock and Awe' bombing of Baghdad in 2003, and in economics, with the uncompromising application of Milton Friedman's free-market doctrine in the UK and the former Soviet Union. The hegemonic imposition of will is clear and the methods are brutal, but the model is comparable to that of cultural provocation.

The second model is one derived from Turner and confirmed by my observations of cultural provocateurs. It consists of three phases: initiating action, liminal phase and reorientation. The initiating action can be tiny compared with the effect that follows. In its milder forms it may be thought of more in terms of a surprise rather than a shock. Either way, it represents a challenge and a disorientation. This first stage contains an element of risk for the instigator, because there may be a backlash, and there may be risk for the centre(s), either in suppressing the challenge or allowing the challenge to destabilise the entity. The second, liminal phase, is where the subject of provocation is in unknown territory, vulnerable during the search for reorientation. This phase is characterised by the alertness associated with risk. The vulnerability may be mitigated by a range of factors: parameters, controls, guidance, new information and the sharing of the experience with others. In the final phase the search is, at least partially, completed as re-evaluation leads to re-positioning, a perspective shift and an enhanced sense of community with others who have shared the risk.

The third model is from complexity theory: internal imbalance may lead to a laminar phase, leading to bifurcations, possibly to oscillations and then, potentially, to chaos. The key moment in this model is the bifurcation, when the internal forces can no longer be held within one entity and they diverge. This moment seems similar to the initiating action, the moment when behaviour is not as expected by the main, original entity and difference is acknowledged. If so, the oscillations of complexity theory can be seen as similar to the way public opinion swings between the 'attractors' of established order/hegemony and disruption/new perspectives. In the socio-political field the oscillations between rebellion and repression are a good example. The oscillation may gradually amplify as far as chaotic behaviour or settle down, by means of a feedback loop. This feedback is the essence of the exploration and experimentation aspects of play. By aligning these models, the liminal phase can be seen as located on the edge of chaos and the final reorientation phase is like the chaotic forces gradually resolving into new configurations. This new configuration is an attractor that may spiral inwards to stasis, becoming increasingly vulnerable to extinction as it does so, or it may retain some imbalance which could engender new bifurcations. Applying this model to the cultural field, the drift from spontaneous communitas into fixed norms, produces orthodoxies that subsequently can be challenged.

Analogies and questions

In this book I intend to establish a concept of an edge, which can be described as a point of transition process moments. These moments differ substantially according to the different contexts, but there are similarities across a wide variety of examples. Although these similarities can only be observed in the detail of practice, taken together, patterns seem to emerge. The provocateur identifies and draws attention to features that are hidden in the assumptions underpinning the paradigm that have become degraded or out of step with developments in the surrounding environment. However, the shift to a new paradigm may not be completed in edge play; the paradigm may be challenged but the moment when a shift could occur may not yet have arrived. Even when there is a reconfiguration into a new paradigm the resolution may remain unstable.

I will approach the multiple complexities of edge processes in terms of three analogies which I will enlarge upon in the main chapters. The fulcrum analogy concerns the shifts between chaos and stasis and thus deals with the destabilisation and formation of structure in many ambiguous combinations, including serious intention/open play, popularity/challenge and the real/not-real. The blade analogy concerns the uncertainty/freedom produced by a combination of risky play and structure. This can reveal contradictions within the system, using the upward–downward movement of empowerment. The border analogy redefines and strengthens communities. These may include marginal communities, formed out of disparate disempowered elements. In Bassi's case the community might be a theatre audience or a loose collection of observers who react similarly to his incitement or a collection of volunteers united by an action. The three analogies could be seen as a linear sequence in the provocative process: destabilisation is followed by changes to internal relationships and thence to the building of new structure. Or they can be seen as a cyclical oscillation between chaos and order, between entropy and organisation brought about by evolutionary specialisation.

So, in writing this book, I was interested in exploring four questions. The first is about the relationship between popularity and challenge. If challenge is uncomfortable, can it only be popular if the challenge is directed at a third party? Is 'popular' just about appealing to a particular cultural community or is it more universal/fundamental than that? The second question considers the power negotiations involved in this kind of provocation. How is popularity used in asymmetric contests with central institutions? What is the mechanism to activate others? How much are ethics and social transformation an aim, and does playfulness compromise ethics in the means and/or ends? How effective are game-changing, ambiguity and creating confusion, and do the de-structuring tendencies of the artists reduce the effectiveness of their challenges? The third question looks at the different sorts of centre that are provoked. What constitutes a centre, how are they formed and what are their various reactions to provocation? The artists themselves form their own centres and I will consider these by looking at the ambiguities between being a leader of group and being a spokesperson for it. Finally I will look at the experience of occupying a position on an edge. What are the formative conditions for taking up this position and what are the outcomes of taking risks over a long period? What are the responses to defensive reactions from centres and is there any evidence for an 'aptitude to evolve' derived from a location on the 'edge of chaos'?

The artists

The three following chapters each focus on a particular artist: the Spanish clown activist, Leo Bassi, the TV/film character actor, Sacha Baron Cohen, and the visual artist, Banksy. All three share the same qualities in their work: firstly, a desire to bring about social transformation by questioning acceptance of established norms; secondly, they work to achieve this aim by means of a playfulness that is widely popular; and thirdly, they work to enjoy, for themselves, the adrenalin stimulation of risk-taking. However, they differ in that they work in different media and, therefore, any similarities between them can suggest more general principles, at least within the modern European context. The diversity is entirely appropriate for this kind of work because any suggestion of an 'ideal' or standard model of practice does not fit with the strident individualism that the artists display. Their distinctiveness is essential to their work, which resists the constrictions of any definition or classification. Furthermore, diversity is the likely outcome of the types of play they engage with, corresponding to similar patterns in the processes described in chaos/complexity theories. In terms of personality, they tend to be very individualist and are not linked by any kind of formal network, nor by conscious connections to a shared tradition. As compared with more theoretically based work, all three began their work with improvised practical experimentation, not only in terms of performance, but also as a basis for their strategies and the formation of their outlook. They have developed their own systems to be able to cope with risk-taking and they have also evolved their individual philosophical frameworks. Comparisons are less about how the artists have interpreted or been influenced by a central set of ideas, and therefore similarities of approach and process across different cultural practices may suggest inherent characteristics of this kind of provocation rather than culturally constructed ones. These similarities are comparable with the unconscious formations that occur in examples of complexity theory. This may have implications for other processes and formations occurring, not only within the field of arts but also in those of politics and economics.

The tension between wide popular appeal and challenging normative attitudes may throw fresh light on the effectiveness of culture as a 'tool' to transform society. The selected artists have all developed expertise not only in maintaining a delicate balance between challenge and appeal, but also an ability to adjust this balance in the moments of practice. This is necessary because their chosen working contexts are susceptible to a high level of unpredictability. This fine tuning of an 'edge' between play and risk will provide the tight focus necessary to precisely describe the processes involved. The 'edge' is not only a point between appeal and aversion, a series of cultural boundaries, but also a point of balance between embodied stress and relaxation, where capabilities may be maximised, and which may produce positive experiences as well as effective results. The 'edge' may also strike a flint that sparks up processes of renewal.

In their different ways, these artists are 'outsiders' and, as such, are able to see excluding normative attitudes with greater clarity as well as having a desire to challenge their particular area of exclusion. Their work is attractive because they play with danger, both physically and in terms of possible retribution. Their practice includes shock but this effect is used, not just for its own sake, but in order to highlight normative values and controls. The irreverent approach usually has a comical side and these aspects together contribute to wide popular appeal. This appeal is developed and enhanced because of their commitment to counter-cultural thinking. Broadly they question capitalist values and controls, especially in their more free-market forms. They appear to have little faith in politicians and the current form of Western democracy, especially its ability to deliver a fair and liberal society. For this reason they take direct action, but not over a single political issue. The roots of their politics tend to be anarchist, with all the emphasis on personal responsibility that is implied within that ideology.

Despite these similarities, there is a difference in approach as a result of the different contexts. Leo Bassi uses a direct inter-personal approach, with live performance providing visceral experiences, and often leading others into unfamiliar locations or situations. His personal accessibility allows for direct action and direct activation of small temporary communities whilst also exposing himself to physical danger. He has refused the seductions of incorporation and thus remains less well known than the other two. He has become increasingly more didactic and less ideologically ambiguous, using established means of production as well as creating his own.

Sacha Baron Cohen has two kinds of spectator: one that he destabilises through game playing on camera; the other that enjoys a superior, empowering laugh at this spectacle. He does not lead or activate others directly and is not interested in creating communities. As compared with Bassi or Banksy, his work is located in the present with less concern for future aspiration or social legacy. As such he is more interested in open-ended play. He has an individualistic discourse that mainly concerns freedom for the self. He uses established means of production and has achieved wide exposure. This has brought him fame, fortune and incorporation as well as a wide dissemination of his subversions of dominant institutions and figures.

Banksy uses surprises and twists to create curiosity, as a means to subtly activate spectators to reconsider assumptions, highlighting what is overlooked or accepted rather than revealing concealed knowledge. His street work confronts a wide range of spectators who have not invited his images. He generates partisanship by challenging the dominant, and by confirming the ideology of the counter-cultural community. Although he aims to lead by example he does not interact with a wide community. Having created an alternative means of production he is able to avoid some of the negative outcomes of fame and fortune by opting for a state of semi-'exile', so that although his work has become incorporated he has not.

The chapter on Banksy is followed by an interlude chapter on two examples of provocative practice by women, Pussy Riot and Burlesque. These examples expand the definitions of provocation and popular culture that I use up to that point. The final chapter focuses on different aspects of circus as a distinct cultural 'centre', treating it in the same way as I have treated individual artists: its formative years, the attitudes that were formed out of necessities of practice, as well as the constant shifting edges between popular appeal, risk and providing exotic, challenging spectacle. The consequences of different positions on this edge can be seen by comparing the development and performatives of Archaos and

Cirque du Soleil. This final chapter opens with a single extraordinary incident that I was lucky enough to be present at, which, although not located within popular culture, provided a fine example of the experience of witnessing a provocative act, the more so because it was unexpected. I also begin Chapters Two, Three and Four with short sections on my own practice that hopefully provide some insider insight into the way that ideas can be formed through practical experimentation in an unknown area.

Notes

1 Mason, Bim (1992) *Street Theatre and Other Outdoor Performance*. London and New York: Routledge: 52–66.
2 Cohen-Cruz, Jan (ed.) (1998) *Radical Street Performance: An International Anthology*. Abingdon and New York: Routledge.
3 www.michaelmoore.com.
4 www.lmbogad.com.
5 theyesmen.org.
6 www.beppegrillo.it.
7 infed.org/mobi/augusto-boal-animation-and-education.
8 www.clownarmy.org.
9 www.ukuncut.org.uk.
10 As defined by John Fiske: 'All cultural commodities must therefore, to a greater or lesser extent, bear the forces that we can call centralising, disciplinary, hegemonic, massifying, commodifying'. (Fiske, John (1989) *Understanding Popular Culture*. London: Unwin Hyman: 28.)
11 Mason (1992).
12 Mason (1992): 92–5.
13 Gendarmes forcefully stopped my show at St Jean de Luz, France 1980. In Athens that year we were not only stopped but arrested.
14 Petit, Philippe (2002) *To Reach the Clouds*. London: Faber & Faber.
15 *Man on Wire* (2007) Film; directed by J. Marsh. 93 minutes. London: Discovery Films, BBC and the UK Film Council. [DVD (2008) Icon Film Ltd.]
16 *Man on Wire* (2007).
17 Petit (2002): 49.
18 Ibid.: 12.
19 *Man on Wire* DVD (2008).
20 Petit (2002):7.
21 Ibid.:19.
22 *Man on Wire* (2007).
23 *Man on Wire* DVD (2008).
24 Petit (2002): 104.
25 Ibid.: 114.
26 *Man on Wire* (2007).
27 Carse, James P. (1986) *Finite and Infinite Games*. New York: Ballantine Books.
28 Bakhtin, Mikhail (1969) *Rabelais and His World*. Bloomington: Indiana University Press (1984): 412.
29 Allix, in *Man on Wire* (2007).
30 *Man on Wire* DVD (2008).
31 *Man on Wire* 2007.
32 Blondeau, in *Man on Wire* (2007).
33 Petit (2002): 163.
34 Extra material on *Man on Wire* DVD (2008).

35 *Man on Wire* (2007).
36 Chinn, extra material on *Man on Wire* DVD (2008).
37 Robertson, Ian (2012) *The Winner Effect, How Power Affects Your Brain*. London, Berlin, New York, Sydney: Bloomsbury.
38 Ibid.: 68
39 Ibid.: 79.
40 Ibid.: 117.
41 Csikszentmihalyi, M. (1975) *Beyond Boredom and Anxiety*. San Francisco: Jossey-Bass: 85.
42 Robertson (2012): 109.
43 Ibid.: 215.
44 Allix, in *Man on Wire* (2007).
45 Robertson (2012): 194.
46 Ibid.: 133.
47 Ibid.: 128.
48 Ibid.: 206.
49 Ibid.: 120.
50 Ibid.: 109.
51 Ibid.: 206.
52 Festinger, L. (1957) *A Theory of Cognitive Dissonance*. California: Stanford University Press.
53 Robertson (2012): 216.
54 Ibid.: 208.
55 Ibid.: 122.
56 Ibid.: 224.
57 Huizinga, J. (1938) *Homo Ludens*. London: Temple Smith (1970): 14.
58 Carse (1986): 9.
59 Ibid.: 62
60 Bateson, Gregory (1972) *Steps to an Ecology of Mind*. St Albans: Granada: 155.
61 Larderet, Pascal (2008) Interview with Bim Mason (25/05/2008).
62 Csikszentmihalyi (1975).
63 Turner, Victor (1969) *The Ritual Process*. New York: Aldine De Gruyter (1995).
64 Welsford, Enid (1935) *The Fool: His social and literary history*. London: Faber & Faber (Reprint 1966).
65 Frazer, J.G. (1922) *The Golden Bough*. London: The Macmillan Press Ltd; Welsford (1935); Campbell, Joseph (1949) *The Hero with a Thousand Faces*. New York: Pantheon Books; etc.
66 Bakhtin (1969): 260.
67 Critchley, Simon (2002) *On Humour*. London and New York: Routledge: 35.
68 Campbell (1949).
69 Fo, Dario (1983) Mask lecture, Riverside Studios, London.
70 Welsford (1935): 291–2.
71 Bakhtin (1969): 296–7.
72 Findlater, Richard (1978) *Joe Grimaldi: His Life and Theatre*, 2nd edn. Cambridge: Cambridge University Press: 164.
73 Taylor, Rogan P. (1983) *The Death and Resurrection Show: From Shaman to Superstar*. London: Frederick Muller Ltd: 114.
74 Bakhtin (1969): 81–2.
75 Ibid.: 62.
76 Abercrombie, Nicholas and Longhurst, Brian (1998) *Audiences*. London: Sage: 25.
77 Bakhtin (1969).
78 Gleick, James (1988) *Chaos*. London: Cardinal Sphere Books.
79 Lewin, Roger (1993) *Complexity* London: Phoenix.
80 Ibid.: 149.

81 Csikszentmihalyi (1975): 50.
82 Ibid.: 80.
83 Ibid.: 80.
84 Gleick (1988): 235.
85 Lewin (1993): 51.
86 Jacob, Francois (1982) *The Possible and the Actual*. London: Penguin (1989): 176.
87 Turner (1969): 132.
88 Benjamin, Walter (1928) *Toys and Play*. First published in *Die Literariche Welt*. *Selected Writings 2*, translated by Rodney Livingstone and others. Cambridge, Massachusetts and London: Belknap Press of Harvard University Press (1999): 120.
89 Turner (1969): 132.
90 Critchley (2002): 65–75.
91 Klein, Naomi (2007) *The Shock Doctrine*. London: Allen Lane.

2   Stasis and chaos

Structure and improvisation

This short section looks at open-ended play that has no goal other than the sustaining of the game itself. Despite the absence of a predetermined objective the play is not without structure. This combination of fluidity and structure provides an introduction to the subject of this chapter.

Mirroring

For the last fifteen years I have used an exercise based on the dynamics of the Greek chorus. The potential of this as a teaching tool was first explored by Jacques Lecoq but has since been developed by others such as John Wright in the UK. The exercise is introduced after a grounding in basic mirror work has been established. For Lecoq, the ability to imitate was fundamental to all dramatic performance.[1] Mirroring is the simplest form of non-linguistic interaction; for example, it is used by parents responding to babies. In this case, replicating an action meta-communicates, firstly, that the initial action has been heard/seen and, secondly, that initiating actions will be responded to. So mirroring is equivalent to the kind of feedback loops that can be seen in larger systems studied by complexity theorists: it creates or stabilises a system. If the actions of an initiator are copied it establishes a simple hierarchical unit, with a centre and a system of communication to an other, which is a form of organisation. Since we are dealing with very complex dynamical systems in human culture at very different scales it seems appropriate to start with a reductionist approach to see how very simple systems operate at a human scale. Since provocateurs share a solid foundation in improvisation it seems appropriate to begin with the operation of dramatic improvisation in its simplest form. There is no need to refer to the numerous practical manuals on improvisation (Keith Johnstone, John Wright, Alison Oddey, etc.) because we are only considering one practical exercise and one theoretical interaction.

Mirroring is usually done with a defined leader initiating actions that the other tries to replicate exactly. A development of this simple mirroring is where there is no leader and two actors try to follow each other. In practice this is achieved by agreeing actions by means of micro-negotiations, switching between proposing slight alterations and accepting the other's suggestions. If we take two actors, A and B, and A leads by initiating an action which, hypothetically, is exactly replicated by B, followed by A exactly replicating B's replication, then we have a situation of stasis, no change occurs – the actors quickly get bored, there is no 'life'. This interaction can be represented as a perfect circle, repeating itself endlessly (Figure 2.1).

What prevents this process is two factors. The first is that, however exactly they try to replicate each other, perfect precision cannot be guaranteed, particularly after several repetitions. This lack of precision may be caused by a range of human variables and is the equivalent of subtle, non-linear factors (interference, air resistance, friction, presence of the experimenter, etc.) that prevent perfect results in the experiments of the hard sciences. The second factor is that any human beings, particularly irrepressibly creative ones such as actors, could not tolerate the boredom of exact replication for very long and therefore one of them will make, at its simplest level, a minor alteration such as increasing the size of an action. This alteration can be represented as what can be called a 'nudge' out of the repetitive perfect circle. B will then have three possible options: they can (a) cancel the nudge by diminishing the size back to the original action, or (b) they can replicate the *altered* action, thereby accepting the change, or (c) they can develop the *nudge*, increasing or exaggerating its nature (Figure 2.2).

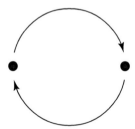

Figure 2.1 Exact mirroring

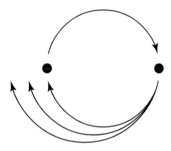

Figure 2.2 Slight augmentation with potential responses

Actor A can respond to these three responses thus:

a   If B's response is to return to the original, they can replicate the original, insisting on stasis, or diminish the exaggeration past the original, setting up a diminishing progression.
b   To the replication of the accepted alteration they can replicate again to confirm and settle a shift to a new position of stasis or, more likely, nudge again to increase the development into an augmenting progression.

Thus, from the neutral starting point there are three possible directions: an augmentation (slow or fast), a diminution, or the maintenance of the neutral position. This third possibility is theoretically possible but hard to sustain, even in such a simple system, because of the non-linear factors and the boredom threshold. If the latter option is represented by a circle the other two can be seen as spirals, either decreasing inwards with diminution to a point of immobility (Figure 2.3) or augmenting outwards (Figure 2.4).

In terms of human physical action, what is augmented or diminished can be one of a whole range of factors: duration, tension, or more precise movement qualities, such as staccato/sustained or bold/hesitant. Gleick uses the example of a swinging pendulum to illustrate attractors in a simple dynamical system. The two extreme positions at the end of the swing are one kind of attractor and the central point is the other, because this is where the pendulum will come to rest.

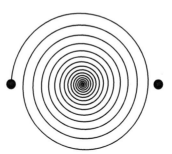

Figure 2.3 Diminution leading to stasis

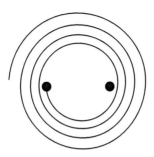

Figure 2.4 Augmentation leading to chaos

If it is not given nudges of energy to counteract the non-linear factors of friction and air-resistance, energy will dissipate, obeying the concept of entropy, an adjunct to the Second Law of Thermodynamics.

> [pendulums:] in phase space the dissipation shows itself as a pull toward the center, from the outer regions of high energy to the inner regions of low energy. The attractor ... is like a pin point magnet embedded in a rubber sheet.[2]

In mirroring, the augmenting circle cannot continue to widen indefinitely; for example, there are limits to the size of action that a human can accomplish and the energy required; large actions cannot be sustained. Therefore, when a limit is reached, the system will begin a sequence of diminution. This could continue back to stasis or, more likely, another quality of movement is selected to be augmented. This creates a pattern of rising and falling as well as a sequence. This rise and fall can be observed in the operation of the choral group.

Choral work

Mirroring with no leader is relatively simple as a duo, even though there may be disparities between the observational abilities of individuals. However, with a small group (e.g. between five and nine) this process becomes much more complex and more powerful. The participants attempt to copy all the others, following and supporting any variations they notice. Because of the fluidity of spatial relationships and direction, visual contact may be interrupted so that a participant may be attempting to replicate another while simultaneously providing variations that are replicated by others. As soon as I introduced the exercise it became clear that students became more 'alive', the level of their performance increased: they were alert but relaxed and it was clear that the pleasure in the playing was self-perpetuating, requiring little intervention or side-coaching. Without steering the process I noticed that patterns began to emerge and these patterns re-occurred over the hundreds of occasions I have observed the exercise. I noticed that the continuous alternation between proposing developments and following them both allowed for self-generated expression but prevented the participants from being restricted to personal habitual norms.

> It's an amazingly freeing space to be in as a performer and creates and promotes a sort of hyper-aware but completely calm state, allowing a new level of reality and grounding to performing ... it is a wonderfully wholesome, collective and grounding experience and has helped build a much more underlying physical confidence in me.
>
> (Participant, 2011)

I noticed that some participants, despite attempting to follow the rest of the group, are more passionate in their expression and they tend to attract attention, thereby having greater influence. However, in order to function well, any initiating action needed to be subtle and the initiator needed to check whether it had been validated (acknowledged and replicated) by others.

> You let the others' presence enhance yours and in return enhance theirs to find places that would be extremely difficult or take much longer on your own. I would say sometimes even impossible to find as you are, in a way, downloading cultural code off of other people.
>
> (Participant, 2011)

The system is simultaneously both open, 'infinite' play, and organised. I also noticed that those participants who are unconfident become less afraid because they share responsibility with others and, initially, they can simply follow what is occurring. Usually the dynamics of the group mounts in both physical and emotional energy and these individuals are encouraged to share the internal life of the group and thereby 'carried' along to more extreme behaviour. By 'getting into the spirit' of the developing culture they help to vitalise it and to lose self-consciousness.

> The reason it's freeing as a group is because you become others, so the group doesn't consist of separate entities forced to do what each other want to do but one entity expressing itself as one entity. So within choral you are constantly creating games, figuring out the rules without ever talking about them and then playing that game for the sheer fun of it, whether that's crying profusely, taking your clothes off, dancing, chasing each other or acting out a love scene.
>
> (Participant, 2011)

In this sense, the group incites itself. Without any discussion, each group will have a noticeably different 'culture' from other groups, for example, by being more forceful or light, more theatrical or dance-like. These mini-cultures naturally emerge from the combination of previously acquired movement and vocal habits of the individuals within it. A group of individuals whose tendency is only to follow tend to arrive at stasis; a group of individuals who tend to lead results in chaotic dispersal. However, with good awareness of others, this does not happen because the system engenders self-similarity which, according to complexity theories, can stabilise a system. However, an over-emphasis on structure could kill the life of the activity; regular rhythms of steps or gestures proved to be an effective way to cohere the group, but I noticed that, without variables, development ceases: the actions become 'stuck'. I concluded that if the structural aspects became over-dominant it led to a stasis of endless repetitions. Similarly, I noticed that, if the level of individual emotional engagement was low, actions would gradually reduce in size and intensity and eventually lead to another form of stasis: inaction.

It also became apparent that different spatial relationships encouraged either cohesion or individual exploration. For example, the inward facing circle was useful if the group had poor feedback because all could see each other. In this case, the emphasis shifted from physical mirroring to sharing the spirit of the action. However, this symmetrical arrangement tended to lead to very linear augmentation of one feature (such as speed, volume, tension), leading to a pattern of rising and falling, oscillating between exhausting hyper-activity and stasis, with limited variation because the body is located in one place and in one direction. The moments immediately after a climax were particularly interesting in that, after a period of mounting cohesion around a single idea, there was uncertainty about the direction of new development and a decline in energy. Individuals became aware that something new must be found so they desperately switched their focus to their internal state, each proposing different starting points. At this moment they needed to watch and mirror very carefully in order to balance diversification with cohesion and stabilise the system.

> You can usually tell you are in the flow of things and connected to the group when the responses are others pushing what you have done further, being 'into it' and from basic primal tools like reading people's faces and body language. At the same time you can also push the energy in a direction that is opposite or not 'in synch' with the group and this quickly deflates the creative energy or stifles it. Like when spinning a ball on your finger you just need to tap it lightly and just in the right place for it to pick up faster and faster speed and therefore become more balanced, but if hit slightly wrong it quickly loses a lot of speed and balance because of this.
>
> (Participant, 2011)

Any starting point was viable; unexpected automatic actions, such as coughing, smiling or adjusting clothing could occur at any time and needed to be incorporated; there was no separation between 'correct' actions that are allowed and actions that are 'unofficial', outside the game. This privileging of non-linear features means that even very subtle natural activities, breathing, for example, or a shift of weight, could be validated by mirroring, exaggerated and thus lead into an emerging development.

The exercise is useful as actor training (to increase awareness and cooperation) and to provide one model of ensemble creation. However, it also serves as a 'Petri dish' in which to explore seemingly endless complexities of cultural process.

> There is Evolution in it, social structures, cultures and their behaviours, rituals, etc. For me it's an explanation of why there are so many dialects, so many cultures, so many opinions. And knowing that one thing can develop into a next thing, but that next thing can literally be anything is a great way of being more relative about things (it could go this way or another and doesn't really matter). When I observe social situations, I see a lot of patterns in it that are similar to choral.
>
> (Participant, 2011)

Although it is an 'abstract' exercise, removed from the 'real' world, it deals in the real personalities, habits and culture that participants embody from their previous lives. Any theatricality that arises is unstable and very temporary.

Within choral you are constantly creating games, and there are rules to these games but they constantly shift. Choral in itself is the most free state I have experienced … The games just form so organically though, and it's amazing to think we could just carry on for hours. I felt I could have carried on for longer. But now I'm exhausted … Hyper aware, internally and externally.

(Participant, 2011)

The interplay between the binaries of individual and group, leading and following, structure and chaos, release and containment is clearly very complex, not simply a matter of oscillations between the two but involving both simultaneously. As Turner puts it:

Spontaneous communitas has something 'magical' about it. Subjectively there is the feeling of endless power … On the other hand, structural action swiftly becomes arid and mechanical if those involved in it are not periodically immersed in the regenerative abyss of communitas. Wisdom is always to find the appropriate relationship between structure and communitas under the *given* circumstances of time and place, to accept each modality when it is paramount without rejecting the other, and not to cling on to one when its present impetus is spent … Spontaneous communitas is nature in dialogue with structure, married to it as a woman is married to a man. Together they make up one stream of life, the one affluent supplying power, the other alluvial fertility.[3]

The fulcrum analogy

Complexity theories indicate a dynamic between a state of stasis and a state of chaos, between stability and instability. They suggest not only that the fixedness of stable systems makes them vulnerable to collapse if there are internal or external variations[4] but also that patterns and forms eventually emerge out of chaotic behaviour. This suggests a two-way process which may appear as a simple oscillation between extremes of chaos and stasis. One of the three ways to consider the nature of edge processes is in terms of a fulcrum in between these two extremes. However, the processes involved are much more complex than that. Bateson used the analogy of a tightrope walker to note the importance of flexibility to maintain equilibrium:[5] in an unstable position stability is maintained through constant adaptation. The complexities can most easily be approached through focussing on one of the directions: the transition from stability to instability. This transition can be examined in terms of taking risks and it can be applied to a range of scales, from individual humans to large organisations, even nation states.

Csikszentmihalyi noted that humans are attracted to both safety and to excitement; in extremes the one becomes boring and the other becomes stressful.[6] He also noted that risk-takers, if they are repeating a challenge, add extra variables to maintain an element of unpredictability. In turn, this encourages a search for higher levels of challenge. He quotes a mountain climber:

'When you run into something you've either done before or experienced the equivalent to … you're going to concentrate more on form than achievement'. By a variety of such measures, the individual, in effect, 'changes the rules' and alters the evaluative criteria.[7]

Although provocative artists may use the power they gain from successful risk-taking to disturb bigger structures, they do not tend to operate within the norms of political organisations because they prefer to retain elements of open play and risk in their practice. Bateson noted the impossibility of distinguishing between operating with a purpose (closed play) and open playing for its own sake, between pretending to be something and being it, so that the real and the 'not real'[8] merged. From the combination of these ideas, I have conceived a continuum between serious, closed play and light, open-ended play, which spans a range of emphases given to norms, morality, structure, reality and purpose (see Table 2.1). This chapter looks at why and how provocative artists use their power and thereby begins to address questions concerning power negotiations,

Table 2.1 Continuum between finite play and infinite play

	← *'Finite play'* ↔ *'Infinite play'* →			
	'Invective'	*'Parody'*	*'Carnival'*	*'Bouffon'*
Rules, frame, logic	Linear		Non-linear, frame distortion, illogic	Abandonment of frames, including logic
Social norms	Within social norms		Extension of social norms	Beyond social norms
Direction	Target, contest	Oppositional, downward movement	Inversions – both up and down	Includes self-deprecation
Meaning	Single meaning		Multiple, fractured meaning	Refusal of meaning
Morality	Moral	Playful morality	Temporary morality	Amoral/cynical
Reality	Real	Parodied is real, parodist is ludic	Fantastical	Not real

Direction: Goes from a contest with a targeted opponent through to turning the direction of the mockery onto the instigator themselves.

Rules & logic: Moves through a point of 'crazy' logic, that makes sense in its own terms, but is not the same as 'real' logic.

Social norms: 1) Social norms are context specific, e.g. in war, extreme violence is acceptable.
2) In practice it is hard for most people to go beyond social norms without experiencing a stressful conflict within themselves that inhibits the freedom of their play. Therefore, the 'bouffonesque' infinite play is an extreme, unsurpassable region.

and the dynamics between play and serious intention, popularity and challenge. Leo Bassi is a prime example of an artist who works with these dynamics.

Leo Bassi: clown activist

'Clowns and fools … were the constant, accredited representatives of the carnival spirit in everyday life out of the carnival season … they were not actors playing their parts on a stage, as did the comic actors of a later period … but remained fools and clowns always and wherever they made their appearance. As such they represented a certain form of life, which was real and ideal at the same time. They stood on the borderline between life and art, in a peculiar mid-zone, as it were; they were neither eccentrics nor dolts, neither were they comic actors.' – Mikhail Bakhtin[9]

'The art of provocation is to bring the people along with you and give them the pleasure of getting close or over the edge.' – Leo Bassi[10]

'Prophets and artists tend to be liminal and marginal people, 'edgemen', who strive with a passionate sincerity to rid themselves of the clichés associated with status incumbency and role-playing and to enter into vital relations with other men in fact or in imagination. In their productions we may catch a glimpse of that unused evolutionary potential in mankind which has not yet been externalized and fixed in structure.' – Victor Turner[11]

Over the last twenty-five years Leo Bassi has accomplished a wide range of work, both as an entertainer and activist, from small-scale street shows to

Plate 2.1 Leo Bassi in *La Vendetta* 2005 (courtesy of Leo Bassi and Theatre Bristol)

hoaxes and large-scale direct actions, on buses, on television, in nightclubs and at various kinds of festival. Although he is well known in Italy and Spain (where he is based), there has been very little documentation of his actions outside of those countries. He is not interested in keeping records so it has not always been possible to be precise about dates. My information is derived from lectures, courses, informal conversations, formal interviews, internet sources as well as seeing five very different performances over a period of twenty-two years (1989–2011).

The Bassi family has been in the circus business since at least the mid-nineteenth century. Leo Bassi grew up steeped in the family traditions and those of the wider circus culture. He was trained as a foot juggler by his father (to be precise, in a Risley act[12]) and worked as part of the family show as a teenager (1969–74) before branching out on his own, working for agents. This led to a year in East Asia performing in restaurants and cabarets. When he returned to Europe (1976/7) he began performing on the streets, linking up with other artists, such as funambulist Philippe Petit. A key moment came when, during one street show, there was a nearby minor accident between a car and a bicycle which drew attention away from his finale routine (see p. 43). Following this he became increasingly interested in recreating the tensions of real life; for example, he arranged for himself to be knocked down by a car as a way of gathering a crowd for his show.

In 1982/3 he was offered public funding for the first time by a clown festival in Barcelona; he created a circus show replacing performing animals with bulldozers and JCBs (this pre-dated the use of motorcycles by Archaos). Gradually he adapted his main act by using techniques, such as slapstick, fire-eating and other 'fakir' stunts, as a vehicle for ideas, which were usually specific to the cultural context of each event.[13] These justifications became a larger feature of his shows and were increasingly serious in intent, so that some of his more recent productions (e.g. *Revelacion* 2005–6; *Utopia* 2009) are more like a lecture interspersed with illustrative physical routines. Alongside this development, he has staged 'one-off' enactments specific to issues arising from current events, increasingly often with a political dimension. He has been described as being 'to Spain what Michael Moore is to the U.S.'[14] The Big Brother action (2000) and the *Bassibus* (from 2004) fall into this category. The *Bassibus* is based on tourist coach tours, a familiar sight in Madrid, and therefore he includes uniformed hostesses, duty-free offers and sing-along music. However, instead of visiting cathedrals and monuments, it takes its occupants to sites of corruption and scandal. Alongside these politically overt performances he has also created more playful, interactive work such as using scores of spectators to launch a vast inflatable rubber duck (2010–11).[15] He has won numerous theatre and comedy awards in Europe, Canada, Chile and the USA.[16] He has performed extensively on Italian and Spanish TV.[17] He has been regarded as the pre-eminent solo performer at European outdoor theatre festivals and has pulled off an impressive number of hoaxes and large-scale events.[18]

Bassi is of particular interest in this area of work both because he integrates popular entertainment with political action, and also because, unusually in circus and street theatre, he is exceptionally articulate about his work. Because he has made a long journey through a wide variety of performance and cultural contexts, he is more able to view his work self-critically than similar artists. Being self-taught through practical experimentation and personal research he has been less directly influenced by recent developments in academic cultural theory.

Bassi challenges himself and others through risk-taking. He uses unconventional, non-linear means, such as humour, absurd juxtapositions and game-changing. He creates some work that is simply entertaining and some that is serious, even didactic. The focus of his work is with direct, inter-personal relationships, often leading others into risk activities. Therefore, he works in live performance, often in the relatively intimate context of a theatre, so that he can mingle, touch, intimidate or otherwise use volunteers, fluidly adapting to and improvising with individuals and integrating specific local/contemporary issues. He uses his corporeality as a site of ambiguity, alternating dignity and physical skill with degradations such as undressing and being spray-painted.

Personal risk, popularity and power

Risk underpins all forms of edge. Personal risk is, in some ways, the most obvious and easiest to examine. All the provocateurs under discussion have been formed by early experiences of personal risk and, to a greater or lesser extent, risk provides the motor for all their provocative work. Bassi's background in the circus will have provided him with a strong grounding in risk-taking. 'My great grandfather balanced with one hand on the edge of the Tower of Pisa and he did this so people would be impressed and come and see the show in the evening'.[19] Juggling, whilst not carrying the risk of injury, nevertheless has a higher frequency for potential failure. The failure (dropping) is more clearly evident to spectators than in, say, acrobatic and aerial skills, in which mistakes can usually be concealed within the choreography. However, Bassi's departure from his family's circus suggests that risk of failure within this context was insufficient for him. Street performance provided both greater unpredictability and the intrusion of 'real life' into his performance, deflating his sense of the relative importance of his ludic skills.

> So I was doing this show in St Michel and had a big crowd of 300 people and, just when I was at my best juggling moment, a car hits a bicycle just next to where I am performing. It wasn't that anyone was injured, just that a bicycle ended up on the floor. And what happens? In three or four seconds all my crowd has gone looking at the car and the guy on the bicycle and I lose everybody. And apart from that I was losing money after working for twenty minutes getting a really big crowd. It was a revelation – real accidents are more entertaining than fine arts.[20]

Such real incidents force active responses by placing observers in a situation where they have to make decisions. This will not work if the actions are perceived as only play.[21] Like all street performers, Bassi discovered that what appears to be real tension is far more attractive than apparently simulated tension. Although modernity challenges easy differentiation between what is real and what is simulated,[22] the simplicity of the kind of the circle show clarifies the relationship between the two. As well as through daring to accomplish difficult feats, real tension can be achieved through daring use of language and daring interactions with the public. He went on to use the incident as the basis for attracting a crowd through invisible theatre.

> And then I thought if the same guy fell over every night at the same time the audiences would stick with me ... So we sort of rehearsed it out of people's view to get the car going at a decent speed without hurting me. So we do it as planned and, bump, I'm on the floor next to the wheel with my head sticking out and the person in the car points out of the window and he's looking at me and a crowd forms, as I expected, and then the guy says 'You've smashed the front of my car' and I say 'I'm sorry I didn't see you, I wasn't looking properly' and he says 'Well, you've scratched it now'. And it did start the show very well and the people loved it and I moved the people off to the area where the juggling equipment was and we went on from there.[23]

I have suggested that the attraction of risk is comparable to the 'lure of the edge of chaos'[24] because the increased activity there is 'a favored place to be'[25] for the evolution of a system. Evolution, in terms of the short span of a human life, is of course not a matter of biological transformation. As with biological evolution, there is nothing entirely new, and cultural traits, such as values and behaviours, may be 'inherited'; adaptation to changing environments is universal, not exceptional. So how fundamental an adaptation from these inherited traits may have occurred? The term 'evolution' might be appropriate when behaviours and attitudes are shed as a human life journey undergoes a fundamental shift from one phase to another. We would recognise this as a 'back to the drawing board' moment, or 'turning over a new leaf', often as a result of ruptures with the past, such as trauma, loss, breakdown or conversion. Many people do not undergo this kind of radical transformation because the framework they grow up in remains intact. Bassi, on the other hand, grew up amidst the collapse of the old circus way of life and some of the values it represented. His departure from Europe for work in Asian restaurants and nightclubs was certainly a major rupture, but perhaps not exceptional at his age and in that decade (the 1970s) which saw many young people adopt 'alternative' lifestyles. However, his transformation from clown–juggler to serious, political spokesperson is exceptional. So, can he be said to have evolved?

The bicycle incident appears to have caused a fundamental shift from one way of thinking about performance to another and occurred at a moment of high adrenalin, at the climax to his show, during a period when he was searching for another model after having rejected variety/circus entertainment. In terms of complexity theory, this period was marked by an internal turbulence that precedes a bifurcation event, oscillating between the certainties of the old circus values and the less structured, open play of street performers in the 1970s. In terms of physiological changes it may well be that repeated success in risk-taking developed the facility of hormone receptors in his brain, as Robertson suggested occurs in the 'Winner Effect'.[26] So, this moment can be seen as an 'edge of chaos' moment, both in terms of the phase he was in and also in terms of his emotional/hormonal state in the moment. As well as the immediate value of risk-taking, his longer-term creative evolution may also convey a sense of achievement, both in terms of self-esteem and also in the eyes of others, and this encourages a sense of personal power. The quantity of his work in the first decade of the twenty-first century suggests a dynamism, its concurrent range on the play continuum suggests a freedom of expression and fluidity of genre; this is not someone who is stuck in a rut, therefore suggesting that Bassi exemplifies an exceptional aptitude to 'evolve'.

An example of Bassi's bravado[27] was when he was invited to perform as part of the South Street Arts Festival in Philadelphia, USA (1988). After performing his indoor show there, he wondered why there were hardly any black members of the audience, since Philadelphia has a substantial black population. Not wanting to exclude that community, he stated his intention of going to the centre of the black neighbourhood in order to perform on the sidewalk. The organisers strongly advised him against this plan out of fear for his own safety but, when pressed, offered to drive him there. However, having off-loaded him, they refused to stay in the vicinity and said they would pick him up in an hour. The locals were surprised to see this portly, middle-aged white man in a suit amongst them and were more surprised when he began setting up a street show and even more surprised as he began his frenzied break-dancing routine. Their suspicion and derision turned into wonder and amusement at his attempt to do black dance, thereby making fun of his whiteness, and he gathered an enormous crowd. Suddenly, some men grabbed him from behind and proceeded to beat him up. He tried to protect himself as they kicked him onto the ground, destroying his props, breaking his ribs and pulping his face. The audience were hostile to these self-appointed guardians of the black ghetto but were too fearful to intervene, except for one woman who screamed at them that all he was trying to do was make them laugh; she cradled him on the ground and with the help of a few others possibly saved his life. In this example, it appears that his bravado in seeking higher levels of risk came up against the real-life tension that he had discovered with the bicycle incident. Despite these injuries, his refusal to be easily intimidated has empowered him when faced with death threats, either by right-wing Catholic extremists (as a reaction to *Revelacion*, described below, p. 62) or by 'the mafia' behind the tourism industry in the Canary Islands (as a reaction to one of his *Bassibus* expeditions) or by security guards shooting rifles into his encampment at the *Big Brother* action (see p. 54). Empowerment may also be derived from speaking or behaving in ways that are disapproved of, releasing from internalised prohibitions. The scope and force of these can be indicated by the experience of embarrassment. As Fiske points out: 'Embarrassment is a popular pleasure because it contains elements of both the dominant and subordinate, the disciplinary and the liberating, it occurs when the ideologically repressed clashes with the forces that repress it'.[28]

Bassi makes good use of this aspect of popular appeal in the climax to *La Vendetta* (2005). The show was introduced as a vendetta between himself and pigeons. After a series of acts linked by a serious theme of mind control, consumerism and globalisation, he removed his suit and tie, stripping down to his underpants, but retaining his spectacles. He then ritualistically poured litres of honey upon his head and rubbed it all over his bulky body. Taking a feather pillow, he entered a large vertical transparent tube, dramatically lit from above and with an industrial fan below. Tearing the pillow apart, he danced joyously to thrashing rock music while the fan blew the swirling feathers around him which then began to stick to his body. When he emerged he was covered in downy feathers looking like a fat chick, resolving the vendetta by being 'reborn' as a pigeon. From the reactions of the audience it was clear that this final sequence provoked astonishment at the combination of actions, laughter at the absurdity and shock at the disturbing level of transgression. Many commented after the show that it provoked feelings of wonder at the beauty of the image, admiration at the bravery and joy at the release from inhibition, particularly as he displayed no urgency to return to a less 'foolish' state. At the end of the particular performance that I witnessed, he returned to the microphone after taking applause, in order to outline subsequent events during his visit, talking seriously, as himself, whilst remaining in this foolish appearance. Without the mask of a performance persona he remained at ease, seemingly unconscious of his appearance. That suggested that he was unconcerned with how he, as himself, was perceived. By providing this image, he presents himself as an exemplar of free expression. As Carse puts it:

> Since culture is a poiesis, all of its participants are poietai – inventors, makers, artists, storytellers, mythologists. They are not, however, makers of actualities, but makers of possibilities. The creativity of culture has no outcome, no conclusion. It does not result in art works, artifacts, productions. Creativity is a continuity that engenders itself in others.[29,30]

In Carse's terms, Bassi presented an image of infinite play because its implications were far greater than the narrow, and ridiculous, justification concerning antagonism towards pigeons.

In the honey-and-feathers example there is a finely balanced interplay between three aspects of the popular as outlined in Chapter One: shared community, risk and empowerment. Communitas was experienced by the audience by means of the 'superior laugh' at the foolishness of his actions. Risk involves uncertainty and this can be exciting if it is also understood that it is not necessary to be in control through, for example, understanding what is being observed. Not understanding culture can have the effect of making people feel inadequate but, in the honey-and-feathers example, the audience, as a whole, appeared to find the general level of challenge acceptable, even though individually it would vary. They were predominantly white, middle-class aficionados of unusual performance. I knew that a good proportion of them had studied arts subjects in higher education. Like all good street performers, Bassi is acutely aware of the importance of targeting work at the likely audience; every performance, whether indoors or out, is adapted to suit local conditions, but the 'otherness' that he was manifesting could well have stimulated an aversive reaction if performed to a more general audience.

The third source of popular attraction is that of empowerment. I have indicated that a sense of empowerment may be gained in two ways: firstly from those with power being brought down. Bassi again:

> Any street artist knows, if you are really good, that when the policeman comes along and tells you [to stop/move on], you can make a joke of his authority without him really knowing it and then have all the audience who understand what is happening roaring with laughter because they know that you are touching his power and the guy maybe feels he is losing his power but doesn't know how to react because you are a step ahead of him. This is basically touching the energy that the authorities have given to this person as a policeman and you are weaving round them with your energy.[31]

Secondly empowerment may be derived from transgressing internalised hegemony or witnessing someone who does so. Paradoxically the 'foolishness' of the honey-and-feathers image may be empowering to observers because they witness a person who appears unafraid of appearing in this way even after the ludic justification had ceased. To be able to observe that a human can be so unconcerned with conventions, such as dignity, opens up cultural space for greater freedom of expression.

> The image of the liberated human psyche can be communicated by art not necessarily through literal representation of the utopian dream, as in socialist realist work, but in the emotions such work is able to elicit … This is why at times art is perceived as subversive, not simply because it presents a world that appears immoral or licentious, as is frequently thought, but because it reminds people of what has been buried – desires their deepest selves dream but cannot manifest within the existing system.[32]

In this example, Bassi may be compared with those participants in choral work who are more passionate in their expression and thus tend to attract attention. These participants instinctively feel the direction the group wishes to take and by doing so unreservedly, in its fullest expression, they cannot help but have greater influence and thereby encourage the group. By doing so, they take up the role of 'spokesperson' for the group, the one who is better able to articulate the desires of the group. I shall return to this theme in the following section. However, the audience experienced Bassi's relish of the honey-and-feathers activity at the same time as they experienced the communitas of the 'superior laugh' at his expense. The superior laugh is simultaneously subverted because Bassi is demonstrating that the audience's norms are also a limitation. His anarchic behaviour suggested that being closer to the edge of chaos is more enjoyable than 'normal' behaviour. There is also an implication that witnessing the experience is a poor, second-hand substitution for being free enough to act in this way. Because the chaotic behaviour is associated with empowerment, the structuring tendencies implied by the superior laugh are challenged. So there is a complex play with ordering and dis-ordering, affirming and challenging, occurring simultaneously. This rich complexity potentially enables a wide range of interpretations. As Fiske states: 'By "showing" rather than "telling", by sketching rather than drawing completely, popular texts open themselves up to a variety of social relevances'.[33] In this example, I heard a range of reactions, from treating it as a clown show to seeing it as a visual spectacle or as a piece of avant-garde theatre, depending on the points of reference of the viewer. Leaving the viewer more scope for interpretation is obviously more empowering than the more didactic approach of the lecture format used in *Revelacion*.

So by means of risk-taking Bassi gains power in two ways; he gains popularity and creates for himself greater freedom of action. In his case, there are at least two outcomes from this acquirement of power. The first is that he is able to use it to challenge dominant power; this has the potential to further raise the level of bravado and also address his sense of social injustice. The second is that he could inspire others to take risks, drawing them into activities in which their own limits are expanded. The two outcomes are not mutually exclusive but they do provide different emphases in different aspects of his work that I will explore in the following sections. His solo shows *Utopia* and *Revelacion* have a David and Goliath quality, challenging dominant power in a contest in which both sides seek supremacy, which is therefore symmetrical and has an emphasis on structure.

Another example, from a *Bassibus* expedition, illustrates the way he combines this challenge with the frisson of a direct personal interface. It also demonstrates the way his sense of personal freedom and power is useful in refusing to be intimidated by authorities.

> The Vice-President [of Spain] ... was making his last week's political campaigns for the elections outside and we turned up, four hundred people. On board these buses we had all this stage equipment, like big generators with enormous amplification, and we set it up on the buses. We circled round where he was so we were more massive than their amplification and we put on the words that he had used the year before saying 'I can assure the Spanish people that there will be weapons of mass destruction in Iraq and that it's a legitimate war' and we put these words on perfectly clear, drowning out his own words and so all the TV cameras, who were filming,

turned on us and he got so angry he came down, surrounded by body-guards and pushed up towards me yelling, red in the face ... It had got to him in an unexpected way and he got angry and he pushed so hard that my girlfriend, Lara, fell; she was dressed as an air stewardess with the *Bassibus* and he pushed up and in front of the cameras. He saw that hitting a woman was not a very good image for a Vice-President so he picked her up and said: 'Are you OK?' and she said 'Oh yes, we are always OK on the *Bassibus*'. And I felt we had real power at that time. And then all of a sudden, they started to push, all these people, security guards, coming up behind and kicking me. I had six stewardesses for that trip; Lara said 'Get round', and they all come and linked arms, all these blue uniforms in front of the cameras and it was a surrealistic moment when the real power, talking about life and death and wars, gets confronted with a street performance and with the techniques we have learned about; how to handle a crowd and how to determine the energies and how to confront direct aggression.[34]

The advocacy of risk-taking also de-structures and destabilises; its chaotic quality is both an advantage in terms of confusing those he challenges, but also, occasionally, a disadvantage as will be seen in the next section on the *Big Brother* intervention. It means that there is a continuous intermingling of the consistency and structural organisation necessary for confrontation with the fluidity and rule-breaking of play. This is not only a matter of means but also of attitude, so that actions are motivated by both a serious moral intention and also a sense of having fun; the game is taken seriously and the intention is de-stressed by the levity of play. The constant delicate shifting of how much weight is given to either, at any moment, provides the image of the fulcrum.

'Pure' infinite play has the potential to be nihilistic and cynical, but playfulness, because of its interactivity, has an important role in the serious business of nurturing ethical awareness. Ethics concerns relationships, and provocation reveals and explores the nature of relationships. An attitude of playfulness means that expressions of ethical values are never exempt from challenge by means of ridicule. Through provocation any serious statement can be ridiculed immediately, not because of the statement itself, but for the certitude with which it is made. Provocation is a form of feedback that constantly refreshes and refines values by challenging their application in respect of unfolding situations; fluidity is privileged over consistency. However, the choices Bassi makes are inevitably determined by his own values, which will tend towards consistency. This kind of work cannot be accomplished without some strong sense of self-confidence. That is to say, he has a sense of some independence from norms established by others.

The phenomenon of 'political correctness' presents a problem for the playfully serious provocateurs like Bassi. Not because they dispute, for example, the importance of language in the formation/maintenance of ideology, but because there is often an imposition of restrictive orthodoxy associated with it that discourages independence of thought in relation to the limits of acceptability.

One of his grandfathers was an anarchist and the theme of self-responsible freedom of action runs throughout all his work. The freedom demonstrated is from restrictions imposed by others; but also he is very conscious of the restrictions he imposes on himself. He sets his own rules according to a value system that he has formulated during a process of self-tuition. So, his use of language is informed by general principles of respect and sensitivity. 'You have to have a safeguard and that is you have to love people and, it's a very general thing, but I want to do something positive'.[35] Hence, he takes care to avoid making fun of the less powerful, isolated outsiders; for example, he criticised Sacha Baron Cohen for ridiculing the marginalised and foreign in his choice of main characters. I will explore this subject more fully in the next chapter.

Power negotiations in the *Big Brother* intervention

Having examined the empowering effects of personal risk-taking, this section looks at how Bassi leads others into situations and actions in which they may have the same kind of empowerment. This is a form of incitement that is exciting, attractive and positive. I focus on his intervention into the production of the first *Big Brother* series in Spain (2000), considering the incident in terms of what Bassi terms 'piggy-backing' on dominant culture and the use of the spectacle of contest to activate those not directly involved. It is evident that, in liberal democracies, the collective voice of large numbers of people cannot be easily ignored by dominant forces so how can this expression be stimulated? The *Big Brother* intervention produced a contest with dominant power and had some potentially very serious consequences but had a strong emphasis on open play. Since incitement is de-structuring, in the sense that it is a release from social norms, the issue of controlling the extent of group behaviour becomes important. This requires the application of structure. In turn, this raises issues of his ambivalent relationships with groups as both co-operator and leader.

Incitement

As stated above, risk is one of the three aspects of the popular and it relates to the 'edge of chaos'. It is clear from Bassi's statements that he believes that moving people from stasis towards chaos is beneficial for them and may be more important than any stated purpose of a particular event.

> I want to ... really excite people and it's this feeling that I communicate, the excitement, and they decide if they want to know more about the poetry or the politics; ... that's their business. Although I have done, and will do, political events, to be really sincere, even when I use politics I use it to obtain this magic moment rather than to solve world problems or to change political minds ... If you show the person the possibility to feel that he can stand up for himself ... he doesn't want to be a sheep, always boring. I don't know where I stand politically, I know where I stand when

I find a passionate person. And [if] I find this passionate person is really exciting to be next to, I tend to agree with them wherever they are.[36]

This seems to suggest that he wants to provide audiences with the adrenalin-filled experiences that he, as a performer, enjoys. He says that the task of the provocative performer is to find out:

> how to surprise, to get a person to come out of their normal life, to bring a person into another field, where this person is more receptive because he's been surprised, because he's been taken off guard. Then it's all up to you: you can do what you like with him. You can talk about beauty, you can dance, sing, but it's this moment, this instant of getting attention.[37]

In terms of the provocative process that I have outlined (p. 25), this can be seen as the initiating action. It leads spectators into a state of attention and uncertainty, in which they may become active in finding order in the confusion.

> Leo Bassi knows how to goad people, get under their skin. The Electrical Union of France have a big festival down near Bordeaux – political stalls, Cuban Solidarity, etc. There are thousands of them, all of the one union. Ten years ago Bassi came on as the EU Minister for privatisation and gives them this whole speech about how the electrical industry is going to be privatised; people were dumbfounded and shouting at him ... Then he sets up his own stall and people are shouting at him and then he appears on this little motorbike trying to kill people and they can't make him out. They don't know what he is, just this madman; the people were really irate. There was this reality shift but done straight. You've got to make people believe you are that thing.[38]

On another occasion he was invited to perform at a rock festival where he played on the scarcity of space for tents. He set up a fence around an area he claimed as his own and taunted the festival-goers to the extent that they rioted and tore down the barrier.

> Theatre cannot exist if it is not provocative; it makes the difference between something that is boring or something that is not boring. It can be provocative in that it makes you think or in that you have to dodge something that is thrown at you.[39]

Despite the potential for ensuing violence in these examples, Bassi does not suggest that he considers violent actions either justified or effective. Indeed, as was shown in the confrontation with the Vice-President, and is borne out in the *Big Brother* and *Revelacion* events below, stimulating a violent reaction from his opponents may be useful to him in a wider political contest with the perpetrator.

Big Brother *description*

Bassi was incensed when the reality TV show, *Big Brother*, first appeared in Spain. *Big Brother* seemed objectionable to him because it treated humans like laboratory animals, normalising a model of control from an invisible and unchallengeable centre, using surveillance as entertainment. It appeared to mutate the villainous oppression of Orwell's vision into a paternalistic benevolence. The following description of this event relies entirely on Bassi's own description because, for reasons that will be made clear, press and media coverage of it was suppressed.

He discovered that the programme was being filmed at a house in an isolated rural location and rented fields adjacent to it from a sympathetic farmer. He then invited others into this game with dominant powers.

> I switched round my internet page to saying 'Camping site near Big Brother stars, Big Brother Convention' and all of a sudden loads of people started to show up and I put in chemical toilets, tents, a press room and I put up an enormous scaffolding with steps so you could see Big Brother directly and follow it live. And in a few days it became an incredible story, more and more people coming, and we had flamenco people playing on the scaffolding all the way through the night and we were talking to the people in the show and then after two days they stopped the people in the show from going outside and they were confined so they wouldn't be able to interact with us because it was fucking up the show. It was no longer isolated ... They began to hire more and more security guards. Then they built an enormous scaffolding and put tarpaulins on it so that we couldn't look over, because they couldn't send us away; so we moved our scaffolding and they built another part and then we started building higher above – it was incredible. So the story went on and I was on the front page of the newspaper – 'There was a big Leo Bassi assault on the *Big Brother*' – and now we had 24-hour press coverage.[40]

As is clear from the popular interest in sport, the spectacle of contest has wide popular appeal and draws people into partisanship. As such, it is useful to provocateurs that aim to activate people. The *Big Brother* action had two phases of contest: one on the ground with the production company and its security guards, and the second with the wider media organisations over the reporting of the events. The first phase was like a game with clearly defined, overt rules with each side pushing the boundaries of those rules. A sense of shared community is likely to have developed among Bassi's supporters by camping together in a remote mountainous region for some weeks and by being defined in opposition to an increasing number of security guards and visits from the police.

In this example, Bassi had selected an issue that is unlikely to have been taken up by political activists. It does not concern economic iniquity or matters of war and peace but power negotiations in culture. As Fiske says it is 'Not about "how to change the world" but rather in what ways should one resist or yield to its demands in order to make life bearable in order to preserve some sense of identity'.[41] He also suggests that popular culture 'attempts to enlarge the space within which bottom-up power has to operate'.[42] He goes on to indicate that an aspect of popular culture is the way that it takes commercially driven culture and reuses it for its own ends. This correlates with Bassi's notion of 'piggy-backing' on whatever is of wide current interest. Of this event he said: 'I have to be there, I have to show the people that this is all fake and to call their bluff in one way or another and by that to piggy-back on the situation and make the people laugh by pin-pointing something'. Fiske provides a parallel terminology:

> Excorporation is the process by which the subordinate make their own culture out of the resources and commodities provided by the dominant system, and this is central to popular culture, for in an industrial society the only resources from which the subordinate can make their own subcultures are those provided by the system that subordinates them.[43]

As in a game of sport, the experience of shared community was focussed into one climactic moment, shared by Bassi's supporters, including his family, colleagues, lawyers and journalists.

> Then it comes to the crunch; there was only a few people left in the house, a big day coming up, whether they would send one guy out or another guy out. It was like the whole of Spain was waiting to find out the final decision who was going to be evicted ... I had lawyers with me and whatever I do I have a lawyer already on hand ... And then comes all my family to help and they're all circus people and my brother-in-law ... has these big sea horns from ships, ex-Soviet army horns from the Polish navy base ... And the lawyers are all going like, you know, 'Yeah!'. We had journalists there and we had at that time eighty, ninety people helping us ... everyone was running about preparing the sirens and then ... the announcer said 'Ladies and Gentlemen the winner is ... the people being evicted is ...' and we put it all on: BLEAHRRRRR!!!!! And they were just like this. All the people, eighty people in the cabin and outside the park, we were all jumping with hands on their ears. And they couldn't hear anything and then we stopped and on the TV they said 'I think we have some problems with the microphones, OK, anyway the winner is ...' BLEAHRRRRR!!!!! And they made out it was from the studios, not from outside, and we were so happy ... All the kids who had helped me and had done this on a voluntary basis, I was providing food for them but they were working for free ... They were all going to town, there was a disco and so most helpers went off to the party.[44]

It is clear from this description that the shared experience of fun, at this moment, predominated over ideological concerns.

The example demonstrates similarities of pattern to those observed in choral work. There is symmetry of mutual escalation as each side built up the height and numbers of supporters. On Bassi's side, although the activities were more varied than in choral work, the group coheres around the achievement of a single climactic moment. This is similar to the symmetrical build-up produced by the inward facing circle, the group incites itself. Because this moment is unsurpassable it is followed by a period of disintegration and dissipation, similar to that within choral work. Both these examples suggest a pattern of 'natural' structure formation and disintegration.

However, the producers continued to escalate the level of force from their side even though Bassi's supporters were relaxing and dissipating after the end of their 'game'.

> at one or two o'clock in the morning, I went to the tent to sleep. Then the most incredible thing – stones falling on the tent, then big stones and then I hear firing air rifles and I look out and it was a scene from the war – all these private guards with dogs and rifles, maybe a line of ten, fifteen people with guns firing on us. I had lighting rigged up and they pulled down all the electrical equipment because I had loudspeakers, amplifiers and microphones and they ripped the whole tent area. It's the first time and only time I have felt real terror in Spain. For a few hours I didn't move from my tent, thinking hopefully they don't know there is someone there and if I go out there they'll shoot me and so I'm there in a situation that reminded me of the Civil War.[45]

The second phase appeared to be less symmetrical because the rules and boundaries were not clear to Bassi. A film crew from a national television station had been sent to cover events from Bassi's side of the fence, but was suddenly withdrawn prior to the siren blast. Control of the reporting was not within Bassi's domain. The CNN cameraman, sent to film on Bassi's side, told him:

> Our company is with the company that makes *Big Brother* and I think this company won't want to have any more news about what happened ... You have got beyond your depth in this situation ... by wreaking havoc with this system, you were putting the company half a million [euros] in jeopardy, I don't know how many millions, and it's not a joke any more. They will defend themselves using anything.[46]

Privileged knowledge began to tip the balance of power in favour of the dominant. Bassi and his followers had expected to use the broadcast to create a nationwide 'splash' but were disappointed:

> The newspaper, *El Pais*, sent me a journalist who was very sympathetic and took pictures and listened to all I had to say and the next day I looked in the newspaper for the article and it didn't come out ... In fact, a long

time afterwards, after the story had gone stale, a little article came out ...
and the way it came out I was like a loser not accepting what had happened
to him, etc. ... And for about a year later I was facing people in the street,
saying 'All this big thing and you go there and why was it? You were paid
to go away?' ... It was very negative for me because it was the first time
I had moved so far and so many fans; I had got ten, twelve thousand hits
on my internet page. Thousands of people, during the week it happened,
were interested and wanted to give their help and feeling how much
energy you could tap into but, at the same time, disappointing everybody
because the real information didn't come out and: 'He got his publicity
and he let everybody down.'[47]

Bassi's intervention can be seen as open play in that, despite its ideological
starting point, there was clearly an emphasis on having fun. Apart from creating
a 'splash' to publicise his objections there was no clear objective beyond that.
The 'piggy-backing' on the huge public interest in the TV series suggests that
he was simply exploring the limits of freedom of action. His ability to impro-
vise and adapt to the unfolding situation suggests the fluidity of open play as
he adapted to different competitive games being played: logistical, legal, publicity and ludic. However, each of these games required organisation. He, too,
was applying structure. The production company, the security guards and the
police were clearly surprised and wrong-footed by Bassi's organisational abilities.
The ludic open-playing nature of Bassi's intervention masked his logistical
expertise and legal preparation. However, to the wider world, *Big Brother* was a
hugely popular ludic entertainment and so, with his ideological objections and
structural abilities, he could be presented as a spoilsport[48] out of step with the
public mood, by companies who aim to mask their self-serving commercial
interest. The first phase of contest can be considered as a victory for Bassi in
that he succeeded in disrupting the broadcast, but the publicity contest can be
considered as a victory for the commercial networks.

So clearly in this example there is a complexity of relationships mixing open
and closed play, the ludic and the ideological, on both sides. Just as Bassi had a
loose temporary coalition of journalists, lawyers, circus artists, the farmer and
volunteer 'kids', the producers had formal agreements with the security guards
and other media organisations.

I remember these guards were all talking on walkie-talkies and they were
speaking back to the base. They hadn't done this on their own initiative,
they were told to do this by the security company who was involved. And
for the security company to do something like this, to risk their contract
and reputation ... the real boss behind them had given them the go-ahead
and so it was real people with real responsibilities in the TV company who
had been so pissed off by me, who had felt that I was doing this intelli-
gently and organised it in my way to not get kicked out by the police, to
have my lawyers to cover me. So probably in some meeting somewhere:

'OK, what do we do? We'll frighten the shit out of him and we'll frighten the owner of the land, we'll destroy'. It was a real commando, secret service operation.[49]

It also appears that the local police were sympathetic to the producers,[50] suggesting some sharing of ideology between different groups. This is an example of 'clustering' of different but overlapping interests, a subject I will return to in the next section. The escalation of force from this cluster out-matched Bassi's cluster, because he did not feel he was in a position to prevent his loose coalition dissipating at the moment they needed to be there to prevent or witness the attack on the camp. This raises the question of applying structure and controls to a group, shifting the relationship from co-operator to leader. I will now discuss controls as a way to approach the ambivalent and often contradictory relationship between leader and a group.

Controls and adaptability

On occasion, participants may abandon all self-control if they feel they have been released from them by permission. Bassi is very aware of the dangers of uncontrolled anarchy when controls are lifted. He described organising a cream-pie fight in a town square in Germany (1986). He prepared 5000 cream pies and a 20m by 20m ring surrounded by grandstands seating 2000 spectators. Groups of children put their names down days in advance in order to take part and helpers were dressed as chefs, who handed out plates of cream pies to contestants who were organised into teams. The bouts were intended to last three minutes at a time, with a winner being declared.

> It worked in the beginning ... everybody got very excited and then I stepped out of the ring to talk to the audience and in two seconds everybody left [their seats] and we had hundreds of people. We had like a kitchen with cooks preparing, and it was aesthetically well organised and then the audience started running and then people began to fall, kids started to cry, people started to run in the streets, kids went so wild hunting down people in the streets, people who had nothing to do with the cream-pie fight ... We were lucky that nothing serious happened.[51]

So, inducing spectators to break free of their usual limitations may ultimately lead to an outbreak of violence. So how is the release to be managed? The unpredictability of outcome that is inherent in provocative actions means that there must be careful preparation and controls placed on the proceedings. Levels of risk are factored in by Bassi according to the level of unpredictability and how high the stakes are. It may not be clear at the outset how high the stakes will be raised. For example, in the *Big Brother* action the stakes were raised on both sides; the ships horns and guns could not have been foreseen by either side.

During the period of the *Bassibus* expeditions he increased the level of controls over his events because of the higher stakes involved. At the tomb of Franco, Bassi had to make full use of his crowd control techniques, acquired through street performance, to calm the excitement of some of the *Bassibus* participants who were ready to start 'smashing the place up'.[52] At other times right-wing infiltrators have attacked property in order that the *Bassibus* events can be portrayed as hooliganism. Hence, identity cards are inspected by members of his team prior to the expeditions. Similarly Bassi is accompanied by lawyers, who advise him on the legality of particular operations. For example, during a *Bassibus* invasion of a golf course to re-establish public access, he was advised it was legal to enter the property but not to touch the fence, so they prepared a system of ladders and platforms to cross over. The other method of control is media management. He has described how he will discuss camera angles with journalists prior to an event so that he can manoeuvre an unfolding situation towards satisfying their requirements. His relationship with the media has gradually shifted since the *Big Brother* action to become less dominant–submissive and more equal. He excludes some reporters and works on a collaborative basis with those whom he selects.

As well as the structuring strategy of limiting potential adverse consequences through the application of controls, there is the open-playing strategy of adaptability. Carse makes the distinction between the two approaches: 'To be prepared *against* surprise is to be trained. To be prepared *for* surprise is to be educated' (his emphasis).[53] Bassi's ability to gauge the limitations of a particular audience and adapt to them had been developed through his experience of street theatre, in which the crowd is never fixed or totally committed. Street performers need to think on their feet, improvising with individuals and adapting to make use of the physical environment. If they are clever, they are not only responsive to site-specifics but can incorporate themes that are significant to a particular audience (another form of 'piggy-backing'). The *Big Brother* intervention is an example of this ability to be responsive to a situation. Within two weeks Bassi created an outdoor festival with all the necessary facilities and legal safeguards and then adapted to the unfolding situation with the security guards and the press. Adaptability is effective in dealing with central institutions that have a slower response because of their size and their tendency to categorise and prioritise in more systematic ways than erratic artists.

So, because Bassi wants to invite others into risky situations, he must provide management in order to prevent adverse consequences backfiring on him or the group he leads. This opens up questions about his relationship with the groups he works with: whether he speaks with them or at them, how much he controls them or is in equal cooperation with them. Risk-takers are attractive because they seem more free of fear than others, and the resulting charisma establishes them as a centre. 'If a performer looks like they don't care about the audience it is attractive because it seems they have no fear or don't have to respond to the public'.[54] In considering this question it is useful to review Bassi's relationship with his team as symptomatic of his relationship with the wider circle of his supporters. These may number from hundreds who actively participate in some way, to thousands who may attend his live performances, to the millions who are aware of his work by means of its coverage on TV. Bassi at various times plays the role of leader, exemplar, guide (both physically and ideologically), party host, entertainer, teacher and orator. By establishing himself as a leader he places others in the complementary relationship of follower;[55] the more he leads the more they are reduced to following. The passivity and delegation of responsibility implied in the role of the follower conflicts with the provocateur's aim of stimulating debate and activism, with their open-ended outcomes, which is a form of privileging fluidity over consistency. Like Banksy, Bassi sees himself as only different from others in the sense that he is the one who dares to speak out and that by doing so he is only releasing others from the fear of intimidation, thereby allowing them more freedom to be active. Bassi's *Revelacion* can be seen as voicing the opinions of what he terms 'isolated individuals' who are intimidated by the dominance of the Catholic Church. The question, therefore, is whether Bassi encourages others to become active and autonomous or whether, despite his intention, his manner encourages others to defer to him. We can examine this question in some detail by referring to a project he undertook in Bristol in 2005 called *Radical Hits*.

He was invited by street performance group Desperate Men and other professional street performers to lead sessions that would culminate in a public performance after five days. All of the group (approximately twelve) were known to each other and most had worked together professionally prior to the project and, therefore, shared a culture which was, in effect, a loose, informal centre in itself. Bassi's position as both outsider to this centre and leader of the project resulted in problematic relationships as the experienced autonomists, used to being leaders themselves, felt uncomfortable in a submissive role. They were also used to a director–performer relationship that was more equal and cooperative than is common in the rest of Europe. Bassi, however, felt his job was to lead, teach and, to some extent, challenge what he perceived as a lack of engagement with politics. Despite attempting to draw out ideas and concerns from each member of the group during the week, he had already established the subject of the culminating event without consultation with the rest of the group. Partly because prior commitments prevented attendance when the timing of the event changed, but also partly because the group began to feel that their expectations and performing skills were not given due consideration, most of the participants dropped out of the project. Bassi cancelled the workshop, inviting those who remained to join him in proceeding with the plan, which was a celebratory open-decked bus tour through the city centre, honouring Walter Wolfgang who had famously heckled at the Labour Party Conference, six months earlier.

This example demonstrates the result of Bassi being without a critical mass of support; he spoke down to the group, rather than on behalf of them. This indicates the importance of context and suggests that, contrary to expectations, even though a position of outsider may facilitate a difference of perspective, it may also decrease the effectiveness of a challenge. The strongest provocation was towards the stasis of practice of the group rather than towards the central cluster of institutions. As such, it was effective in activating the participants, raising questions about the purpose of street performance, as well as raising much passionate indignation. Bassi was more interested in connecting with the wider community of left-wing dissenters, those who supported Wolfgang, than in reinforcing the status of the city's counter-cultural performance community. On the one hand, he was attempting to foster a wider communitas of ideology whilst simultaneously challenging a narrower communitas of norms. His self-seriousness, perhaps caused by a defensive response, disconnected him from the group. The consistency of his own aims and means reduced his ability to adapt to those of the group.

In this instance, there appears to have been a mismatch of expectations: Bassi may have been seeking a relationship with the team similar to that in choral work. In that activity, developments occur when there is no instructor. Passionate members of the group attract attention and thus can have more influence, but they continually check whether each of their small initiatives has been registered and accepted by being mirrored. The members retain more autonomy and are thus activated. The *Radical Hits* relationship was equivalent in choral work to a member being outside the group instructing them, which would defeat the object.

> The term 'cooperation', which is sometimes used as the opposite of 'competition', covers a wide variety of patterns, some of them symmetrical and others complementary, some bi-polar and others in which the cooperating individuals are chiefly orientated to some personal or impersonal goal.[56]

In the *Radical Hits* situation he may have expected that the shared ideology would be accompanied by shared norms. They appear to have expected him to check whether his suggestions had been registered and accepted. Because of the gap in norms of practice[57] a leader–follower relationship ensued. In the *Bassibus* situations mentioned above, Bassi had to apply management controls to prevent injury or arrest so the need for leadership was clear, but in the *Big Brother* episode the situation was more ambivalent. The fact that supporters felt 'let down' suggests that they expected him to deliver a result for them; they had deferred responsibility to him. So Bassi's desire to activate others through inviting them into risky situations may contain a contradiction. Carse uses the phrase: 'Whoever *must* play cannot *play*' (his emphasis).[58] This could usefully be adapted to: 'Whoever is told how to be autonomous cannot be autonomous'.

In other contexts, Bassi seems much more of a team player. His background in circus provided him with a sense of community that extended beyond his family's company. Circus professionals have traditionally considered each other as part of one international 'family', with whom they operate by means of an economy of favours and barter, even between commercially competitive companies. On top of this, his grandfather's influence, as a socialist internationalist, would have nurtured a sense of connection which would have extended to workers outside the circus community. Bassi continues to enjoy a sense of solidarity with circus performers, comedians and activists around the world. He received an award from the Russian clown company, Licidei, in 2007, and has long-standing working relationships with international comedians such as Jango Edwards, Teatro de Anonimo clown company in Brazil, as well activists across Europe, in Palestine, Brazil and the USA, including a woman in India who works on micro-credits. Although he refrains from becoming a part of the official Spanish political left, he is not concerned with competing against other performers or activists and is increasingly interested in cooperating in alliances with others in the eco-socialist movement. Therefore, Bassi's work demonstrates both speaking on behalf of communities as well as speaking down to them and the kind of relationship is determined by the context in which he operates.

As well as being determined by the context, the distinctions between leader and co-operator are defined by the degree to which the provocateur takes themselves seriously. Bassi is in the unique position of creating work that spans a wide range on the play continuum, from the playfulness of a popular entertainer to the seriousness of a political activist. Because he covers this range it is possible to see whether and how he can make serious points whilst avoiding the dangers of becoming a new authority himself. One of the keys to unlocking these questions is whether the mockery has a single direction towards one opposing target or is multi-directional, targeting *all* seriousness, including that of the instigator. Seriousness suggests a privileged knowledge of 'the truth', an elevation of one perspective over many others and, therefore, indicates a dominant–submissive relationship. The problem for provocateurs aiming to be ethical players is to avoid this kind of relationship whilst also not compromising their desire to make serious points. How much they consider this an issue is indicated by the amount of self-deprecation and self-parody they employ. By making fun of their own position, they indicate their awareness of how they must appear to outsiders and suggest it is possible to ridicule the speaker whilst avoiding ridiculing the statement. They also indicate that their perspective is only one of many, avoiding a dominant–submissive relationship.

> the second important trait of the people's festive laughter; that it is also directed at those who laugh. The people do not exclude themselves ... They, too are incomplete, they also die and are revived and renewed. This is one of the essential differences of the people's festive laughter from the pure satire of modern times. The satirist whose laughter is negative places himself above the object of his mockery.[59]

How seriously does Bassi take himself? Are there signs of self-mockery, which would suggest that he can laugh at his aspiration to be a major player in the transformation of society? In the final section I will cite examples of self-mockery but, in general, he does not make fun of himself as much as, say, Banksy does. This may be because, as a person who presents himself as a clown so frequently, he may not feel it is necessary to self-deprecate. It also may not be obvious how a clown can self-deprecate.

So, the shift between controls and adaptability, and between leading and activating, are both forms of the dynamic between structure and fluidity. The fine adjustment between the two is like straddling a see-saw, the emphasis on one side or the other is finely adjusted according to changes in the context. This aspect of the edge as a fulcrum conveys advantages and disadvantages to the provocateur. On the one hand Bassi's privileging of fluidity over consistency enables him to surprise and confuse an organisation with far greater power. On the other hand the fluidity means that he cannot sustain this advantage. As Carse indicates, infinite plays are vulnerable when faced with finite players because they do not have hard outcomes.[60] For Bassi, the outcome of the *Big Brother* intervention was that he lost work opportunities with TV companies and he lost friends. He took risks and paid a price for doing so. In the next section I will cover a situation in which the risks were far more serious – his life was threatened.

Centres and their reaction to *Revelacion*

In this section I will develop the themes of incitement, enlarging personal freedoms and contesting with dominant power by examining an example where Bassi's emphasis is more on leading through didactic oration rather than directly activating others. Rather than emphasising the upward movement of his supporters, it is more concerned with the descent of the dominant. The example differs from the *Vendetta* or *Big Brother* examples in that Bassi promotes an ideological standpoint, emphasising a serious purpose rather than the playful qualities. Therefore, it privileges 'communitas of ideology' over the fluid ephemerality of shared experience.

Bassi's theatre show *Revelacion* (2005–7) targeted monotheistic religions, challenging the basis of their dominance over their host societies. He drew attention to the similarities between the historically antagonistic religions of Judaism, Christianity and Islam and showed how these shared a common root in previous belief systems. For example, he referred to evidence showing that many important Christian churches were built on sites of pagan worship and how the date of Christmas had been set to fit in with the Celtic midwinter festival. Like many of Bassi's shows it interwove serious monologue with foot juggling and comic sketches, including one in which he is dressed as the Pope dancing to rock music, in front of a huge cross lit up by flashing disco lights. Despite the playful form he made it clear that he intended to promote one idea and confront another. 'I made this show as a celebration, a glorification of humanistic, agnostic and atheist thinking, debunking the bible and going against what I think is a whole load of bullshit and hypocrisy'.[61] Unlike the finale to *Vendetta*, there was less ambivalence over meaning: it was intended to be interpreted in one way. The head-on attack has similarities to the *Big Brother* confrontation, but differs in that, in *Revelacion*, he was a single voice rather than the leading representative of what he described as a '*Big Brother* festival'. The single voice and the un-ambivalent negative message differentiate it from his more carnivalesque work. The lack of ambivalence in the attack stimulated a counter-attack. The singularity of his voice focussed the counter-attack onto a narrow target: himself.

The show provoked outrage in conservative sections of the Spanish Catholic community. Priests participated in demonstrations against the show.[62] In his sermon on the 12 March 2006, the Archbishop of Toledo, Antonio Cañizares called the show 'blasphemous, anti-Christian and a true insult to the Church'.[63] Conservative local politicians demonstrated allegiance to the church by cutting funds to the theatre festival in an attempt to prevent performances of Bassi's show.

> An immediate consequence of the statements of Cañizares was, inter alia, that the City of Toledo, PP,[64] withdrew the grant to the T+T Festival programme. Leo Bassi, was finally enabled to perform last night through a loan from local unions CCOO and UGT.[65] This unique representation, scheduled for ten o'clock last night, had to be delayed half an hour because a dozen ultras[66] gathered at the gates of the premises to try to prevent representation. Their cries were answered by those who wanted to enter the theatre. The voices of 'Inquisition!' and 'Freedom of expression!' crossed … as the tension grew a young woman was hit by the ultras and had to be taken to the hospital with a fractured skull.[67]

The controversy around issues of freedom of speech and causing offence was specifically played out in the courts and in the press, but more generally it tested the extent of the power of the Church to affect matters of state in modern Spain. The contest for public opinion intensified when Bassi first received death threats and subsequently an active bomb was placed in the theatre while two hundred people were watching his show at the Alfil Theatre, Madrid.[68] This act was preceded by separate protests from conservative Catholics alongside neo-Nazis[69] so that the Archbishop's remarks were linked by a chain of association with violent extremism. In 2011 a version of the show caused Bassi to be indicted for blasphemy.[70] By means of the sensational headlines and other debate in the media, Bassi was able to activate a much larger and wider section of the population than were present at the performances and ensuing demonstrations. When I asked him five years later what examples of his work would he consider as having changed the wider society he replied:

> The bomb in the theatre, because the atheist show brought home to many people in Spain that the Catholic Church is still linked to a fascist element in society and what is left of Catholic society most probably made people think that the Catholic Church seems more extremist. So maybe [they] have broken away, maybe I have made one million people break away.[71]

Centres

In the previous two sections I have focussed on Bassi's actions, but this section is more concerned with the reactions to his provocation. In order to discuss the repercussions it will be useful to think of those affected in terms of 'centres'. Comparisons can then be made between the dynamics operating at a large scale and those dynamics and patterns observed at the micro-scale of choral work. Centres have centres within them – formal or informal groupings and individuals within those groupings. It is only from a more distant perspective that what is shared can be identified. Thus 'Spain', for example, is both an environment composed of many sub-centres and also one centre amongst others in the wider European or global contexts, with its own national interests and culture. So, in considering the effects of Bassi's provocations, one must include the wider society; he is both within the society, but is also in a liminal position with regard to dominant Spanish culture. Although carrying personal risk for Bassi, this controversy succeeded in revealing the relationships within the cluster of central institutions: the networks between them, the level of intolerance within parts of the Church and its desire to be the national arbiter of limits to civil liberties. The centres involved were the Catholic Church (in particular the Archbishop's office), the conservative organisations such as Alternativa Española (who demonstrated against the show), the Hazteoir website (a forum for conservative Catholic views), the centre-right Partido Popular (which controlled local government in Toledo) and the festival organisation. Without going into details, it is evident that the relationships between these centres were very close, with some individuals belonging to two or three of the centres and with various levels of financial and political patronage. For example, in the Youtube compilation of the events around the Alfil Theatre protests[72] a priest can be seen addressing protesters next to another speaker who finishes with the Nazi salute, indicating a close relationship between the two. This is comparable with centres involved in the *Big Brother* intervention – the producers, the media companies, the editorial boards of newspapers, the security guards and the police.

Another comparison to this interconnectedness between seemingly unrelated centres is the understated and somewhat surprising connection, cited by McKenzie, between university Performance Studies courses and a society based on capitalism. He argues that the courses must adhere to the 'norms of the academy, norms that are themselves tied to extra-institutional forces'.[73] He quotes Foucault: 'Once a student has spent six or seven years of his life within this artificial society, he becomes "absorbable": society can consume him. Insidiously he will have been given socially desirable models of behaviour'.[74] Similarly, in the *Revelacion* example, there were no formal links between the Catholic Church and the Partido Popular, despite a shared ideology. Even so, the violent actions of ultra-conservatives had an effect throughout the network of relationships; the Catholic Church could be associated with the violence and, as a consequence, each centre was keen to emphasise the separateness of one from the other, reinforcing the distinctiveness of their identity. Thus the provocation created turbulence that emphasises defensive cohesion at one stage and separateness at another. This has parallels with the pattern of behaviour, observed in choral work, when individuals diverge after arriving at a shared climax. The bomb can be seen as an unsurpassable moment which is then followed by a period of dispersion. In the next chapter I will approach the subject of centres from a different angle, examining micro-centres in their simplest form, in order to widen the concept of centres and edges. To prepare for this it is useful to identify the ways that centres react to provocation. The resistance of structures to destabilisation demonstrates one of the dynamics between stasis and chaos.

The first problem for the centre is how to perceive the provocation: the provocateur may use confusing signals as to the reality or otherwise of the action. The playful appearance of an action may conceal a serious intention or, conversely, the appearance of seriousness may conceal a hoax. If the action appears to be merely playful, or can be portrayed as such, the centre can afford to dismiss the activity. Despite its ludic qualities, *Revelacion* was correctly identified as being a serious attack. If the action is perceived as a real challenge there are two main reactions possible: defending against the feedback or opening up to it. There are at least four main kinds of defensive reaction. The first is the application of suppressive controls by means of legal restrictions, censorship or even intimidation through violence. If the initiating action is mis-perceived, or if the instruments of suppression are not fully controlled, the reaction may be inappropriate, risking a public backlash onto the centre. The use of guns on the *Big Brother* camp carried a huge risk for the production company. The bomber of the theatre is an example of an agent of suppression being out of control, the less structural approach being associated with the less rational forces within many religious organisations. Clearly, the crudeness of this kind of reaction is not something that sophisticated central organisations in a developed society wish to be associated with.

A second defensive strategy is that of protection; feedback from the edges is blocked off, the core values are re-articulated and the perimeters of the centre are more closely defined and strengthened. In this instance, the strategy is exemplified by the refusal to listen to Bassi's historical evidence on the roots of Christianity and, as is typical in these cases, the refusal of protesters to see the show they were protesting about. More generally, this can be observed in the reaction of the Catholic Church to the advance of secularism. Core values are frequently restated and the Church is forced into ever more precise instructions and contorted ideological positions – for example, on the acceptable conditions for condom use. The concept of consistent universal 'truth' becomes harder to sustain in a world where technology and culture flows on with ever greater speed. As Bassi observed:

> Conservatives are always wrong … because the world that they are trying to conserve has already gone. The only way to be conservative is to believe in renewal and so the real conservatives are taking risks and going against the system … we are the ones who are giving society the possibility to maintain itself through change.[75]

The closing down of feedback increases isolation from the environment. The defensive barriers may become prison walls and its inhabitants increasingly institutionalised and unable to countenance change. This strategy, whilst comforting to those within the Catholic community, ironically may make the church seem increasingly irrelevant to a growing proportion of the rest of society.

A third way centres may react is by marginalising the provocation or provocateur, either by simply dismissing them or by actually excluding them, or both. Bassi's opponents can easily dismiss him as a buffoon because of the clownish aspect of his work. In describing the confrontation with the Vice-President of Spain, Bassi recalled: 'he turned to me and he says "with clowns like these, with an opposition that can only find clowns to oppose us, there is no way that this can be a threat to us"'. However, capitalist-related institutions are not the only source of marginalisation strategies: 'I'm most dismissed by left-wing intellectuals; they don't like seeing someone like me on their turf, because they "own" the issues and because I'm aware of trying to get over to the mainstream'.[76] Exclusion, on the other hand, is a form of suppression. The pressure put upon the T+T Festival to withdraw *Revelacion* is a good example. When threatened with being black-listed by commercial TV entertainment after the *Big Brother* action, Bassi abandoned that avenue of work rather than submit to being controlled in this way. However, this risked him being marginalised from the mainstream. I will explore the intricacies of this subject more fully when examining the work of Banksy and Sacha Baron Cohen.

As well as these blocking strategies, centres may switch to accepting or adopting the challenge. This may appear to be an act of tolerance and openness or it may be an act of incorporation. Often it is not clear which is which; both may be happening at the same time. For example, legal toleration may enable the commercial potential, caused by controversy, to be exploited, 'piggy-backing' on its popular appeal. Initial connections with cultural or media institutions, political parties or commercial enterprises can suggest that they are open to the controversial and they may appear to endorse the provocative stance. This initial act of patronage can quickly evolve into a relationship of dependence and redefinition of values towards those of central institutions.[77] Bassi has succeeded in avoiding much of this problem by his lack of interest in financial or career advancement. However, it is a reasonable supposition that, if he had avoided his challenge in *Revelacion*, more career opportunities might have opened up. He takes great pride in his ability to obtain many minutes of prime-time TV coverage, by means of the appeal that his work has to news editors. This circumvents the expense of conventional publicity routes and reaches greater numbers than those available through Arts features or advertising. He also aims to avoid commodification by refusing to exactly replicate his productions, shifting between genres, between types of audience and between kinds of location, preventing the simplification that can result in facile packaging by the media and other cultural centres.

Opening up to provocative feedback carries risks for an entity because there may be too much contradictory feedback coming from different directions. As

Gleick states: 'Feedback can get out of hand, as it does when sound from a loudspeaker feeds back through a microphone ... Or feedback can produce stability, as in a thermostat'.[78] Democratic nation states are often forced into the role of arbitrating between competing communities with their increasingly sophisticated lobbying organisations. The danger for governments is that in trying to accommodate the concerns of different interest groups they become driven by feedback, dominated by whichever lobby group can be most vociferous, at the expense of cohesion. So, for a centre to accept provocation is potentially de-structuring, whereas the defensive strategies tend towards structure. As McKenzie points out: 'liminal practices can lead to either schism or reinforcement of existing social structures'.[79] For any centre, from the large scale of religious organisations, political parties or even nation states down to the small scale of individuals, the problem is about achieving a balance between control, by closing down provocative feedback, and opening up to it. As complexity theory suggests, this 'edge of chaos' is the most favourable point to be, allowing feedback, yet not to the point of the entity becoming unstable.

So, as well as schism and re-enforcement, there may be a positive outcome to provocation. Combining complexity theory with Bakhtin's notion of renewal, it can be argued that the increased internal connectivity at the edge of chaos can have a rejuvenating effect that maintains the health of the system. The advantages of engaging with provocations are the renewing effects they may have on the whole society. As Bakhtin says: 'The essence of the grotesque is precisely to present a contradictory and double-faced fullness of life. Negation and destruction (death of the old) are included as an essential phase, inseparable from affirmation, from the birth of something new and better'.[80] These advantages are twofold: society is helped to evolve, both through the activation and adjustment of internal relationships and also through sharing the development of the centres external to it, for example their technological advancement. This second point means that ideas, organisations or systems that are no longer relevant are identified and can be discarded to make way for new developments. There may be contention around the decision to do so but, by means of the provocative action, previously accepted components are questioned and thus brought into play.

This process can be seen throughout Bassi's recent work, but most significantly in his challenge to the Catholic Church. Its centuries-old influence over public life was reinforced in the Fascist era so that the continued strength of such links in the early twenty-first century went largely unnoticed by much of the general public until his provocation drew attention to it, questioning its acceptance. In this example, the relative power of each side of the debate was revealed by demonstrating the diminishing support for the Catholic Church's influence in Spain in 2006, a different relationship to one which had existed, say, twenty years previously. As such, Bassi's provocation can be seen as part of a feedback loop, identifying and challenging an element of society and helping to readjust its societal relationships to ones more appropriate to the modern context. I will develop this theme of revelation in terms of the blade analogy in the next chapter.

Activation

As well as the discarding of the old, the health of an entity is improved by the increased connectivity. The 'public' observe the contest between the centre and the provocateur. They may be present at the event or constituents of the wider public. Although attendees at the performances were likely to have been of a similar political orientation to Bassi and thus unrepresentative of the wider public, they nevertheless can be considered as an inner ring of a ripple that widened out through word of mouth and sympathetic media outlets to reach a national audience in Spain. The heterogeneity of 'the public' means that there will be many different responses to a provocation: they are centres in themselves. Generally, those who are in a weaker or a more insecure position will feel more vulnerable during transformation and are thus more inclined to seek a reduction of unpredictability by means of the application of tighter controls. However, the more this occurs the less potential there is for evolution. Other members of the public may not feel themselves to be weak or insecure within the structure but may have more to lose. Bassi believes that his primary task is to tackle widespread apathy that is caused by the pervasiveness of trivia throughout the media.

> I think spending four or five hours a day in front of a TV atrophies the sensual communication, people are less able to communicate sensually and it affects the brain, in my opinion. People are more easily conned today than before, like sheep they don't stick up for themselves, don't argue; not only because of cynicism but it's worse than that, it's psychological, there are some aspects of the brain they are not using any more and this is no longer interacting with other cognitive parts of the brain so they are less able to act on reality and are more passive in that way.[81]

The insistent reiteration of consumerist values encourages a passivity of thought and may reduce activity to the narrow field of acquisition. The emphasis on individual choice encourages a focus on the personal experience of pleasure, atomising and creating a feeling of isolation that needs to be alleviated by virtual communities of soap operas and internet games. From this position, provocation can seem like an annoying distraction from pleasure unless it is presented as entertainment and its destabilising factors are concealed. In this context, the initial challenge for the public is to be open to some level of engagement with the provocative process, to allow activity to occur. The second challenge is to sustain this activity by not retreating either to deferral to a prior position or to defer to a new centre. If the latter is the case, a mere replacement has occurred rather than adapting a less passive relationship with centres. As has been suggested above, charismatic spokespersons can easily become leaders and new authorities. The rapidity of change in the twenty-first century means that we live in a world of fluid parameters rather than the more rigid certainties of previous generations. This can encourage an active process of questioning as new issues emerge, but it can also be so confusing that the certitude of the opinionated is attractive, particularly if complexity is reduced to facile simplification. So contemporary life in the developed world presents individuals with a challenge to accept living in an uncertain context and a responsibility to be active in locating oneself within it.

By means of Bassi's *Revelacion*, members of the public not present at the live events are brought *into* play by the provocation and situate themselves in relationship to it. We can imagine that a topic of public concern, such as the power of the Catholic Church in Spain, is a matter of some relevance to most of the population and this will lead to the formation of a personal opinion in respect of it. The act of thinking about complex issues and voicing an opinion is empowering to a previously passive individual and means that citizens can become more responsible for their own decisions rather than being controlled by others. By this means they gain a greater sense of themselves as a centre, increasing intellectual autonomy, and therefore begin to extricate themselves from complementary relationships with the central cluster such as dominant–submissive, active–passive, succouring–dependent. As such, there is less danger of unquestioning adherence to charismatic leaders and a greater sense of self-responsibility in relationship to others in society. At this scale it is hard to identify a direct process of this kind occurring and it may well be that the majority of the population remain controlled by the influence of commentators, columnists and editors but at the least these opinion-formers are challenged to think in fresh terms.

Thus, paradoxically, opening up to provocation may diminish the need to resort to authoritarian controls. It is evident that states ruled by repressive regimes are less culturally dynamic and that hidden scandal and corruption bleed the state. In addition, increasing amounts of energy must go into internal controls, blocking feedback (e.g. via press censorship) as the state becomes increasingly separated from its context. In our complex societies, centres can co-exist without hardly being aware of each other; as Jacob has found in studies of evolution: 'Each species thus lives in its own unique sensory world, to which other species may be partially or totally blind'.[82] As well as activation of individuals, the myriad of sub-centres that comprise the internal ecology of society will have encouraged an awareness of different perspectives around the issue and thus may foster a greater sense of being part of a larger entity. As is clear from the *Revelacion* example, disparate elements form temporary alliances under threat from opponents, increasing connectivity between isolated individuals and sub-groups with diverse ideologies.

Bassi's unequivocal didactic message invoked defensive strategies of suppression and protection. The heated passions and head-on power struggle, exemplified by the violent confrontation, were negative and destructive for both sides. Temporary alliances were made up to a point of climax, followed by a phase of disassociation, similar to the pattern observed in choral work. The tightening of controls, necessary in a conflict, reinforced structure and ideology for those directly involved. However, for those observing from a safe distance, some activation is likely to have occurred and ideological fluidity was introduced. In this example there is an edge, not only between different cultural perspectives, but between chaos and order, fluidity and consistency. As in any spectatorship of contest, partisanship is encouraged and this creates a reconfiguration of allegiances.[83]

Ambivalence and the *Bassibus*

In this final section on Bassi I will examine a third form of activation that he employs – that of creating uncertainty through ambivalence. Creating uncertainty is a part of a process of bringing structure towards a state of chaos. I will use specific moments from a *Bassibus* tour as examples of ambivalence, both in terms of Bassi's practice and the way it is received. Creating uncertainty through ambivalence is a more subtle strategy than that of incitement, releasing audiences from limitations by 'getting people off balance'. In relation to risk, his use of the bicycle accident deliberately confused the meta-communication about whether to receive his actions as real or not-real. His adeptness at playing with perception was later developed in his indoor work. For example, in *La Vendetta* he performed a hypnotism act using two 'volunteers', who appeared to be unable to accomplish simple physical tasks such as moving their hands. The expert way he handled these volunteers meant that their responses were entirely credible, effectively creating a feeling of uncertainty in his audience. In other shows he uses another conjuring trick to give the impression he is soaking the stage with petrol while holding a lighted fire-torch. (Because his deceptions are usually revealed within the show, his intention appears to be to create temporary uncertainty rather than sustaining the kind of permanent deception sometimes used by Sacha Baron Cohen).

He also uses his appearance to destabilise expectations. For example, he is often costumed with a formal suit and tie and, with his glasses, bald head and portly solidity, he looks like a bank manager, a business man or a politician.[84] His performance at Cabaret Kazam, Bristol (30/10/2005) was typical of the way he uses this appearance to establish expectations that he later confounds. As often with his shows, from the moment of his first entrance he used the appearance to convey an air of solidity and seriousness, moving slowly and somewhat threateningly, assessing the public who were dressed casually. His opening discourse presented himself as a foreigner; he complimented the British for their sense of humour but ironically suggested that it was not well represented by the previous acts. After this hint of intimidation he elevated his high status further by referring to his greater age and experience as a performer ('fresh from a tour of Paris, Berlin, New York, Tokyo') making fun of the parochialism of the venue. Having established his persona, status and a serious linear discourse the music changed to a thumping techno style to which he began to move rhythmically, gradually enlarging his movements, doubling the speed to a frenetic pace. He then removed his shoes and socks, using parodic striptease moves, pulled out his back support and lay on it with his legs in the air. Baseballs were tossed to him, which he manipulated skilfully between his hands and feet, increasing the quantity until a finale cascade. Because of what he had established at the beginning this illogical, fast-paced, physically adept routine, performed with youthful agility to youthful music, was a great surprise; assumptions were exploded. The audience laughed, of course, but became more excited and alert to having other assumptions undermined. The genre shift took them into a zone of unpredictability.

> Art is all about being able to understand the meaning of things and then just swapping them around: if you do like this it's normal and if you do like that it's not normal. Artists can see this and know the reasons for this and then can surprise people and open up spaces for the collective mind of people to go forwards.[85]

He has used this look for decades and it has enabled him to convince security guards, politicians and audiences that he was, at different times, the Bulgarian Ambassador, the Italian Consul, or various EEC ministers.[86] When he speaks to a crowd or a TV camera about serious matters, dressed in this way, he appears credible as a real politician. His appearance also works as a contrast, for example, to distinguish him from the casually dressed *Bassibus* participants and its wider circle of supporters, thus providing a visual focus and suggesting intellectual credibility (see Plate 2.2). The *Bassibus* format itself has a similarly deceptive

Plate 2.2 Bassibus tour, Arganda 2011 (photo: Bim Mason)

appearance. The mystery tour on tourist buses has a ludic appearance and provides a playful experience but conceals a serious, well-researched purpose.

The Bassibus

After being marginalised by TV companies as a result of the *Big Brother* episode and suffering serious intimidation with the *Revelacion*, the *Bassibus* has provided him with an alternative means of production which is not dependent on other organisations and avoids being controlled because it is mobile, unrepeated and unpredictable. It began as a means of informing and activating by means of exposing privilege.

> I want to show you where these frightening politicians live, how dis-connected they are from the reality of everyday life because they live in completely closed surroundings and they are completely rich and they own their own golf courses. The idea is to get people to feel this indig-nation by showing how these people are, who they are really ... Bringing people on a five-hour tour and trying to get to see, but without them doing anything illegal, going to ring the bell to see if anyone is in the house and singing to them.[87]

On one occasion he took the occupants to one of the most expensive restau-rants in Madrid, where they ordered simple items such as water and nuts and then drove a few miles to a gypsy shanty town on the outskirts of the city where they shared the titbits with the residents, who were incredulous at the prices on the restaurant menu. On another occasion they took buses to The Valley of the Fallen, the tomb of Franco, where they placed a photo of the occasion when Franco met with Saddam Hussein and they presented a proposal to turn it into 'Francoland': a sort of Fascism-themed Disneyland. Another trip was to a secretive NATO base whose purpose was officially stated as research into 'extra-terrestrial biology'. In response to the guards demand that they go away, all the participants put on ET masks and the greeting tones from *Close Encounters of the Third Kind* were broadcast from the bus as Bassi asked to be taken to their leader.

As part of the *Bassibus* tour that I attended (15/05/2011), spectators were led to an isolated field and walked down a track, with assistants carrying ladders and platforms. Arriving at a long wall, there was a strong smell and, climbing onto it, spectators looked down at a lake of solid oil that had been dumped by a firm that was being paid to dispose of it properly. The land had been sold to the municipality without the presence of this dump being disclosed and, therefore, the municipality was faced with the large cost of decontaminating the area using public funds. Bassi and his assistants donned protective dust suits and climbed over and down to the edge of the lake, where they floated an election poster of the conservative Partido Popular, which was alleged to be connected to the scandal. This event provided a powerful metaphor for playing on an edge-as-border.

The spectators watched from the summit of the wall, smelling the stink from corruption, as the provocateur openly, and partly for their amusement, partly as their representative, transgressed the physical limit in order to draw attention to the concealed excrement of society, an abuse of nature perpetrated by dominant organisations. Playfully, he physically rubbed the (pictorial) nose of a representative in the ordure (oil contamination) of their own making. The metaphor can be widened to include the whole *Bassibus* mystery tour: the provocateur literally taking others into uncertainty, placing them in a liminal situation on the edge of legality (the trespass).

There were two specific incidents on this tour that demonstrated the nature of Bassi's ambivalence. The first is when he addressed participants who were walking between two city-centre organisations associated with scandals. He chose a raised area in front of a monument and, as the group assembled, he improvised a series of comic heroic/demagogic poses before making a serious speech, slipping easily between parodying the politician persona and 'becoming' it (Plate 2.3). The second moment was immediately after the oil-lake trespass, when he gave a serious TV interview while dressed absurdly in a disposable dust suit (see Plate 2.4). To add to the absurdity his nose was red, bleeding slightly from a scrape climbing over the wall.

Plate 2.3 Bassibus tour, Madrid 2011 (photo: Bim Mason)

Plate 2.4 Bassibus tour, 2011 (photo: Bim Mason)

The first example suggests that Bassi is very aware that he is *playing* the politician, not only physically but performatively. Although he may believe very sincerely in what he is saying it may also be, to him at that moment, a game. By contrast, in the second example he looked ridiculous, but talked very seriously, either without an awareness of his appearance or with a disregard for its importance. This suggests that he was either not conscious of playing or more likely, in view of the first example, he refused to accept the norm of dignified appearance for political TV interviews. Having chosen to play at 'politician' he was unwilling to play by the established rules, even though it had the potential to undermine his visual credibility as a serious commentator. In order to disentangle this complex interweaving of levity and sincerity, it will be useful to look at the matter from three perspectives: Bassi's intended communication, the reception of that communication and his personal enjoyment of playing a role. To begin, it will be useful to refer to some of Bassi's statements on the matter of what and how he intends to communicate.

Bassi's circus background provided him with an awareness that an entertainer must try to 'please' the public, but he is also aware that pleasing them does not necessarily imply a subservient attitude.

> It's not what they want rationally; it's what they want in their sub-conscious. Sometimes you give the audience what they didn't want to want but they [do] want. So you are playing to the audience on that level. It's saying: OK let's really go to the basics now – what do these guys want? What do they really try to see even if they will think it is taboo or whether it is immoral and how far they will accept.[88]

The attitude expressed in this statement marks a shift of emphasis from entertainer, a provider of popular experiences, to guide/educator. Indeed giving people what they don't know they want could be regarded as potentially despotic, so to what extent is he concerned with social transformation? This question can be approached by examining the structure and purpose of his actions in relationship to different types of play. Pure play, as described by Carse and Huizinga, must be un-constricted by moral considerations, direction and any purpose beyond the continuation of itself. The *Bassibus* examples cited above suggest he may indeed be refusing to circumscribe his freedom whilst playing a game. Moreover in 2005 Bassi hinted that he had no moral purpose to his actions, despite having just premiered *Revelacion*.

> Entertainment is not only what you do but it is a desperate attempt to try to smash through the barrier of information that reaches people and generate information that makes people want to come and see you. I'd like to think we, all performers, are information generators … We are living in a world where there is a whole industry to take information from A to B, but if there is no information, it all goes to boredom and, in fact, they need desperately people who have the circus spirit, that can be entertaining. I want to maintain a totally open mind, I would say amoral mind, to producing news.[89]

This statement appears to suggest that not only the form but also the content of his work may be no more than an attention-seeking ploy. However, Bassi clearly has short-term goals, such as exposing specific malpractices. He does appear to have a consistent political/moral purpose to his actions even though he does not support the political practices of either left or right. He is unwilling to become a member of a specific political party, to toe a party line. Indeed, he comes into conflict with his 'natural' allies on the left because they consider that he encroaches onto their territory. They do not like his independence and want to draw him into being a part of their centre rather than establishing his own.

> I've been to [Socialist-governed] Barcelona this summer and going round seeing the corruption there and the Socialists were saying 'Hey I thought you were one of us' and I said 'I'm not a card-carrying member of any party and so there's corruption here and we'll show it'.[90]

His 2009 show, *Utopia*, was a critique of the contemporary form of socialism in Spain and was consequently seen as a betrayal by some on the left.

Up until 2011 he had not proposed a long-term political agenda, but focussed more on abuses of power and privilege. In more recent work he has begun to 'stand for' a particular ideology (humanism and atheism). In his 2011 interview he acknowledged support for social-democracy and was considering aligning himself with 'people to do with ecology, urbanism, architects, lawyers, writers, film-makers. I thought it was necessary to form a coalition of thinking and to listen to other opinions in completely different ways'. Although his political orientation is becoming more defined, he does not propose specific goals in his performance work. Despite the lack of defined objectives there are clearly principles that provide a motivation for his actions. The *Bassibus* action

> started as a gut feeling against the Iraq war … the elections were coming up and I thought the only way it is going to be effective is if they [the conservative Partido Popular] lose the election. I also had the feeling that the Socialist Party didn't want to win the election and I had the feeling the political organisation [of the party's election strategy] was not very organised, there was no energy.[91]

As well as weaving together play and seriousness, Bassi uses real/not real confusion. This is 'a more complex form of play; the game which is constructed not upon the premise "This is play" but rather round the question "Is this play?"'.[92] Because he is able to view politics as game-playing, he can confuse those he opposes, presenting himself as a serious political activist at one moment and then clowning around on his inflatable duck at another moment. In terms of reacting to his *Bassibus* interventions, making a serious suppressive attack on a clown makes the attacker look foolishly heavy-handed, but dismissing evidence-based accusations of corruption[93] as a joke (marginalisation) seems like an evasion. Prior to 2011 the shorthand description he was assigned by the media and press was as 'the clown Leo Bassi' or 'the buffoon'. In 2011 this began to shift to 'the clown activist',[94] linking the two aspects of his work. In some respects the ambivalence works against him because it makes him easier to marginalise.

Bassi refers to comedy as an 'enhancer',[95] a way to help get the message across, not as a goal in itself. This suggests that, for him, levity is only a means to an end and therefore can be considered as not really play; as Huizinga put it: 'Play to order is no longer play'.[96] As well as using comedy as an 'enhancer', levity is also used to de-stress the moments of anxiety caused by stress. At the outset of the *Bassibus* outing there was much joking and even a sing-along which used the physical release of laughter to relax the occupants from the stresses of unpredictability. Another example occurred during this tour when Bassi donned a clown nose and led the group to the outside of a theatre. Here there was a short parodic performance given by the tour's five hostesses with Bassi playing the theatre's director. He produced an over-sized letter that he had written to the theatre and then, removing the nose, he moved to the theatre's entrance, to deliver a real letter asking the director to resign. The theatre's security guards nervously watched this large unexpected group, but appeared somewhat reassured by the jocularity of the proceedings. They were disarmed and reassured by what was clearly a protest but bore the signs of comedy: the red nose, the laughter, the circus music. The confusing genre shifts are all forms of frame-breaking that are likely to have the effect of making spectators and participants more alert and active in seeking sense and order. These can also be seen as another effective strategy in his contest with opponents in the central cluster, a form of camouflage or dis-information that gives him an advantage in what would otherwise be very unequal in terms of power and resources.

He destabilises his opponents by developing unconventional methods, such as using the ship's horns at the *Big Brother* action or, conversely, surprising them with his use of conventional means, such as the deployment of local laws against the producers. The complexities of play and seriousness can be clearly seen in the *Big Brother* action. The producers were engaged in the real, serious interplay of commercial business, presenting 'reality' but within the ludic realm of entertainment. Bassi, on the other hand, approached this from the position of the playful entertainer, making fun of the situation, but making serious points about the normalisation of surveillance and the exploitation of non-professionals. He playfully added another layer to the surveillance, spying on the watchers, intruding on the intruders, puncturing the illusion of levity and revealing the ruthless, target-centred seriousness of its business interest. The game of politics was being played with serious intent on both sides, but Bassi was *both* having fun and making a serious point.

Bassi clearly enjoys the experience of playing a role in front of observers; he also derives pleasure from the effect he creates in the wider society. The *Bassibus* expeditions prior to 2004 were recognised as contributing to the downfall of the conservative Partido Popular and the subsequent change of policy towards Iraq.[97] Bassi was lauded for his efforts at the Socialists' victory celebration.

> All the socialists were really happy and we came with a whole crew of all the buses; we were twenty in all, and we walked to the party at the central socialist office. It was an incredible feeling and when we got there thousands of socialist flags were waving at the party for the victory of the elections and they saw us and the cameras turned round and people stood back and ten thousand people made an applause for the Bassibus team and that was an extraordinarily emotional moment. Putting this on a circus basis, a clown basis, the clown coming in and actually having some kind of effect and that putting the provocation on a dimension that is not desperate – it is hard hitting, but it is still fun and that's more dangerous.[98]

This statement suggests that pleasure in the effect of the 'splash' was as much an incentive as the achievement of a political goal. One way an individual acquires a sense of prowess is through an awareness of effect on the surrounding environment. Bassi often describes his actions in terms of the success at having an impact that goes beyond the immediate event and its spectators (manifested as media coverage, reactions of opponents/authorities), as against the difficulties overcome (physical and legal obstructions, intimidation, media indifference). Interwoven with his progressive principles is the prowess that can be acquired by 'changing the world'. Demonstrations of prowess have a distinctly male character which may be not only a matter of culturally acquired confidence, but more contentiously may be the result of inherent hormonal differences in the neurochemistry of the two genders. During the *Bassibus* expedition to the Arganda oil lake, Bassi simultaneously reinforced and subverted this quality. When offered a pair of rubber boots as he prepared to wade into the lake, he replied:

'I'm a big macho and don't need them', both making fun of macho values, but at the same time, by not accepting them, reinforcing his male prowess.

At the beginning of this chapter I offered a continuum between play and seriousness. Bassi's work suggests that this taxonomy is not appropriate in his case. Although his performances have a range of emphases on the continuum, it is clear from the intention, reception and experience that placing specific examples at a particular point on this spectrum is to ignore much of their distinctive character-istics. There is an inseparable combination of real/not real, clown/activist, playfulness/seriousness, leader/spokesperson. So this is not so much a matter of finding a context-appropriate point between binaries but a combining of con-sistent ideology with a fluidity of form. Bakhtin suggests that in general, if not in a specific moment, the combination is synergetic.

> True ambivalent and universal laughter does not deny seriousness but purifies and completes it. Laughter purifies from dogmatism, from the intolerant and the petrified; it liberates from fanaticism and pedantry, from fear and intimidation, from didacticism, naïveté and illusion, from the single meaning, the single level, from sentimentality. Laughter does not permit seriousness to atrophy ... It restores this ambivalent wholeness.[99]

However, at the two moments on the *Bassibus* tour, described above, it is hard to distinguish the seriousness from the play. Who can say if his ideology is not partly as a result of his projection of himself as an opponent of the dominant, a role that he likes to play, or conversely whether his playfulness is a calculated strategy to mask his consistent, sincerely held views? Both propositions could be true, even within the same moment. To be entirely accurate it would be necessary to also bring into consideration the mood of the performer, how they are affected by the atmosphere and the distraction of practical considerations. However, this level of dissection is unnecessary; the point is that two or more considerations are 'in play' more or less simultaneously with subtle shifts of emphasis occurring as events unfold. These shifts of emphasis are like the subtleties of a tipping point suggested in the image of a fulcrum.

Notes

1 Lecoq, Jacques (2000) *The Moving Body.* London: Methuen: 21.
2 Gleick, James (1988) *Chaos.* London: Cardinal Sphere Books: 134.
3 Turner, Victor (1969) *The Ritual Process.* New York: Aldine De Gruyter (1995): 139, 140.
4 Gleick (1988): 292
5 Bateson, Gregory (1972) *Steps to an Ecology of Mind.* St Albans: Granada: 125.
6 Csikszentmihalyi, M. (1975) *Beyond Boredom and Anxiety.* San Francisco: Jossey-Bass.
7 Ibid.: 80.
8 Bateson (1972): 36, 47–8.
9 Bakhtin, Mikhail (1969) *Rabelais and His World.* Bloomington: Indiana University Press (1984): 8.
10 Bassi, Leo, Lecture at Circomedia (27/10/2005).

11 Turner, Victor (1969) *The Ritual Process*. New York: Aldine De Gruyter (1995): 128.
12 A Risley act is one where the juggler lies on their back and manipulates people or objects with their feet. Bassi uses footballs/baseballs and large objects such as a fake upright piano.
13 Selecting a member of the audience to receive a custard pie in the face was presented as an example of democracy – satisfying the wishes of the majority at the expense of those in minority. For a fuller description of a performance from 1989 see Mason, Bim (1992) *Street Theatre and Other Outdoor Performance*. London and New York: Routledge: 60–3.
14 https://jaberbock.wordpress.com/tag/leo-bassi/. Accessed 22/01/2010.
15 'I have the world's largest inflatable duck. I brought it to Rio … It was in all the Brazilian TV and newspapers, headlines. It is 48 metres in diameter and you can have fifty or sixty people on it' (Interview, 2011). Even these more open-playing populist events are sometimes accompanied by a message: 'Before the Pope comes to Madrid I want to have the duck out, its yellow is the same colour as the Pope. In Spanish a duck is 'pato', which rhymes with 'patologia', like a sickness. [It can be] a symbol of children, innocence, family, non-aggressivity against militarism and there is a possibility the duck will go to Gaza as part of the flotilla' (Interview, 2011).
16 The Off Broadway OBIE Award (New York 1989) and the Golden Nose Award (Barcelona 1994).
17 *Prove Techniche*, Rai 3, Italy, 1990–1; *The + Plus*, Canal+, Spain 1998; *The Martian Chronicles,* Tele5, Spain, 1999–2001, as well as appearing on many talk shows (e.g. *The Ruby Wax Show*, BBC2, UK, 1997). In 1995 the German theatre festival, 3SAT, produced a forty minute TV special on his *Hidden Instincts* show.
18 As listed on website: dma.nl/cybercus/biography.html (accessed 08/07/2011), these include: Conning the Italian air force into having a squadron of 104 Starfighter jets dive bomb an open-air stage during one of his shows while two companies of soldiers with armoured vehicles rounded up and arrested the bewildered audience (Nogara, Verona 1986). Posing as the vice-minister of the Ministry of Laughter for the EEC during a tour of the ex-Soviet Union and getting away with it, to the point of giving a lecture on 'Laughter and the Free Market', in front of 3000 students at the University of Tashkent (Kazakhstan, Uzbekistan 1991). Selling hundreds of small bottles of normal tap-water for two dollars each to eager buyers though he had told them beforehand that it was, in fact, normal tap-water! They reasoned that if he was selling it for one pound [sic] it couldn't just be tap-water and so they imagined that the bottles contained some miracle treatment … They were wrong (Barcelona, Madrid Spain. Many occasions!). Juggling an upright piano on his feet and hanging from famous buildings, every Sunday for the Italian RAI TV (*Prove Tecniche*, RAI, Italy 1990). Having been challenged to liven up, a bit, the city of Bielefeld, Germany, getting 200 Hells Angels to wreak havoc, artistically, on the historical downtown for a weekend. One of the highlights was their rendering of *Carmen* by Bizet, using, mostly, the revving ups of their bikes' engines (Bielefeld, Germany 1986). Organizing one of the biggest cream-pie fights in the world with more than 5000 pies and about 500 participants for an audience of 10,000 (*Just for Laughs*, Montreal, Canada 1993). Left for dead after being battered and clubbed, by a few hostile members of the audience, escaping with broken shoulder and ribs (South Street, Philadelphia, PA, USA 1988). Convincing the mayor of Montreal that receiving a cream pie in the face would be a graphic illustration of democracy (Canadian TV 1992). Creating a commotion and being followed by a crowd wanting to be cured from various illnesses, after successfully hypnotising eight people (Archangalsk, N. Russia 1992). Getting into a potentially dangerous theological discussion about the nature of comedy with the fourth highest spiritual leader of Islam, the Rector of the Islamic University of Bukhara (Bukhara, Uzbekistan 1991). Inventing the first elastic band powered dragster and being propelled on it at 60 km/h over 700 m at a car

show, in front of 50,000 people. The elastic band had been powered by 30 people (Motor Show, Bologna, Italy 1984). After having been presented to Mr Ralph Klein, Premier of Manitoba, as the Italian Consul, jumping into a small lake, fully dressed and inviting the bewildered politician in with him, in front of all the press, as a gesture of friendship between Canada and Italy (Calgary, Canada 1993).

19 Circomedia lecture (2005).
20 Ibid.
21 Bateson (1972): 152–3.
22 For example: 'Politicians employ the tools of the marketplace to ensure that their image is recognizable, distinct, and attractive; they use discursive manipulation to craft a reality conducive to their policy recommendations; they create pre-packaged pseudo-events which are easily portrayed on the evening news; and they use their influence over journalists and editors to mould reporting and determine the content of the news ... the ebbing divisions between "real" political actors, the media, critics, and entertainers is more evident with each passing year as political candidates build their brand by appearing on the talk show circuit' (Saunders, Robert A., 2008, *The Many Faces of Sacha Baron Cohen.* Lanham, Maryland and Plymouth UK: Lexington Books: 58).
23 Circomedia lecture (2005).
24 Lewin, Roger (1992) *Complexity.* New York and Ontario: Macmillan: 149.
25 Ibid.: 186.
26 Robertson, Ian (2012) *The Winner Effect, How Power Affects Your Brain.* London, Berlin, New York, Sydney: Bloomsbury.
27 Bassi, Leo, in conversation (01/11/2005).
28 Fiske, John (1989) *Understanding Popular Culture.* London and New York: Routledge: 65.
29 This is a good description of one of the aspects of choral work.
30 Carse, James P. (1987) *Finite and Infinite Games.* New York: Ballantine Books: 67.
31 Circomedia lecture (2005).
32 Becker, Carol ed. (1994) *The Subversive Imagination.* London and New York: Routledge: 117–18.
33 Fiske (1989): 122.
34 Circomedia lecture (2005).
35 Interview (2011).
36 Circomedia lecture (2005).
37 Ibid.
38 Brian Popay, Natural Theatre, interview (07/12/04).
39 Circomedia lecture (2005).
40 Circomedia lecture (2005).
41 Fiske (1989): 34.
42 Ibid.: 56.
43 Ibid.: 15.
44 Circomedia lecture (2005).
45 Ibid.
46 Ibid.
47 ibid.
48 The 'spoilsport [who] shatters the play world itself': Huizinga, J. (1938) *Homo Ludens.* London: Temple Smith (1970): 11.
49 Circomedia lecture (2005).
50 'I phoned the police and the military police came about seven-thirty, eight in the morning and I said: "This is a disaster" and they were all like smiling and laughing. He said: "Oh yeah, what do you want to do?" I said: "Make a formal complaint, let's say the effect of firing." He said: "You would do anything to get publicity." I said: "What?" He said: "It's true, I mean", he said: "look, the holes come from the inside". I said: "There were witnesses who saw the whole thing." He said: "Yes

but you put the whole organisation together, they're all gonna say the same thing."' (Circomedia lecture, 2005).

51 Circomedia lecture (2005).
52 Bassi, Leo, Provocation Workshop at Circomedia (30/10/2005).
53 Carse (1987): 23.
54 Circomedia lecture (2005).
55 Bateson's 'complementary' and 'symmetrical' relationships. Bateson (1972): 294.
56 Ibid.: 97 footnote.
57 One member felt inadequate and indignant when asked to whip up a crowd in the Saturday morning shopping centre and lead them half a mile to where Wolfgang was due to speak.
58 Carse (1987): 4.
59 Bakhtin (1969): 12.
60 Carse (1987): 39.
61 Circomedia lecture (2005).
62 Youtube: LEO BASSI Una bomba en el teatro Alfil. www.youtube.com/watch? v=47ebZn6_ndg. Accessed 12/05/2013.
63 *Guardian* (18/03/2006).
64 PP stands for Partido Popular, the conservative political party.
65 Confederación Syndical de Comisiones Obreras and the Union General de Trabadores.
66 Shorthand for ultra-conservatives.
67 *El Pais* (19/03/2006).
68 *El Pais* (02/03/2006); *The Guardian* (18/3/2006).
69 LEO BASSI Una bomba.
70 "'I entered the hall dressed as the Pope, and explained that Ratzinger was changing his mind about condoms", Bassi said at a recent news conference. "I told the audience that a bomb had been planted at the theatre where I had last done this. I wanted to illustrate what the far right is prepared to do". Bassi soon had an example of how far the far right is prepared to go: the charges have been brought by the Association of Christian Lawyers and other Catholic Church fringe groups deeply concerned about the truth. They say they warned the rector of the university, Marcos Sacristán – who also faces charges – , that Bassi's conference could "involve crimes that are clearly detailed in the Penal Code".' http://iberosphere.com/2011/03/spain-still-doesnt-understand-the-separation-of-church-and-state/2492. Accessed 22/01/2010.
71 Interview with Bim Mason (16/05/2011).
72 LEO BASSI Una bomba.
73 McKenzie, Jon (2001) *Perform or Else*. London and New York: Routledge: 48
74 Foucault, Michel (1989) *Foucault Live (Interviews 1966–84)*. Trans. John Johnston. Ed. Sylvene Lotringer. New York: Semiotext(e): 66.
75 Interview (2011)
76 Ibid.
77 This ambivalence will be more fully explored in the chapters on Baron Cohen and Banksy.
78 Gleick (1988): 61.
79 McKenzie (2001): 51.
80 Bakhtin (1969): 62.
81 Circomedia lecture (2005).
82 Jacob, Francois (1982) *The Possible and the Actual*. London: Penguin (1989): 410.
83 This analysis of the reaction of centres is backed up by the example of Kazakhstan's sequence of reactions to the character of Borat. As Robert Saunders outlines (2008), there was initial confusion about how to respond to a ludic false portrayal and use of its name. The 'attack' could not be taken seriously because it was clearly deliberately inaccurate, using a film location in Romania and Macedonian music. After a period

of ignoring and dismissing the character (marginalisation), the imminent release of the film prompted an attempt to suppress it through legal action. This backfired because it reinforced a false perception of a totalitarian state and boosted Baron Cohen's publicity. Following this there was internal activation that led to a redefinition and restatement of the values and identity of the country. This adjustment meant that the country was able to recalibrate its position in the wider global environment. 'The movie has already created unprecedented interest in Kazakhstan. Not only has Borat promoted our name and flag, he has also indirectly fuelled a great wave of patriotism', Gauhar Abdygaliyeva, a Kazakh student studying in America (Saunders, 2008: 121).

'The original condemnation [of Borat] prompted more questions from the world media which in turn led to further opportunities to discuss Kazakhstan. If we had laughed it off or ignored it, we wouldn't be anywhere near where we are today in terms of recognition and public visibility'. Roman Vassilenko, press attaché at the Kazakhstan embassy in the USA (ibid.: 125).

84 'I'm 53, I look like a portly gentleman, if I put a tie on and so on. And if a portly gentleman starts doing crazy things this is going to be exciting, make people ask questions, what happened to this man? Why does he do this? When I was younger I looked different and used it in a different way. It's just a question of being opportunistic. Looking at what you are – not through your eyes but through the eyes of the audience, using yourself as a puppet. I use this puppet: what would I like it to do? And so it's funny if this puppet looks like a politician make him clown about and jump about or ride a little motorcycle. If I was doing this with a red nose on or big shoes there wouldn't be much importance.' (Provocation Workshop 30/10/2005).

85 Provocation Workshop (2005).

86 www.dma.nl/cybercus/biography.html. Accessed 21/01/2010.

87 Provocation Workshop (2005).

88 Circomedia lecture (2005).

89 Ibid.

90 Provocation Workshop (2005).

91 Ibid.

92 Bateson (1972): 155.

93 'I work in collaboration with ATTAK, an environmentalist group and other NGOs. They give me information and workers that I need to do all this … I have a lot of friends who are journalists who give me information … in the newsrooms you will find they are full of frustrated journalists, so many young people have gone in with the hope of writing something important and after a few months they have to toe the line and don't make waves', Provocation Workshop (2005).

94 *El Pais* (16/05/2011).

95 Provocation Workshop (2005).

96 Huizinga, J. (1938) *Homo Ludens*. London: Temple Smith (1955): 7.

97 The bombing of trains in Madrid and the government's unsubstantiated accusations of ETA as being responsible caused a rapid shift in public opinion away from the conservative Partido Popular, led by Jose Aznar. He had sent Spanish troops into Iraq in 2003 to support the alliance against Saddam Hussein. Within weeks of the 2004 election of the socialist PSOE, led by Jose Zapatero, Spain was withdrawing them.

98 Provocation Workshop (2005).

99 Bakhtin (1969): 123.

3 On the edge of chaos

The Bigheads

I created the Bigheads for my indoor theatre play *The Joy Society* in 2003, but they were then used as street theatre at festivals and other outdoor venues in the UK, as well as in Belgium, the Netherlands, Spain, Austria, the USA, Canada and Singapore (2003–8) (Plates 3.1–3.6). The piece was intended to work within the parameters of the street-theatre industry, but it also attempted to push the extent of those parameters by challenging the growing tendency of such work to present safe, 'cute' images designed to suit the 'family audience' norm. They were designed to be un-ignorable. The objects themselves are large, latex heads, one metre high, with rotating eyes, extendable tongues and the facility to squirt water, either from the mouth, or the ears or between the legs. The performer's body is concealed except for the legs; the arms can emerge from slits near the ears. The aperture at the base of the head is wide enough for the performer to be able to squat down, so that the feet are concealed. We normally used them as a trio, connected by walkie-talkies to a 'controller', who looks out for potential opportunities or problems, because the performers have limited vision through small holes in the eyebrows. The controller can cue choreographed actions, so that the heads can move in unison. They usually move along a pre-arranged route, looking for opportunities for interaction either with spectators or with architecture and street furniture. At certain points they stop, sit or squat, in order to accumulate enough focus from spectators to perform more subtle gestures with the hands, enabling longer, non-verbal interaction with spectators. Spectators have a constant choice of two ways of engagement, as inter-actors or as secondary watchers of the interaction.

For spectators the combination of signs contained in the image of the Bigheads set off an oscillation between two reactions. The most obvious was between attraction and repulsion. The image had a fairground/carnival aesthetic, reminiscent of figures from Disneyland, football team mascots and high-street store promotion figures. Conversely, the image is slightly nightmarish and the spitting, dribbling wet tongues, used irreverently, produce reactions of disgust. Because spectators would often physically engage in the game that they thought the Bigheads were proposing, the way that they interpreted the game could be observed. The poking out of the tongues had a particularly confusing double sense: it appeared to be

Plate 3.1 Bigheads at Delft, June 2005 (author's collection)

Plate 3.2 Bigheads at *Juste pour Rire* Festival, Montreal, 2005 (photo: Bim Mason)

interpreted as cheeky fun by some and as erotic sensuality by others. The positioning of the tongue near the top of the legs has a phallic resonance. The licking of objects and spectators is very libidinous, and doing so in a public space appears transgressive, even deviant. Similarly, the image oscillated between low-status, vulnerable victim and high-status threatening tyrant, both in a real and not-real way. Frequently children would 'adopt' a head, leading it by the hand, feeding it, showing it things. Other children might attack the 'monster'. Adolescents would become nearly hysterical when a wet tongue touched their ankle. Adults would often express their opinion of the performer inside, either in terms of foolish self-humiliation or admiration at the courage and endurance of such an act.

Similarly, the surreality of the image was able to make the ordinary absurd through juxtaposition, putting behavioural norms into a position of relativity. A frequent tactic was to mirror mundane human activities, such as sitting at restaurant tables, entering (with difficulty) a public phone box or waiting at a bus stop (Plate 3.4). The contrast was more apparent if the environment was very mundane, such as in the undecorated shopping streets, rather than within the context of a festival site. The juxtaposition had the disconnected quality of dreams, denying the primacy of logic or of making sense in any other way. The extraordinary appearance propelled the observers into a liminal zone of active questioning, as I was able to observe at the Montreal comedy festival, *Juste pour Rire* (2006). A river of people flowed down the street with the Bigheads moving slowly in the opposite direction. The density of the crowds meant that people could not see very far in front of them. As controller, I was often ahead of the team looking for possibilities. In this position I was very close to people at the moment they caught their first glimpse and, from their physical responses, it was easy to see a sequential pattern of reactions: surprise, disbelief, questioning (What is it? Is it safe? How does it work? What is it for? Is it for children or for adults? Is that tongue cheeky or erotic?). The initial reaction was followed by either laughter or fear, or oscillations between them.

The fact that the faces were not recognisable as those of any public figure avoided them being interpreted as a 'statement', political or otherwise. The purpose remained unstated and, therefore, more available for projections by spectators. Because there was less opportunity to categorise, spectators seemed to sustain their openness longer. As well as by means of creating uncertainty, the risk factor was augmented by raising the stakes with a sense of threat. The equivocal tongues were used as weapons, as water was dribbled down them from inside and then flicked off or squirted at specific targets or, if the watching crowd pressed in too tightly, it could be squirted out of the ear slits as the heads rotated, sprinkling it in every direction; the consequent opening up of the space, as people backed away, would enable the team to make an exit. The sense of threat would also be created by one Bighead creeping up behind spectators who were watching the other two. The tongue tips could be animated so that they moved like sensitive insect feelers, targeting a particular area of the spectator's body and approaching slowly, providing secondary spectatorship for others. The tension would mount until the shock of the discovery, with the resulting shriek by the target and laughter from others. In this moment the secondary spectators share and thereby endorse the 'conspiracy', identifying with the risk-taking without having to take risks themselves, creating a bond amongst themselves and with the performers.

Walkabout work is developed through repeated improvisations with the public: it is discovered rather than pre-determined. For example, in creating a piece it is necessary to select only two stimuli, an appearance and an attitude, before trying it out. The dramaturgy emerges out of repeated experiments. For the performers, the experience was one of high alertness; the heat and humidity inside meant that they had to be minimally dressed and this, combined with not being able to see well, made them feel vulnerable. They became adept at being able to assess a situation with very limited visual information and only intermittently audible directions. Because of heightened alertness the pace of learning was very rapid. The primary concern was seeing how far you could go, both in terms of the performers' daring and also the spectators' limit of acceptability. For example, younger children might be fascinated but on the edge of terror, or police officers in their car might 'play along', but begin to show signs of unease as doors were opened or windscreen wipers were tampered with (Plate 3.3).

In each case, there needed to be acute observation to detect signs of the shift from excitement to alarm. The reaction would, of course, depend on context. Whereas in the UK it is possible to go as far as licking uniformed policemen or security guards, the suggestion of a similar approach in Spain resulted in the performer's hand within the tongue being discreetly crushed by a policeman's boot. Similarly, the tongue approaching from behind, threatening both men and women became a standardised tactic but, at a festival in Belgium, a young

Plate 3.3 Bigheads at Harbourside Festival, Bristol, 2003 (photo: Matt Smith)

Plate 3.4 Bigheads at *Juste pour Rire* Festival, Montreal, 2005 (photo: Bim Mason)

man of Middle-Eastern appearance reacted violently in defence of the woman he was with, presumably because of different attitudes to women and sexuality to those we were used to. In Singapore, performing near open-air, shore-front restaurants, the Bigheads became caught between order and play. Customers seated at tables beckoned the performers to approach for interaction but the restaurant owners told the festival stewards to instruct the team to keep their distance. In a city that actively imposed large fines for spitting and littering, the transgressive behaviour of the Bigheads was unwelcome to the authorities.

The piece aimed to 'get something going' with the spectators by establishing an open-ended play that had a sense of an event with a life of its own. Many street performers seek these moments of 'lift off', stimulating and sustaining spectator activity, but also withdrawing to a very minor role if that activity sustains itself. An example of this withdrawal occurred at an international rugby final in Cardiff. Asked to entertain the crowds as they arrived at the match, we found ourselves in the middle of a high-spirited throng of people, fresh from the surrounding bars, pressing in on all sides, with the vulnerable performers being playfully slapped and pinched. We retreated up a few steps to the raised entrance of an office; the heads squatted or sat, presenting a visual image to the river of people passing. The image alone stimulated a carnivalesque reaction that surprised us; women as well as men, would mount the steps so that they were in full view of hundreds of people, and present their front or back sides to the tongues, requesting to be licked, dancing in a grotesque parody of the erotic. Because of the already heightened atmosphere, the level of provocation required to achieve this 'lift off' needed to be only very slight, as if the mere image triggered a release into transgressive behaviour.

Plate 3.5 Bigheads at Delft, June 2005 (author's collection)

Plate 3.6 Bigheads at *Juste pour Rire* Festival, Montreal, 2005 (photo: Bim Mason)

Because the 'rules' of this open playing were not defined, the game could get out of hand, leading to chaos. Fortunately, although a persistent battering was alarming, the heads themselves provided a protective barrier for the performer. The main threat was to the delivery of the performance: tongues could be seized and pulled away, leaving the performer visually exposed through the open mouth. Very occasionally, the Bigheads would be shoved from the side, sometimes knocking the performer over, always shocking them. When the situation escalated in this way, water tactics could be deployed and the location changed. However, this was sometimes interpreted as part of the chase-me, chase-you game or as a retreat of outsiders in a real power game. If pursued, a frequent tactic was to use the walkie-talkie communication so that all three Bigheads jumped simultaneously, rotating to face in the opposite direction. The ability of these 'blind', disconnected creatures to act in concert was most disconcerting; the sudden switching from creating chaos to using (an invisible) structure refreshed the game by changing the rules. The tactic could reverse the status as well as direction, with the pursuers becoming the pursued. This was one of many ways we learned to control events. If this simply raised the excitement, we discovered that the best strategy was to terminate the pursuit game by squatting down in front of families with small children and using small, gentle actions, to encourage mirroring and other inter-actions. The gentle atmosphere and the presence of responsible adults sent a signal to the pursuers that a different kind of game had commenced, involving (passive) spectatorship. In this way we found we could control chaos through a control and release mechanism and thus determine a point of creative adaptation rather than having no system. The sense of order was so strong on one occasion that a baby, enchanted with the big face, allowed itself to be placed on the extended tongue and 'eaten', closely monitored by the trusting parents and the performer.

Although we toured this piece for five years it remained an exploration in progress, not only because of the variety of contexts, but also because of the complexity of processes at work. The piece was clearly very popular, both with promoters and public. But why were they so fascinated and excited by the challenges of both the threat and disorientation? Was this because so much organisation, effort and personal risk had been put in the service of an apparently non-sensical purpose? How were we triggering such an extreme (because of being in public) release of violence and eroticism? We felt we were on an acute edge between attraction and repulsion/alarm, but were surprised by how much we could get away with. It seemed as if this was to do with a combination of chaotic behaviour and structure. But how did that work? To unlock these questions the application of the blade analogy seems useful because its two key features are the release of suppressed behaviours and the confusing combination of risky play with careful planning.

The blade analogy

The blade analogy has two main interrelated aspects: the personal, where a provocateur places themselves in risky situations, and the process of cultural transformation that the actions and method of the provocateur contribute to. In order to be effective the provocateur must take risks as well as being playful. Both these aspects can be viewed as a form of being 'on the edge of chaos'. According to complexity theories, the absence of structure in the state of chaos threatens the cohesion and survival of an entity. In Chapter One I cited Klein,[1] who described social chaos being initiated by shock tactics, so that populations become willing to adopt alternative political systems as long as they promise effective structure. In her examples, a new order is imposed, but there are parallels to the 'natural' emergence of new structures out of breakdown, suggested in complexity theories.[2] Together with Bakhtin's notion that unlocking fixed structural relationships brings about 'rebirth', this can be viewed as a sequential process of breakdown and reconfiguration, triggered by a provocative action. With the Bigheads, the initial appearance is a 'shock' moment that initiates a search for meaning. Unlike in choral work, where fluidity is constant, this is a sudden jump from one set of rules to another. The provocation reveals and tests whether norms and ideology remain fit for pur- pose, acting as a part of a feedback loop. In this sense, the action acts like the application of a blade, either in the sense of a sculptor's chisel cutting away what is superfluous, revealing what is concealed within, or as a scalpel, a painful but necessary part of a curative process. In both cases the blade must be very precisely targeted and, literally, incisive to be effective. This model is intended to be applicable at both the large scale of societies as well as to individuals. Having touched on this subject at the large scale with Bassi's *Revelacion*, this chapter looks at the precise moments of this occurring with individuals. In terms of the three aspects of the popular, the blade analogy is associated with the appeal of risk and transgression. Within the last few decades, one of the most adept performer–creators to employ extreme risk and transgression for the sake of popularity is Sacha Baron Cohen. In particular he is adept at switching from one set of rules to another. Whereas with Bassi it was ambivalent as to whether he was playing at politics or playing for politics, Baron Cohen appears to be conscious of playing two or three games simultaneously. He is particularly interested in recording the moments of transition as observers realise that established rules no longer apply.

Sacha Baron Cohen: the joker

> 'In everything, in meaning and image, in the sound of sacred words, parody discovered the Achilles heel that was open to derision, some trait that permitted linkage to the lower body stratum ... The serious aspects of class culture are official and authoritarian; they are combined with vio- lence, prohibitions, limitations and always contain an element of fear and of intimidation ... It was the victory of laughter over fear that most impressed medieval man. It was not only a victory over mystic terror of God, but also a victory over the awe inspired by the forces of nature, and

most of all over the oppression and guilt related to all that was consecrated and forbidden.' – Mikhail Bakhtin[3]

'A well-orchestrated lie is more of a turn-on than the naked truth.' – Philippe Gaulier[4]

The body of Baron Cohen's work shows that he is particularly interested in an inter-personal edge, often game-playing on a one-to-one basis. The more powerful the figures or organisations he deals with the greater the satisfaction of hoaxing them, identifying and exploiting their weaknesses, contradictions and prejudices. Like Bassi, Baron Cohen works with two audiences: firstly, those he interacts with and secondly those who observe this interaction, as in walkabout performance. However, Baron Cohen's secondary audience is remote from the initial event as they watch from the comfort of their cinema seat or sitting-room sofa. They enjoy a 'superior laugh'[5] at the expense of his interlocutors, much in the same way as described above in the Bigheads' surprises. He delights in desta-bilising his opponents with shock and confusion and has made full use of the comedic, and hence commercial, value of recording this status drop. As well as bringing others towards an inward state of chaos, he clearly relishes placing himself in vulnerable situations, relying on his wits (and careful pre-planning) to survive.

His work can widen understanding of the blade analogy in a number of ways. Firstly, the quantity and breadth of his targets helps to define the nature of centres. His filmed work allows for a close observation of reactions to provo-cation, providing examples of the different ways centres respond to an outsider perspective. Secondly, by means of this close observation, we can see how he employs complex layers of game-playing, concealing meticulous planning behind outlandish behaviour. Thirdly, because he has achieved substantial popular appeal for work that pushes the limits of cultural acceptability, we can observe the link between transgression, popularity and the process of incorporation. Finally, his training with Philippe Gaulier has given his work direct links to a body of knowledge and historical practices, especially regarding the carnivalesque, that are highly relevant to this subject.

I focus mainly on the material he created between 2000 and 2009, the period in which he was developing a novel format and which gave his three main characters, Ali G, Borat and Bruno, their fullest expression. All three were developed in the *Ali G* TV series (2000–4) and each was the lead character in a feature film that Sacha Baron Cohen wrote and produced. These were *Ali G Indahouse*,[6] *Borat, Cultural Learnings of America for Make Benefit Glorious Nation of Kazakhstan*[7] and *Bruno*.[8] In this period, he gained critical acclaim, widespread popularity and financial success. *Borat* (2006) alone made over US$260 million[9] and he has been a subject of the *New Hero of Comedy* TV series (2009). He won two BAFTA Awards in 2001 for *Da Ali G Show* and, in 2007, a Golden Globe Award for the Best Actor in a Comedy or a Musical, as well as numerous other awards and Emmy nominations. By means of his comic interviews he made transparent the political attitudes that underpin many social interactions.

Although difficult to quantify, the wide popularity of his comedy raised awareness of connections between politics and everyday personal choices for many who were disengaged from formal political processes.[10]

Compared to the interviews with Bassi or the written work of Banksy there is very little exposition, by him, of his work.[11] There are relatively few interviews in which he is out of character and even some of these are subject to suspicions of obscuring the true facts of particular events, for publicity purposes. Instead of looking at his work from the perspectives of film/media composition or aesthetics, I focus on those sections within the films and TV programmes that appear to be recordings of one-off interactions with unsuspecting interviewees or members of the general public. It is impossible to ascertain, through simple observation, how much the impression of verisimilitude has been artificially created through pre-arrangement, editing, subsequent additions and the participation of actors. As is well established, a camera, or any other form of observation, alters behaviour: interviewees, either consciously or unconsciously, 'act' a version of themselves that they want to present or that they think the audience want to see. Much of Baron Cohen's work is about using the powerful effect of the camera's presence to encourage this desire for approval or to reveal a more accurate impression of individuals than the mask they wish to present. Because there are degrees of simulation by all involved in an interview dialogue, it may be more useful to think in terms of 'contrived' or 'spontaneous', rather than terms such as 'real' or 'artificial'.

Baron Cohen grew up in a conventional upper-middle-class Jewish family in suburban London. His grandfather was a Holocaust survivor and his mother is Israeli. His sense of cultural identity was strengthened by being active in a youth cultural group, Habonim Dror, that integrated Socialism, Judaism and Zionism. He also spent a year in Israel (1989–90) on a kibbutz and participating in the programme Machon L'Madrichei Chutz La'Aretz, which was founded in 1946 to train youth leaders to promote Zionist values in Jewish communities around the world. He studied history at Cambridge University (1990–3); his dissertation on the American Civil Rights movement focussed on the 1964 killings in Mississippi of activists, two of whom were Jewish.

> When I was in university, there was this major historian of the Third Reich, Ian Kershaw, who said, 'The path to Auschwitz was paved with indifference.' I know it's not very funny being a comedian talking about the Holocaust, but it's an interesting idea that not everyone in Germany had to be a raving anti-Semite. They just had to be apathetic.[12]

The combatting of apathy as a prime goal has parallels with Bassi's desire to 'wake people up'. A photograph from Baron Cohen's student years shows him with Ken Livingstone, then the socialist Mayor of London; Baron Cohen is holding a placard that says: 'Never again! Nazis off our streets'. As Ali Hines, the director of *Ali G* said: 'Prejudice is personally very important to him and he takes an active interest in exposing it'.[13]

As a creative performer, his main influence is Phillipe Gaulier with whom he trained (1993–4). Gaulier is especially renowned as a teacher of clown and *bouffon*. Baron Cohen indicates the nature of this influence in the Preface he wrote for Gaulier's book, *The Tormentor*:

> I was always interested in comedy, but it was Gaulier who helped me understand how to be funny, how to be open in the moment, how to keep the performance light and playful and how to act with the pleasure of a four year old pretending to be a cowboy ... I owe my career and the discovery of my own inner idiot to Philippe Gaulier. He has and always will be the inspiration for my work.[14]

The style of *bouffon* came out of Lecoq's curiosity about 'people who believe in nothing and make fun of everything'.[15]

> I noticed it became quite unbearable seeing someone dressed in a suit making fun of someone dressed the same way: it rapidly turned very spiteful and so difficult to handle that I decided that the person making fun had necessarily to be distinct from his victim. He had to be different ... In a bouffonesque body, the person who mocks can say the unsayable, going so far as to mock what 'cannot' be mocked: war, famine, God ... Their function was not to make fun of a particular individual, but more generally of everyone, of society as a whole.[16]

Gaulier studied at Lecoq's school and subsequently became a teacher there, developing his own direction of *bouffon*. He draws the analogy with those who were forced to live outside the city walls in the Middle Ages: 'The outcasts were hunchbacks, the legless, freaks, queers, prostitutes, Jews, witches, heretical priests, madmen, depressives, Down's Syndrome sufferers, cripples and so on'.[17] Relating this world to the present day he cites the victims of racism, prejudice and xenophobia. He cites the real example of Amazonian Indians, enraged about the murder of one of their group by 'skinheads' (presumably loggers/settlers). Gaulier also emphasises the importance of *Le Jeu*, the game of pretending. He makes it a requirement that actors find the pleasure in this game, even whilst acting melodrama or Greek tragedy. *Le Jeu* releases the imagination so that acting is a continuous creative process. As Gaulier puts it: 'Truth kills the joy of imagining ... When the imagination opens up, it enjoys making us believe the time of the game is real ... There is nothing of reality and everything seems so believable'.[18] Gaulier also gave Baron Cohen the notion of pushing interplay to the limit. As Peter Baynham (writer for *Borat, Brass Eye* and *The Day Today*) put it: 'The big thing that he took away from [Gaulier's] clowning class was the theory that any more stupid and you die, which is like the implication that if you went one chop further you'd just be killed'.[19]

However, the influence of Gaulier on Baron Cohen can be overstated. He is not a teacher of physical technique and dislikes comic 'gags', whereas Baron

Cohen uses some standard slapstick in his clowning.[20] Despite this difference, Gaulier's definition of the clown seems like a blueprint for Baron Cohen's three main characters.

> The clown has the laughter and joy of someone who hoodwinks the administration, of someone who is disobedient. The clown comes from very far away, like the Wandering Jew or the Gypsy. He talks with a special accent which has never been heard before. He comes from nowhere in particular. He brings the freedom of someone who is rootless and so laughs better. He helps us dream because he isn't from round here.[21]

Like many people of dual culture, Baron Cohen may have experienced some degree of outsider status both in his relationship with the Israeli kibbutz culture and also to the British cultural mainstream. His knowledge of the *bouffon* style explains his use of outsider characters both to make fun of social attitudes and also for a certain amount of self-mockery. For example, he has described being taken by his mother with fellow teenagers to perform street dance at Covent Garden, London, in emulation of black youth culture.[22] His early character of Jocelyn Cheadle-Hume used and made fun of this attempt by a member of the suburban middle class to ingratiate himself with urban street culture.[23] Similarly, the character of Bruno both draws upon and makes fun of his early work as a fashion model. Gaulier's pedagogy demonstrates that being able to acknowledge and share unattractive or embarrassing sides of one's personality is liberating for the performer and also the observer. As Baron Cohen laughs at the sexual obsessions of Ali G, one is also laughing at that part of oneself that cannot refrain from being interested in sexual display. Similarly, one can identify with the outsider status of Borat and Bruno, either as visiting foreigner or cultural outsider. The ability to laugh at an aspect of oneself is not only liberating but also disarms anyone who attempts to ridicule that particular aspect. The more that inadequacies, such as physical imperfections, weaknesses or obsessions, have been explored and are acknowledged by the object of mockery, the less power they have to induce feelings of humiliation, fear or guilt in them. Those who would seek to intimidate by drawing attention to difference from central norms are disarmed and this gives the provocateur power in the asymmetric struggle with central institutions.

Borat at the rodeo

The scene in *Borat* in which the main character addresses a packed rodeo stadium and then proceeds to sing a parody of *The Stars and Stripes* is one of the most remarkable filmed examples of provocation of this type. So I consider the event from three different angles: in terms of power negotiations, in terms of the experience of risk and the effects on the risk-taker and, thirdly, using complexity theory, to try to explain the processes that led to the collapse of a horse and rider carrying the national flag.

The rodeo scene is one of several incidents when Baron Cohen uses incitement to destabilise a crowd so that its reactions can be captured on film. In *Bruno* he incites a stadium full of homophobic spectators of cage-fighting by kissing and undressing his fellow combatant. In the same film, he confronts a predominantly African-American TV chat show audience with a whole range of issues around gay parenthood. In each case he begins by showing respect for the values of the audience, enlivening them by stimulating cheers of approval, and then gradually moving step by step, as if naively, towards an extreme position. This technique of exaggeration can also be seen in the '*Throw the Jew down the Well*' sequence (*Da Ali G Show*). From this extreme point, he either exaggerates to the point of absurdity or inverts the sentiment by demonstrating an opposing action. In the rodeo scene he does both. The speech to the crowd starts with a proposition that can easily be shared by the crowd, 'We support your war on terror', and gradually he increases the extremity of the proposition as far as annihilating the Iraqi people. Having praised the USA, he sings a fictitious national anthem of Kazakhstan to the tune of the *Stars and Stripes*, which includes lines such as 'all other countries are little girls'. This inversion technique is used by other provocateurs, but these filmed examples demonstrate very precisely the effect of him transgressing the limits of acceptable behaviour. Baron Cohen is also interested in creating a similar effect with the audience in the cinema. Ken Daviditian, Baron Cohen's co-actor in *Borat*, recalled their discussion of the naked bed fight: 'I said, "people are going to cover their eyes if they see me naked" and he said: "No, no, that's what I want"'.[24] The result was that, in the cinema, 'people are screaming, yelling, squirming'.[25] In *Bruno* he tries to exceed the impact of the previous film, pushing the boundaries of acceptability even further and filming the response. The sequence, in which he shows to a focus group a video clip of a singing penis, derives comedy from the horrified reactions. I observed similar reactions to this sequence in the cinema, so that this audience was both horrified and able to laugh at the horrified reaction, in effect, enabling them to laugh at themselves. This provides an example of the way play (signified by laughter) eases the stress around an edge (the display of male genitalia) thus subverting prudish norms.

Power play in the rodeo scene

Turner states that: 'In closed or structured societies, it is the marginal or "inferior" person or the "outsider" who often comes to symbolize what David Hume has called "the sentiment for humanity", which in its turn relates to the model we have termed "communitas"'.[26] In the rodeo scene the singing of the national anthem simultaneously invokes all three of Turner's notions of communitas: the shared norm (the ritual), the shared ideology ('the land of the free …', etc.) and the shared experience (through communal singing). The event had three phases: in the first Baron Cohen is clearly in a very weak position relative to the large crowd. He is seen alone, striding with difficulty through the churned-up mud, into the centre of the arena. He is introduced as a foreigner, but his costume demonstrates that he is attempting to fit in with the norms of the event: he wears a stars-and-stripes shirt, cowboy hat, boots and denims. He is seen to be aspiring to become a member of the community from a low position in the hierarchy. He confirms this impression by vocalising his support for the USA and its war, stimulating cheers and applause after each statement. By means of this rhythmic, ritualistic call-and-answer technique he nurtures an experience of shared communitas, harnessing the power as it combines with the communitas of norms and ideology. He appears to have become part of that communitas as well as strengthening the cohesion of the mass. There appears to be structure as he sets the rhythm and leads them into greater cheers with each statement. The structure is not normally associated with rodeo events, but is a familiar enough norm from evangelical Christian forms of worship. As they follow his lead he gains power so that, at the end of this phase, it is difficult to perceive Borat as remaining in as liminal a position as he had been at the beginning. He has been increasingly effective the more he appears to adopt the shared norms and ideology of the group.

In the second phase, he uses this newly gained leadership to fracture the cohesive structure. As his statements become more extreme, most spectators gradually cease vocal endorsement while others continue. Their assumptions, which have been derived from the prior endorsement of norms, are dispelled and they appear uncertain, as the structure weakens. The cheering falters and the spontaneous communitas dissipates as the differences in norms and ideology are brought to light by the gradations of extremity. However, by means of these extreme proposals, he encourages dissociation from the barbarous sentiments expressed, such as inflicting full military power on 'all the men, women and children [of Iraq]'. The use of this phrase to an audience with traditional family values stimulated a suggestion of a shared humanity and arguably engendered some distant sense of communitas with families in Iraq. In the third phase, he reunites them with his parody of the national anthem. What at first appears as a homage to the USA, by using the tune of *The Stars and Stripes,* becomes increasingly obvious as a travesty, with statements denigrating notions of US supremacy. Because the singing of the national anthem is a norm that has taken on a semi-sacred quality in the USA and is also an expression of shared ideology, he was able to use its substantial power to threaten the whole community. As Turner says: 'danger is one of the chief ingredients in the production of existential communitas'.[27] Through this action, Baron Cohen had reverted to a liminal status whilst reinforcing all three forms of communitas in the crowd and restoring structure. So it appears that there is an alternating correspondence between the strength of structure and the liminality of the provocateur. The crowd is at its most fractured when Borat has led the ideology to the excesses of its logical conclusion. They are at their most cohesive when he places himself in liminality. So whilst it can be said that the liminal person engenders communitas, it is not necessarily by means of engendering feelings of empathy or 'the sentiment for humanity', but conversely may be by engendering hostile feelings against others. This 'tribal' reaction is compounded because the cinema audience enjoys the discomfiture of the rodeo audience, setting up one community against another, breaking up any sense of universal *communitas*.

Risk and its effects

In the extra material, provided on the *Borat* DVD, the rodeo producer indicates that if Borat is ever seen again in the locality he will be violently assaulted. Clearly, it would take substantial courage to walk, alone, to the centre of the stadium and to embark on a plan that will lead to inciting a crowd against oneself. How has Baron Cohen arrived at being able to undertake this extreme venture and what are the effects on him personally of this kind of event?

In the *New Hero of Comedy* programme, dedicated to him, the most prevalent comment from other comedians is about Baron Cohen's outstanding courage.[28] His ability to continue playing a role, apparently being unaffected by high levels of intimidation, is extraordinary. For viewers there appears to be as much of a thrill from watching him dare to disregard social conventions or hierarchies in his conversations with prominent figures as from watching him take apparent physical risks. As Jay Roach puts it: 'There's this cathartic vicarious thrill of watching him step into danger. You like to think you could but you never would. It's a high-wire act and yet it's simultaneously hilarious'.[29] Yet, there is also a question about the extent of his risk-taking. As Jamie Glassman, writer of the *Da Ali G Show*, says: 'It's good to make comedy, it's good to make people laugh, but is it really worth dying for?'.[30] This suggests that, for Baron Cohen, there is a personal objective beyond entertaining or revealing prejudice. He seems to be continuously challenging himself as to whether he can 'get away with it', be that by hoaxing and destabilising interviewees or avoiding being arrested, sued or physically attacked. During his early work on children's TV, he elected to film himself interacting with ordinary people in the street, while dressed, for example, in a bird costume. As was outlined in the discussion of the Bigheads above, the effect on the performer of this kind of walkabout performance is empowering, because people do not know how to respond. The act of lowering one's status unapologetically by means of an absurd costume demonstrates a self-confidence that people find unnerving. In walkabout performance, the fluidity required in order to be able to respond creatively to each situation increases with frequency. Stress decreases rapidly as expertise in the game-playing is acquired, so that increasing levels of challenge may be sought. This might be by abandoning controls provided by pre-planning (e.g. prepared texts) or by seeking out more unpredictable and intimidating situations. As Garry Shandling put it: 'Not knowing what is going to happen until the next beat … that is where all of his work, his strength is … That he can pull off a character that appearingly seems broad but is so real that people right in front of him don't realise it's an actor. It's really quite shocking'.[31] This ability to remain in character in the face of intimidation suggests an intensity of activity similar to that of the mountain climbers described by Csikzentmihalyi.[32] Daring to go to such extremes provides him with an edge in terms of the blade analogy. Because those he interacts with appear unable to conceive that anyone would place themselves in such a situation, they expose aspects of their personality or ideology that they might otherwise be more reticent about. It is the reactions of spectators at public events and the vox populi interviews that reveal most prejudice, either because they become less inhibited, as a result of Borat's excessive expressions of prejudice, or because they become alarmed by Bruno's difference, such as when he flirts with homophobes. The risks are managed both in terms of his own stress and in terms of controls put in place. The organisation behind the camera must purport to be less sophisticated than it actually is in order to be able to outmanoeuvre others. False companies and websites were created in order to give credibility to requests for interviews; innocuous looking disclaimer forms outwitted the unsuspecting targets and provided the basis for legal defence in cases of litigation. The presence of the camera also mitigates against the potential for immediate physical retribution. With this array of defences Baron Cohen was able to reduce the level of risk. It is also possible that many of the recordings have been enhanced to make them appear more dangerous than they seem, as has been revealed in the case of the interview with the supposed 'terrorist' Ayman Abu Aita in *Bruno*. [33] Baron Cohen also gained control by testing out his interventions; many of the sequences in *Borat*, including the rodeo scene, were reworks of experiments tried out in the *Ali G in da USA* series.

With the increasing frequency of such exploits during the production of the *Ali G Shows*, the 'Winner Effect',[34] as outlined in Chapter One, will have become activated and led to an escalation of the level of risks undertaken. As the film director, Richard Curtis, put it: 'He tried to keep that element of fear'.[35] This can be seen in the progression of Baron Cohen's work from the more studio-based interviews of *Ali G* to the outside interventions of *Borat*, to the more confrontational style of *Bruno*. A specific example of his interest in maintaining his position on an edge is the decision to terminate the UK version of the *Ali G* Show because prominent figures, such as Mohamed Al Fayed, were offering themselves as targets for their own self-promotional reasons. As Al Hines, director of *Ali G* put it: 'for Sacha and myself it lacked that kind of edge'.[36] The frisson he had experienced when, for example, interviewing Tony Benn[37] was missing and so he sought out the bigger challenge of George Bush's USA. He would have gained a sense of his own power in being able to dupe large centrist organisations such as the FBI and NASA, as well as hoaxing high-profile political figures of the superpower. Baron Cohen's experience of performing in the street will have provided him with a confidence derived from the (what can seem surprising) ease with which one is able to encourage spectators to respond vocally. This street theatre technique quickly conveys a sense of power to the instigator, as can be seen in the first phase of the rodeo sequence, enabling Baron Cohen to move, with just a few phrases, from weak outsider to leader. The empowerment may lead to the kind of arrogance that is not uncommon among solo street performers.

The consequence of a high level of confidence is a confirmation of existing modes of behaviour and thus may reduce flexibility. Baron Cohen's conventional childhood and increasingly conventional middle-age would suggest that his provocative work was a temporary strategy, an unconventional means to a conventional end, and that his outsider perspective was only ever an assumed one, acted out as part of a career game. Indeed it can be argued that he was able to take more risks because of the self-confidence provided by his privileged education and secure family background, a position which is very different from the reality of, for example, the Amazonian Indians, cited by Gaulier. Conversely, the habituation to edge-play may develop into an 'aptitude to evolve'.[38] Commentators remark on Baron Cohen's unusual energy and dedication,[39] but is it possible to observe more specific examples of rapid 'evolution' in his work? Does there appear to be a correlation between risk-taking and significant changes in behaviour? There are two examples that seem to suggest this. The first is a single incident and the second a longer period of intense adaptability.

Ali G was originally conceived by Baron Cohen as an absurdly fake TV presenter.

> The first was MC Jocelyn Cheadle-Hume, an Ali G-style figure loosely based on the Radio 1 DJ Tim Westwood, who affects a gangsta rapper style despite being white and the son of a bishop. One day, while out filming as this character, Baron Cohen spotted a group of white skate-boarders and went to join them. 'Me and Mike looked at each other and suddenly had this realisation that people believe this character', he says. 'At that point a tourist bus turned up at a bus stop right next to us. I looked at Mike and he looked at me. So we jumped on and essentially comman-deered the bus. I took the microphone and I was like "Yo, check it out. I is here and this is me bus. Booyakasha"'. Giddy with the success of the day's filming, the crew then followed Baron Cohen into a pub where he began breakdancing. In a foretaste of things to come the landlord called the police and had them all thrown out.[40]

Similar to Bassi's discovery of the potential of the real/not real interface in his bicycle accident (p. 43), this incident led Baron Cohen to realise his potential to dupe the unsuspecting with extreme characterisation and also the potential to parody a real-life type without it being recognised as such. The incident provided the basis for his career over the subsequent decade. As referred to earlier, the act of lowering one's status unapologetically is empower-ing, whether this is a matter of dressing in a bird costume or using the character of a 'stupid' outsider, the former being a short-term 'fractal' of a long-term strategy – that of getting himself to the 'edge of chaos'.

Perhaps the period with the greatest demands on him to adapt was during the making of the twelve episodes of *Ali G in da USA* (2003–4). In these episodes the three characters, who are extraordinarily different, have an almost equal prominence. Before and after this time, only one of the characters has the main focus. The format of these episodes is that there is a studio debate with

Ali G, and the rest is comprised of on-location interviews with all of the three characters. This suggests that there was constant change of situation as well as character, each producing the adrenalin-filled experience of pulling off a hoax. The result of this period of work can be seen in the differences between the films, *Ali G Indahouse* (2002) and *Borat* (2006). The former is a fairly conventional light comedy and the latter was a multi-award-winning, ground-breaking film that exceeded all box-office expectations and established Baron Cohen's credibility as being much more than an entertaining comic. Therefore, it seems reasonable to conclude from these two examples that there is some correlation between risk-taking and a rapid beneficial development of his practice.

Complexity theory and the collapse of a horse

Finally, I will use complexity theory to look at the causes and effects of the collapse of the horse and rider, carrying the national flag, which occurs during Borat's rendition of the fictitious national anthem of Kazakhstan. The collapse appears almost out of shot and is unnecessary to the accomplishment of the provocation. This suggests that it was a real accident and, to begin with, I will work under the assumption that it was. It is unclear what caused the accident: the rider may have been inexperienced but, given that rodeos are dedicated to displays of riding expertise and given the importance of carrying the national flag, this seems unlikely. More likely seems the possibility that the vocal hostility expressed by the crowd may have unnerved the horse. Whatever the cause, the occurrence of the accident seemed very odd and it may not be easy to dismiss the idea that there was some connection between the provocation and the accident; that, in some way, Baron Cohen had somehow caused the horse, rider and flag to collapse. Conversely, the collapse can be seen as a random accident, not caused by the crowd to any significant degree. If this is the case, the chance event is only connected to the main event by its timing. However, because of the immense symbolism of the collapse and its timing, the perception of its significance by both rodeo spectators and cinema-goers is unavoidable. So, whether the accident was real or staged, the question it raises is how to interpret it. The absence of any obvious direct, physical connection and the accidental nature of the collapse suggest that there were sub-liminal processes at work. That, although the crowd would not wish for the horse to collapse, the former's reaction to Baron Cohen had triggered it, that the feeling in the crowd, and possibly in Baron Cohen himself, was that the situation was getting out of control as much as the horse. Baron Cohen glances nervously behind him as the horse goes down suggesting that, for him, this was unexpected and, therefore, he, as much as the crowd, were in an unpredictable zone, 'on the edge of chaos'. So how can this sequence of events best be explained?

In terms of complexity theory, the crowd can be treated as a single entity. Baron Cohen has caused the cohesion of the entity to disintegrate as individual members react at different times and at different levels of outrage or confusion. They can be described as being in a state of psychological turbulence. Referring to patterns in differential equations, Gleick states: 'Just as turbulence transmits energy from large scales downwards through chains of vortices to the dissipating small scales of viscosity, so information is transmitted back from the small scales to the large'.[41] If the event is seen in these terms, the collapse of the horse can be viewed as a physical fractal of the structural collapse in the crowd. Arguably, despite its presumed familiarity with large crowds, the horse was more acutely sensitive to strong human emotions and quick to respond physically. The visual impact of the collapse of the flag-bearer also transmits back to the larger entity, compounding the effects by means of a feedback loop. This is an example of where 'Feedback can get out of hand, as it does when sound from a loudspeaker feeds back through a microphone'.[42] This situation demonstrates an oscillation between a single component and the entire system, the small scale affecting the large scale and vice-versa. There is a suggestion of the potential of other, apparently unconnected, symptoms of stress breaking out; the resultant sense that 'anything could happen' indicates a fluidity throughout the structure. The closed, finite play has transformed into an open play of unknowable possibilities. So, at this precise moment, before the destabilisation of structure has coalesced into a communitas of shared perception of danger, the provocation can be seen to be operating effectively and with a complex interplay of conscious and sub-conscious levels. This moment is brief and although it may have been useful as a questioning of norms, it is likely, in this instance, that, rather than causing a repositioning of edges (in the sense of the borders), the reaction would be for existing norms to reassert themselves with more vigour as a means to escape from the fear of the unknown. The subsequent violent threats to Baron Cohen, mentioned earlier, suggest the level of fearful stress that had been experienced by the crowd.

The rodeo example provides an excellent illustration of the way that the combination of risky play and careful preparation provides a sharp edge. Indeed, it suggests that the riskier the play and the more thorough the organisation, the keener the edge. It also demonstrates how the application of this blade combination causes breakdown of structure, both revealing suppressed attitude (prejudice) and releasing expression of it. The other aspect of the blade strategy is precise targeting, which is necessary for the performance to be effective. I will now look at Baron Cohen's targeting of much smaller centres.

Centres under interrogation

Baron Cohen's interviews provide detailed examples of centres encountering a provocative challenge. They provide a clearer definition of the characteristics of a centre, of how centres are formed and of the various reactions to provocation. Whereas Bassi interacts with large-scale centres, Baron Cohen often works on a one-to-one basis. Similarities between the two scales confirm the fractal nature of this model and also provide detail of process that is less easy to identify in larger, more complex processes. In its simplest terms, the process is the interaction between a centre and a surrounding system, which produces structure. In a large organisation, the centre may be a board of management or a central committee; the system may be sub-divided into a hierarchy of departments that interact at various levels. At a micro-scale, the centre and the system can each be one person.

The Paul Wilmot interview

In the series *Ali G in da USA* (2003–4), Baron Cohen uses the character of Bruno to target experts within the narrow field of fashion. This sector is useful for him because it is concerned with the esoteric minutiae that denote what is 'in' or 'out'. It is clear from these interviews that, for those within this industry, being 'out' is a matter of ridicule. Bruno shares a joke that 'foreigners have got no fashion sense'. Another interviewee, a fashion designer, has based her designs upon clothes worn by 'trailer-trash'; she and Bruno laugh at the inability of this poor section of the population to afford to buy their own 'look'. Being wealthy is thereby denoted as being a requirement of being 'in'. As a complement to the fashion industry interviews there is one with Paul Wilmot (Episode 1: *Law and Order*), who had spent seven years in charge of public relations for Calvin Klein and is a person who feels himself able to pronounce on the relative popularity of particular celebrities: whether they are 'in fashion'. Treating them as commercial objects, he declares: 'I'm judge and jury. I can tell you who is "in" or "out".' He then proceeds to identify which celebrities fit into each category.

This precise classification to the otherwise ludic fields of fashion and entertainment is a good example of the emergence of 'the crystallisation of order'.[43] Jacob, writing about evolution, claims 'the living world is evolving in the opposite direction to the inanimate world, steering not towards disorder but toward increasing order'.[44] More significantly, as quoted above, Turner describes the emergence of structure out of transitory, unordered existential communitas.[45] In this incident, Bruno and Wilmot share all three forms of communitas: the playful, pleasurable experience of spontaneous communitas, the shared understanding of a communitas of norms and the complicity of shared communitas of ideology. Wilmot's application of order to the caprices of celebrity culture is predicated on the assumption of a demarcation between exclusion and inclusion in relation to a cultural entity. On one level, Wilmot is only a single person with very defined opinions; on another, through his expert knowledge of the world of Hollywood celebrities, he has given himself the role of a functionary in a system, the arbiter of the arbitrary. He has de-personalised his subjective opinion into an objective statement of fact. Baron Cohen understands and encourages this perception by beginning the interview with: 'What is Paul Wilmot?', suggesting that he is being considered as a phenomenon, an institution, rather than on a personal level. Wilmot, with encouragement from Bruno, is claiming to be able to dictate the location of a border by defining those who are included and those who are excluded. By setting these limits and being accepted in this position he is establishing himself as a centre of the fashion in celebrities.

Baron Cohen seems to have recognised the significance of the interview with Paul Wilmot, because two years later, in the introduction of Bruno in the film of the same name, he says: 'I am the host of Funkyzeit, the most important TV fashion show in any German speaking country, apart from Germany. Funkyzeit is uber-influential; in fact, Austrian fashionistas live their lives according to my "in" or "out" list'. Baron Cohen draws attention to the power of this kind of central arbiter in Bruno interviews with others in the international fashion industry (*Ali G in da USA*). He demonstrates how they crave inclusion within the sub-culture that the arbiter has established. For example, having established himself with them as an 'expert', with his own Austrian TV show, he is able to direct models, designers or 'fashion experts' to impersonate others, or either to make statements that they know to be false or express opinions that they clearly do not believe in or, more spectacularly, to express an opinion that is in complete contradiction to one they have expressed two minutes previously (Episode 2: *War*). It appears that they do this, partly to help an outsider, but also to fit in with a given norm (that of Austrian fashion) and to make themselves look significant within the fashion culture of the USA. As well as illustrating Baron Cohen's premise about the ease with which some people are persuaded to acquiesce in the opinions of others, these examples also draw attention to the need for these people to feel included. The rules of the conventional publicity game implicitly state that any exposure is worthwhile to gain or maintain a public presence and that this presence is a form of power in itself. Because these individuals depend on public visibility for ranking within their sub-culture, they will do whatever is asked.

The film camera conveys status to those in front of it. Many outdoor performers, such as Desperate Men in the UK, have used the power of its presence to induce members of the public to behave in extraordinary ways, even though, in their case, the camera itself was clearly fake. For some the documentation of their behaviour may be seen as exposing them to criticism by their superiors. In the case of the fashion industry, the camera may be seen as an opportunity for self-promotion. By using and enlarging the boundaries of the publicity game, Baron Cohen was able to expose aspects of the centres of fashion that are normally concealed. So, there are at least two aspects to the emergence of structure: firstly the initiative and secondly the recognition. As was seen in the examination of improvised choral work (Chapter Two), for a new game to emerge, an initiating action must be accompanied by recognition, signalled by an imitation. The dialogue between an initiator and a single responder establishes the simplest form of structure, which is clearly hierarchical, unless the responder responds with an equally powerful action, as in choral work. Thus the dialogue between Bruno and Wilmot demonstrates a hierarchical relationship, with Bruno nodding, as if in appreciation of the sagacity of the 'master', as he answers Bruno's questions. In this micro-system, Wilmot is receiving feedback from the 'outside', simply through the outsider's (Bruno's) acknowledgment of his status. This micro-system can be seen as a basic component in a much larger hierarchical system of the fashion industry. It can be compared to other examples cited by theorists of complexity.

With or without chaos, serious cognitive scientists can no longer model the mind as a static structure. They recognize a hierarchy of scales, from neuron upward, providing an opportunity for the interplay of microscale and macroscale so characteristic of fluid turbulence and other complex dynamical processes.[46]

The fashion industry and celebrity culture is useful for Baron Cohen because it is both very fluid, highly susceptible to slight variations, and also has a complex relationship of top-down and bottom-up flows of influence. The position of the designer is paradoxical in that they both must lead but also follow trends. The fluidity means that they must risk finance and reputation in a milieu with high levels of uncertainty. The successful survivors in this highly competitive fluid system naturally acquire a confidence that can appear as arrogance to some. Repetition of successful negotiations cements their reputation but, of course, they cannot allow their designs to become predictable. The hierarchical structure of this tiny community has a fractal similarity to that of a bigger system. Those who have more influence are centres of their own system, as well as forming a cluster of closely associated centres that have strong, if not harmonious, links between them. The stronger the links between these clustered centres the more influence they have over the wider system. Even if the exact pattern of connectivity is hard to discern, this model begins to resemble a molecular model with all its sub-atomic particles providing positive or negative attraction. Or, if one substitutes 'influence' for 'gravity', it could be compared with astronomical models. Using these models, a centre is defined more by its relative position in a system than by its inherent qualities. It is both the centre of its own system and a component in a larger system.

Due to the comparative volatility of the industry, the centres are dependent on being highly attuned to feedback. Compared with other cultural systems, such as the Catholic Church, which has had centuries of sedimentation, the fashion industry is closer to the edge of chaos. As such, its components (e.g. that of Paul Wilmot or Bruno's fiction) need to vigorously assert themselves to gain influence and ensure their survival. Thus the model begins to resemble evolutionary models, as outlined by Lewin: 'Collective adaption to selfish ends produces the maximum average fitness, each species in context of others ... Creatures get better at evolving in the midst of all this activity, that they improve their evolvability'.[47]

Centres in other interviews

From this specific example I will now widen out to compare interviews with Baron Cohen's other two characters. He mainly targets right-wing attitudes: snobbery, xenophobia, homophobia, anti-semitism, patriotism, moral superiority and chauvinism.[48] However, he also targets left-wing figures including peace protesters, environmentalists, feminists and African-American orthodoxy, so that anyone who sets themselves up as an authority or has privileged knowledge is seen as a target for ridicule. Unlike Bruno's targets, Borat's are neither centre-establishers nor aspire to be included: they are gatekeepers. They define and articulate the criteria of 'correct' behaviour appropriate to specific cultural contexts in a wider variety of sub-cultures than the world of fashion. A sample from the *Ali G in da USA* series included a dating coach, an etiquette coach, acting coaches and New Age healers. Borat uses his low status as a foreigner to have these codes explained. Like Bruno, he refers to an alternative culture, of which he is a representative and for which he can define the norms and ideology, that of the unsophisticated culture of a fictitious Kazakhstan. By claiming that various forms of prejudice are the norm in this world, he releases expressions of prejudice that are normally suppressed within the culture of the USA. In effect, his interviewees can enjoy the communitas of feeling included in the fictitious culture rather than feeling excluded from their own. They are ideologically close to a centre rather than being on an edge. As Baron Cohen explains: 'Borat essentially works as a tool. By himself being anti-semitic he lets people lower their guard and expose their own prejudice, whether it's anti-semitism or an acceptance of anti-semitism'.[49]

By contrast, Ali G's interviewees were figures less concerned with conforming to norms established by others. They were mainly those at the apex of their field: a sample from the *Ali G in da USA* series included Donald Trump, Newt Gingrich, James Baker, Marlin Fitzwater, Ralph Nader, Boutros Boutros Gali, Buzz Aldrin, top scientists, film producers, art critics and the director of the Actors Studio. They are confident as centres of their own system, setting their own norms for themselves and for others. From this pre-eminent position they condescend to Ali G and to the culture he represents. Baron Cohen uses the apparent ignorance and stupidity of his character in order to draw out this condescension. At the same time, however, he exposes the weakness of their position because of the narrowness of their day-to-day experience and their ignorance of other sub-cultures. Their insular, elite position is shown to be a disadvantage in respect of the unknown language and behaviours of Ali G's world. They are also led to believe that they or their field of knowledge is unknown and irrelevant to Ali G, who, in these encounters, plays as a representative of the non-specialist mass of the population. Their sense of themselves as leaders of society is thereby diminished to being leaders of the much more limited system that immediately surrounds them. With Ali G, Baron Cohen uses a fictitious alternative culture, not to release excluded norms and ideology, but to challenge their universal application.

> This old authority and truth pretend to be absolute, to have an extra-temporal importance. Therefore their representations (the agelasts) are gloomily serious ... They do not see themselves in the mirror of time, do not perceive their own origin, limitations and end; they do not recognise their own ridiculous faces or the comic nature of their pretensions to eternity and immutability.[50]

In this way the provocateur, from a position on an edge, is able to diminish the sense of importance of those in a central position.

Baron Cohen also highlights cultural differences through the lack of shared senses of humour. Borat painstakingly tries to learn American humour (with Humour Coach, Pat Haggerty, *Borat*) and also to tell jokes from his culture which seem either too cruel or too strange to be funny for a Western audience. Although Borat's sense of humour cannot be easily shared, audiences clearly feel connected to Baron Cohen's and, as such, feel complicit in his hoaxes. In this sense he creates a community of conspiracy against his targets which is shared by members of the audience if they laugh with him. By conveying the values, customs and language of an alien world he places the accepted perspective into a relative position. As Mary Douglas puts it: 'A joke is a play upon form that affords an opportunity for realising that an accepted pattern has no necessity'.[51] For example, when Borat goes to an American patriot festival,[52] he responds to a list of reasons why America is the best country by pointing out its deficiencies in respect of the supposed values of Kazakhstan: it does not have the biggest apple, or the woman with the most pubic hair, or the world's biggest man-made box and so on. Similarly in his rodeo national anthem he sings not about liberty, strength and courage, but about the quality of Kazakhstan's potassium. Ali G effectively uses references to his world in Staines and particularly his girlfriend, Julie, in discussions about feminism, indicating that she does not mind his sexism, which shifts the nature of the discussion into areas of cultural hegemony that are problematic for his interviewees. As well as being destabilised by the norms of Baron Cohen's characters these worldly wise figures would experience a secondary destabilisation once they realise they have been duped. Both the challenge of fictitious norms and the challenge of real deception are a form of feedback on changes to the environment that require adaption of behaviour by the centre or its system, similar to feedback processes in evolution.

Two other examples from Baron Cohen's practice demonstrate the nature of power negotiations in this kind of provocation and provide an approach to consider the question of ethics in the final section of this chapter. The two examples are both from the film *Bruno*, and both demonstrate the destabilisation processes set off by an act of provocation. The first is an encounter between Bruno and soldiers at a military training camp; the second is an interview between Bruno and a Christian counsellor. In both examples the provocation works well as comic destabilisation precisely because the provoked persons are very sure of their norms and ideology. They have become secure because the systems they inhabit are constantly reinforced. The military must instil norms because of concerns about maintaining internal stability in the face of chaotic adversity. The Christian evangelist must do so because of concerns about maintaining cohesion in the face of increasing challenges to religious orthodoxy. Both systems are hierarchical and the provoked persons in these examples are enforcers of the norms of the system.

Bruno at the training camp

In the film, *Bruno*, when the main character enters the training school of the National Guard and is faced with shouting and threats by drill sergeants, his unruffled and unapologetic response to the aggression reveals its lack of effectiveness. He is instructed to put on a uniform, clearly as a way to signify his acceptance of the military norms. The putting on of the uniform, therefore, is a transition moment, a liminal zone. He enters the zone by dressing in the basic outfit, but does not cross the threshold, leaving the boots unlaced, the hat askew and adding a belt and neckscarf. By contrast, the uniform is treated by the soldiers with respect. Bruno proposes an alternative value system by treating the uniform as a fashion item. He offers his version of the uniform as a creative suggestion 'to break up the strong vertical lines'. By offering suggestions and treating the soldiers' intimidation as a personal attack he is relating to them as human beings. In so doing, he introduces an element of communitas, resisting their attempt to dehumanise him through adoption of the uniform. As Turner says:

> Liminal entities are neither here nor there; they are betwixt and between the positions assigned and arrayed by custom, convention, and ceremonial ... liminal phenomena ... reveal, however fleetingly, some recognition (in symbol if not in language) of a generalized social bond that has ceased to be and has simultaneously yet to be fragmented into a multiplicity of structural ties.[53]

He weakens their authority by not responding to intimidation in the way that they would expect, thus transforming the rules of the game, and also takes the upper hand by chiding them for their ignorance of the meaning of D and G on his belt: 'Dolce and Gabbana, come on!'. By suggesting that their aggressive response is 'bitchy' he subverts both their sense of masculinity and their prohibition of 'profanities'. When ordered to do push-ups outside a strictly demarcated area ('the alley'), he refrains from refusing, which would amount to a symmetrical challenge to authority that they would be prepared for. Instead, he transforms the action into a game, playing with the precise placement of his little finger on the line of demarcation, thus lightening the seriousness of the situation. This literal example of playing on the edge is compounded when he shares a joke of innuendo with the viewers in the cinema: 'I don't want to go into your alley ... not yet'. For the soldiers, the adherence to all the minor details of discipline are tokens of accepted subservience; any evidence of disregard for the detail is perceived as a refusal to accept the authority of the whole institution. As in many hierarchical systems (including academia) unnecessary details of observance are imposed to monitor adherence to the central authority. As Turner says: 'from the perspectival viewpoint of those concerned with the maintenance of "structure", all sustained manifestations of [existential] communitas must appear as dangerous and anarchical, and have to be hedged round with prescriptions, prohibitions, and conditions'.[54]

Baron Cohen accepts the detail but clearly does not accept the values of the National Guard and this can be seen to destabilise the soldiers who are at a loss when confronted with these alternative values. Their eyes can be seen to flicker with amazement, incomprehension and an inner turmoil as they struggle to know how to regain control. It is reasonable to assume that their sense of being 'on edge' was heightened by the presence of the camera and its crew. In terms of contest the two sides have different aims. The soldiers want Bruno to demonstrate obedience by putting on the uniform properly. Baron Cohen primarily wants to maximise their confusion for the sake of comedy and maintain his liminality as long as possible but, unlike them, he does not have a specific objective to be accomplished.

The persona of the character acts as a mask, enabling the actor to treat the interaction with more distance. By continually asking himself 'How would the character respond?' he can be more objective in his choice of responses to the outside world. The mask also acts as camouflage, presenting an appearance of stupidity, vulnerability or ignorance that deceives the soldiers into thinking that they are in control of the situation. Thus there are several levels of inter-play occurring simultaneously. Firstly, the actor must manage his/her own emotional reactions as he is faced with aggressive intimidation; he must also manage the interplay with others, manipulating it towards desired aims. Both of these interplays are 'real'. The provoked person treats the unreal mask as if real. However, using Huizinga's idea that all contests, however seriously intended, are forms of play,[55] it appears that the provoked person (the military instructor) is also playing, but without the consciousness of a game. Thus Baron Cohen enables the viewers to become conscious of the game-playing that exists in real situations.

The encounter can also be seen as an inversion: those who are invested with power by the weighty precedents and mortal authority of the military, who have acquired behaviours specifically designed for exerting their control, are quickly reduced to open-mouthed inertia as their expectations of obedience evaporate. Bruno, the physically weak outsider, even in the act of physically obeying, has become master in that he retains an element of autonomy as he opts to play their game. From the film and from extra footage on the DVD, it is clear that in the remainder of the hours spent at the training camp he continued to find ways to maintain his identity and subvert the military norms. However, the encounter is also being filmed and this provides the inversion with another layer. To the cinema audience, the soldiers appear as ridiculous puppets under the control of Baron Cohen, as he artfully triggers their reactions. The incredulity displayed by the soldiers, as they lose control, suggests what Turner calls 'a limbo of statuslessness'.[56] This state resembles 'crossing a no-man's-land where chaos and stability pull in opposite directions' from complexity theory.[57] The rapid flicking of their eyes suggests the intense mental activity required to cope with the difference of norms and unpredict-ability that they are facing. Lewin describes the process in terms of complexity theory: 'As you leave ordered territory and enter the region of chaos you traverse maximum computational capacity, maximum information manipulation'.[58] Within this state, Baron Cohen appears to be intuitively aware of the power of small actions to have large effects, as exemplified with his play of the placement of his little finger. Lewin continues:

the edge of chaos is where information ... gets the upper hand over energy. Being at the transition point between order and chaos not only buys you exquisite control – small input/big change – but it also buys you the possibility that information processing can become an important part of the dynamics of the system.[59]

It is possible to see, in this moment, a simultaneous occurrence of liminality with an arrival at the edge of chaos. Both of these theories, of liminality and complexity, use structure as a key concept in a binary relationship: the former associates structure with norms of behaviour, the latter associates structure with a state of stability. This correlation suggests that the two theories can be closely related even though they concern different fields.

Game-play and resisting conversion

An understanding of power negotiations in this kind of provocation can be widened by another episode from the same film. The character of Bruno decides to renounce homosexuality and, to this end, he visits a Christian counsellor, Pastor Jody Trautwein. A previous scene, in which Bruno has a session with a martial arts instructor, has a physical parallel with the layers of game-playing involved in the counsellor scene. The instructor is teaching him how to defend himself against attacks from gay people. The ensuing physical grappling and writhing seems intended to suggest that Bruno is using the overt purpose as a ruse to enjoy close physical contact and that this enjoyment might also be shared by the instructor. Even if the instructor is not conscious of the game-playing, Baron Cohen is drawing attention to the possible presence of a layer of interaction that is concealed even from a participant. The scene with the counsellor similarly suggests actions with unconscious motives. The counsellor gives an intense speech about how an appeal to Jesus can help Bruno become heterosexual. When it is finished Bruno asks him 'Are you hitting on me?' suggesting that the impassioned speech has been a cover for deep inter-personal contact and, by implication, that the counsellor's choice of occupation – private, intimate, man-to-man conversations about homosexuality – might carry concealed motives. The framing of the speech in this way suggests the presence of more than one game being played. The counsellor appears to remain very sure in his denial of participation in a flirting game and continues with the conversion game. Nevertheless, he is visibly disconcerted by the fact that Bruno is perceiving the interaction as a flirting game.

So Baron Cohen has introduced to the situation a suggestion of parallel objectives and a different set of rules. Carse's notion of infinite play is useful here:

The rules of an infinite game must change during the course of the play ... The rules of an infinite game are changed to prevent anyone from winning the game ... To be serious is to press for a specified conclusion. To be playful is to allow for possibility whatever the cost to oneself.[60]

As with the training camp encounter, Baron Cohen does not oppose but suggests alternatives. He asks a question rather than makes a statement. He indicates that the counsellor's speech about Jesus has been received by Bruno not for its content but the manner of its delivery, privileging the communitas of the personal interaction over the ideology that is being communicated. The counsellor can be seen as a finite player seeking the specific conclusion of a conversion, whereas Baron Cohen can be seen as an infinite player, opening up possibilities. He uses his question as a tactical ambush to gain comic effect, but it is also indicative of his wider strategy of infinite playing with the closed mentality of deeply held conviction.

Baron Cohen's interviews contain a complexity of layers of game-playing. At its simplest level he induces his interviewees to perform for the camera, either literally, as in the case of Bruno's fashion interviewees, or to impersonate others or state opinions that are not their own or to act the role they have created for themselves, as is the case with Ali G's scientists or politicians. Baron Cohen's status play encourages this performing, either by employing the low status of Ali G and Borat to stimulate high-status complementary relationships, such as student–teacher, guest–host or seeker–guide, or by employing the high status of Bruno to stimulate a director–actor relationship. Baron Cohen also changes the rules of the game both on and off camera, for example, in the case of the Ali G interviewees, they are led to believe that the character is another member of the crew until the last minute.[61] This perspective on the world as layers of game-playing may derive from Gaulier. One of his key pedagogical approaches to acting (for example, of melodramatic scenes) is to ask the actors to play concealed trivial games whilst the characters they act play the prescribed scene. In this way, there is a real interaction occurring, actor to actor, that can give life to the scene between the characters. Expertise in this double play enables Baron Cohen to manipulate a real situation whilst remaining in character. His goal is to manoeuvre the situation so that the provoked persons show expressions of uncertainty or incredulity, whether this is a one-to-one interview, a group discussion or the large-scale spectaculars such as the rodeo scene in *Borat*, discussed above. Again, this derives from another of Gaulier's pedagogical methods: to approach the state of clowning, he employs a variety of ways to induce uncertainty as a way to uncover real reactions of confusion, inadequacy and failure which are funny to observers.

The interviews with serious, self-important figures suggest that the manner of the interviewees is merely a ludic act, a public mask that is employed in order to enhance their status in front of the camera and/or as a protection against revealing their 'true' selves. As such, the public persona has no real 'objective' value, despite the invocation of 'common sense', reasonableness or, in the case of the scientists that are interviewed, the logic of their position. However central or serious or validated by popular media these persons are, they may appear irrelevant or unworthy from another perspective. This is not dissimilar to Bassi's challenge of monotheism or Banksy's self-effacing offer of multiple conclusions at the end of *Exit through the Gift Shop*.[62] The consequent implication of multiple perspectives is that any single-sided point of view, such as that inherent in prejudice, is absurd and a delusion. From Baron Cohen's perspective of the world, with his fluid game-playing, the serious intention of Bassi and the oppositional stance of Banksy can seem too simplistic, even naive and, unlike them, he does not offer himself as an exemplar.

So, different aspects of play are an important destabilising factor within these power negotiations. However, to view Baron Cohen's work as one side of a simple binary between open/infinite play and closed/finite play is to understate its complexity. Firstly, he has made statements that suggest his work is intended to enlighten as well as entertain. He described *Borat* as 'a dramatic demonstration of how racism feeds on dumb conformity as much as rabid bigotry'.[63] Although this is not pressing for a specific objective, or at least not an easily quantifiable one, it has a serious didactic intention which is far from the notion behind the carnivalesque attitudes of *bouffons*: 'people who believe in nothing and make fun of everything'. Secondly, he plays many roles within the production of his work: he is a playful improviser but is also, at times, writer, director and producer so, whereas Baron Cohen, the performer, may be interested in opening up infinite possibilities, as the director/producer he will be seriously seeking specific conclusions. In this role, his apparent primary interest seems to be in capturing the frisson that occurs when people are confronted with apparently real events that they cannot understand, or that make them fearful or angry. The entertainment value of this spectacle, combined with the well-established film distribution system, enables him to disseminate his revealed examples of prejudice and 'dumb conformity' to a very wide audience. This clearly illustrates the essence of the blade analogy: the combination of risky play with structure that reveals and releases suppressed behaviour. However, popularity, as well as being useful as a vehicle for ideas, also has commercial value, and distributing the comic discomfiture of individuals for this purpose raises the question of exploitation.

Play and ethical fluidity

In the first section I looked at risk and play. In the second section I explored Baron Cohen's exceptional adeptness at moving from one sort of game to another or playing two simultaneously, and the effect that this fluidity had on centres. This section is about the consequences of his multi-layered approach on the wider public and the nature of his popularity. This will tease out the ambiguities in his work, specifically differences between the ludic fictional character and the ethics of the real artist in relation to the two senses of 'popular' outlined in Chapter One.

Baron Cohen took a different route from provocative comedians such as Bill Hicks, who, in The Comedy Store style (from 1979) of Ben Elton and Alexei Sayle, produced a torrent of invective that, for all its transgression, was didactic. A more closely related comedian is Chris Morris, who in *Brass Eye* (Channel 4, 1997 and 2001) provided an inspiration and model for Baron Cohen's interviews with prominent figures, using the format of a current affairs programme. Although Morris created an effective parody, its main character appeared to be well-educated and sophisticated, well-suited to the culture of news and information programmes. The fact that it remained in its late-night viewing slot suggests that its appeal was somewhat limited to viewers of this type of programme.[64] The character of Ali G, on the other hand, makes a hero of a poorly educated, unemployed wannabe who embodies work-shy cynicism, drugs and low-level criminality. He is located in lower-middle class suburbia with references to New York street-gang culture shared by much of contemporary youth. Fiske cites the example of aboriginal Australians identifying with native Americans in the Western film genre, sharing a communitas of ideological resistance.[65] This is similar to the identification with both the character of Ali G and also Baron Cohen's bottom-up ridicule of powerful and educated figures. As well as celebrating what is normally denigrated, Ali G also refutes or ignores top-down instruction (for example, regarding political-correctness) and is seen to be effective disarming, confusing and coercing his intellectual and social superiors. His combination of official and unofficial traits, derived from mainstream culture, is further complicated by Baron Cohen's original format of subverting figures from politics, diplomacy, business, science, religion, the arts and feminism, and national heroes. Together these represent a fairly complete range of representatives of a liberal democracy. As Fiske suggests, the less-privileged classes interpret given culture in a way that is empowering for themselves. Thus, by means of the celebration of un-official culture and the denigration of official culture, the character appeals to both a particular cultural community and a more general one of the less privileged.

However, the New York street-gang culture has been incorporated by commercial enterprise and thus has strongly influenced the commercial mainstream of fashion and music. Baron Cohen used Ali G to 'piggy-back' on this fashion, but, before discussing his relationship to incorporation, I will consider Ali G in relation to 'popular' in the sense that Bakhtin used that term. This will help to disentangle the convoluted mixture of manufactured popularity and that which is more timeless and universal. For Bakhtin, popular has the sense of emerging from the people, an embodiment of the carnival spirit, with its liberation into an open positive laughter at everything including the self; a love of excess and exaggeration, a multiplicity of perspectives and voices, an inversion of hierarchies, especially the privileging of the 'lower body stratum'[66] and a merging with the crowd: 'The individual feels that he is an indissoluble part of the collectivity, a member of the people's mass body'.[67] In his shows, Ali G uses dance and extravagant gesture; in his studio-based interviews, he frequently makes reference to fast-food consumption, to soft drugs, to intimate details of his sex life and to farts and turds. This highlighting of the 'lower body stratum' in the context of serious discussions demonstrates an inversion over the intellect, the 'upper body stratum'. Fiske identifies embarrassment as the point of conflict between 'the conventional and the subversive, between the dominant and the subordinate, between top-down and bottom-up power … it occurs when the ideologically repressed clashes with the forces that repress it'.[68] Ali G does not present any signs of embarrassment in discussing matters of the lower body stratum with those who appear to be his intellectual and educational superiors, so there does not appear to be any conflict within him. He offers what Bakhtin describes as: 'an absolutely gay and fearless talk, free and frank, which echoes in the festive square beyond all verbal prohibitions, limitations and conventions'.[69] Ali G has popular appeal because he does not appear to be 'ideologically repressed' and this suggests he is more liberated. The impression is confirmed because, in his interviews, he does not seem to betray any trace of intimidation by official status. He meets some of the most powerful men in the world and deliberately mis-states their names (e.g. United Nations Secretary General, 'Boutros Boutros Boutros' Ghali) or their field of expertise ('techmology'), or challenges their very purpose (such as asking the Chair of the UK Arts Council why everything it funds 'is such crap'). Through this kind of ridicule he effects a reversal of status, an inversion, which is potentially empowering to all those who would feel themselves in an inferior position. As Turner claims:

> for those who are normally at the bottom of the pecking order and experience the comradeship and equality of joint subordinates, the liminality of status reversal might provide an opportunity to escape from the communitas of necessity ... into a pseudostructure where all behavioural extravagances are possible.[70]

So that, for some sections of the population, the popular traits displayed by the character are reinforced by identification with the performer. Ali G, with all his 'behavioural extravagances', presents a way of relating to the world that is universally attractive, if suppressed. In Bakhtin's terms he is the Carnival King, celebrating life in excessive consumption. Although this does indicate a stimulation of communitas, it would seem to suggest that he was only popular with those who are less privileged, in effect, one community laughing at another. However, the evidence suggests that his popularity extended across all sections of society.[71] As with most clowning, the superior laugh may be accompanied by a sympathetic affection as observers recognise their own experiences of failure, because even the most privileged have felt themselves to be stupid, ignorant, clumsy or otherwise inadequate.

Ali G at Harvard University

However, it is important not to conflate the character with the creator; although Ali G is carnivalesque, Baron Cohen is an entrepreneur. The ambiguities presented by the empowering quality of Ali G and the superior laugh at the pretensions of the character are well illustrated when he was invited to speak to students and parents at Harvard University in the character of Ali G (09/06/2004). The University authorities seemed remarkably secure in opening the institution to ridicule; one presumes there will have been some anxieties about offending some of the audience with his lewdness, anti-feminism and references to drugs. However, the character is so extremely naive and clownish (from the outset displaying the most rudimentary knowledge of spelling as if a major accomplishment), that he is framed as a mere entertainer in the service of his audience. This deferential lowering of status at the beginning of the act is in direct contrast to Bassi's entrances, which establish a sense of authority and potential threat. So the Harvard event works at two levels: the world of Ali G as the stupid outsider and the world of Baron Cohen as the Cambridge graduate. Whilst the character is irreverent and appears to disregard conventions, the actor is careful to play within the rules of, for example, the use of potentially offensive words. The actor fulfils his given brief of delivering humour, in the form of the superior laugh, as well as the *appearance* of challenge. Although he made fun of sex, drugs and education in this speech, the event can be seen as Baron Cohen being both incorporated and marginalised and demonstrates the link between the two: the provocateur is invited to take up a privileged position within the system on the condition of obeying the fundamental rules of the system. With his independence circumscribed, the provocateur can then be framed in a way that suits the particular system and can thus be neutralised; challenge is reduced to cheekiness. In the period under discussion (2000–9) Baron Cohen, perversely, became more incorporated the more his work became provocative. Moreover, the conservative News Corporation, by investing in *Bruno*, clearly viewed his work as being of service to them in terms of profit. In the context of the USA, he has been transformed from a potentially threatening, clever outsider to becoming a fully incorporated and neutralised member of the Hollywood elite. It is significant that his 2012 film, *The Dictator*, did not target centres within the USA, or their norms, but a stereotypical enemy of them. This shift from a target that is within the dominant culture to one that is outside removes one of the key ingredients of the blade strategy.

Unlike Bassi and Banksy, he is not interested in activating others, he is not part of an oppositional community and he has not engaged in any public acts of solidarity. Baron Cohen seems interested in enlarging his own cultural space and freedom of action but not that of others. Both Bassi and Banksy have a utopian aspiration.[72] The only sense of utopia that is provided by Baron Cohen is the final scenes of *Borat* and *Bruno*, and these are fantasies of self-aggrandisement. Borat is starring in his own sex-and-violence film (*Sexy Drown Watch*) and Bruno is wallowing in the shared glow of fame, singing with superstars. Similarly, unlike Bassi and Banksy, Baron Cohen seems less interested in long-term opposition to hegemony. After *Bruno* he appears to have abandoned the aim of using his work for both its commercial value and to make a social impact, prioritising the former over the latter. Even before this time he seemed more interested in achieving episodes of supremacy that were brief. His interest and participation in the fashion industry provided him with a model of temporary impact and fluidity of form; shape-shifting avoids any requirement for consistency. This example of ideological inconsistency refines the duality of play and intention, outlined in the previous chapter. It would suggest that, if the fluidity of open play is privileged, it ultimately dissipates the force of intention, destabilising its structure.

This fluidity can be identified in the ambivalent ethics in his practice. Despite the ethical dimension to his choice of targets there have nevertheless been instances of questionable ethics in his methods. Most of the victims of his hoaxes are public figures or wannabes, but some are less privileged. The Palestinian, Ayman Abu Aita, has sued for being misrepresented as a member of the Al-Aqsa Martyr's Brigade in the film *Bruno*. As a result of this misrepresentation Abu Aita:

> started to receive countless calls from outraged Palestinians. They ask how I could allow myself to be laughed at in this way, how I could agree to it, he says. 'They are angry that I have embarrassed the Palestinian people, because we are being presented in this false, disgusting way.' Abu Aita is standing in the Palestinian parliamentary elections slated for January 2010, and opposition candidates are already using this incident to discredit him.[73]

Similarly, the villagers of Glod, Romania, who appeared in *Borat*, sued, but were unsuccessful because consent forms had been signed and "'Most of the villagers knew they were taking part in a film, not a documentary." But she [a 20th Century Fox representative] admitted that "maybe not all people who took part in the film understood what it was all about'".[74] It appears that, in these cases, the unsuspecting participants could not match the careful preparation and legal muscle of a multi-national company.

Most of his interviewees appear to be selected in order to reveal their chauvinism or condescension, but others are made fun of simply because they are trying to help someone who appears to be floundering in an alien culture, such as the driving instructor in *Borat* or the guide to the UN building.[75] In other examples he makes fun of generosity or an inability to understand the situation. For example, Bruno asks interviewees to gesture a message to children who are deaf and then to repeat it frequently.[76] In such cases the ridicule is different to the bringing low of the high: it ridicules those that have risked lowering themselves in order to serve others less fortunate. There is no reversal because the laugh of superiority is directed at those who have already lowered themselves. The cynical attitude displayed towards moral acts or expressions of value borders on nihilism. Through such exploitative strategies he may even create public sympathy for those targets who are hoaxed, particularly when they are filmed using hidden cameras. In *Bruno* such a tactic is used on aged Republican Congressman, Ron Paul, who appears awkward and embarrassed as he is trapped in a room while Bruno flirts with him. This appears identical to entrapment tactics used by the police or journalists to prove wrong-doing which, in those cases, may seem justified. To use them on 'innocent' individuals to display embarrassment for the purposes of entertainment seems oppressive. Conversely, this example has the potential to increase suspicion of the power of the camera in particular and the media more generally and, therefore, can be seen as empowering to the viewers. As Tony Benn put it, after he had seen how he had been hoaxed: 'I realised what he had done would be to bring out all these media myths [and] that it was actually a very important piece of political education'.[77]

The ethical intention of parodying chauvinistic attitudes can merge into endorsing them. This is not simply a matter of misinterpretation by the public, in the way that the racism of the character of Alf Garnett in the 1960s *Till Death Do Us Part* unintentionally normalised extreme expressions. In the notorious sequence in which Borat encourages a sing-along to his anti-semitic song, *Throw the Jew down the Well*,[78] the joke is clearly on the shocking acquiescence of the participants. However, the sexism of Ali G appears to go beyond parody into a promotion and relish of sexism. One Ali G sketch concerns a farcical attempt to unite North and South Korea by means of female representatives who undress and then perform sex acts in shadow behind a screen:[79] the emphasis is on the voyeuristic aspect rather than comedy. The *Ali G Shows* certainly parody the character's naivety in his enjoyment of sexy dancing, but the widespread use of it suggests that its commercial value and Baron Cohen's enjoyment were also significant factors in its inclusion.

Furthermore, the use of Baron Cohen's three main characters has been criticised for making them the subject of the superior laugh at outsiders, by those within the cultural system.

> Novelist Jeanette Winterson was asked about Ali G in 2003 and, like the Kazakhstani government today, found him impossible to stomach. 'I don't know what the difference is between him and the Black and White Minstrels', she said. Felix Dexter, the black comedian, agreed: 'He allows the liberal middle classes to laugh at black street culture in a context where they can retain their sense of political correctness'.[80]

In the case of Borat, Baron Cohen claims he is ridiculing how foreign-ness is perceived rather than the reality of Kazakhstan's cultural attitudes. As he said in an interview with *The Daily Telegraph*: 'The joke is not on Kazakhstan. I think the joke is on people who can believe that the Kazakhstan that I describe can exist'.[81] Whilst it may be true that the audience laugh at the ignorance and narrow minds of many of his interlocutors, they also laugh at Ali G's clumsiness, stupidity, naive pretensions and lack of sophistication. Similarly, in *Bruno*, the main target of humour is the homophobes but it is also aimed at the vanity, superficiality and narcissism of the central character. The stereotype is reinforced. While this may strengthen the sense of communitas between Baron Cohen and the wider public (thus increasing his popularity), it is at the expense of reinforcing repressive attitudes towards outsiders and minorities. This may be seen as the unavoidable outcome of not taking an ethical standpoint for the sake of 'making fun of all'.

As well as game-playing with the participants on camera, Baron Cohen is also playing with the viewers of the filmed work. Gaulier often refers to the wink, a sign of complicity between actors or with the audience. Baron Cohen's characters never actually wink at the camera, but the wink is implied as he makes fun of serious and important figures: the viewers may share the conspiracy with him, they are in on the game. However, this is further complicated because the complicity we may feel is also an illusion. Baron Cohen is 'dishonest' with us because in some cases the 'real' interviews or events have been set up, are acted or are not what they appear to be. I have mentioned the falsity of the interview with the supposed member of the Al-Aqsa Martyr's Brigade. Other examples are the attempted kidnapping of Pamela Anderson that provides the climax to *Borat*, which was revealed to have been set up[82] and the supposed disruption of the MTV award ceremony with the faked outrage of Eminem who walked out (2009). The hoax is shared only by a limited circle of celebrities and the film makers. His wider audience is deceived into believing that they share a community of conspiracy with him. Thus the sense of communitas that they may feel with him is false. Unlike the overt fabrications in *Borat* and *Bruno*, these are permanent hoaxes of the wider public, not dissimilar to the effects of propaganda: supposed fact feeds a myth. Arguably this can be justified as part of the game of publicity stunts and reality shows: that notions of authenticity and integrity are just another game of performatives in a nihilistic world of masks behind masks. As Larry Charles, the director of *Borat* said: 'It was pushing at the boundaries of what comedy was, of what film was, of what a character was, of what reality was, ultimately'.[83]

The final scene of *Bruno* is another example of the complexities of the levels of game-playing. The celebrities, Sting, Bono, Elton John and Snoop Dog, act themselves performing a fund-raising song, making fun of their sometime sincerity and worthiness. For making fun of themselves they can either be seen as 'good sports' for their self-deprecation or as dupes and fools who are humiliating themselves for the sake of extra publicity, in the same way as Bruno's fashion interviewees have done. Either way, this play-acting does greater service to Baron Cohen who has incorporated them into his game. Arguably, he can also be seen in the same light, prepared to do anything for the sake of a sensationalism that serves a particular need of the capitalist–consumerist game. So this kind of ideological fluidity, sometimes bordering on nihilism, leads to an ambivalent state that is closer to 'the people who believe in nothing and make fun of everything',[84] rather than Bakhtin's description of the carnivalesque individual who 'feels that he is an indissoluble part of the collectivity, a member of the people's mass body'.[85] Paradoxically, during the period under discussion, Baron Cohen's methodology became more structured as his ideology became more fluid. The *Ali G Shows* and much of *Borat* were comprised mainly of improvised interviews, but most of *Bruno* and all of *The Dictator* are scripted. This can be understood as a necessity because of the increasing scale and complexity of production with each film, but it does also beg the question whether fitting in with an established means of production demanded a loosening of his earlier ideological standpoint. Less conjectural, however, is the fact that the abandonment of improvisation with unsuspecting individuals removed the element of risk which is a major component of the blade strategy.

Despite the clear evidence of incorporation, the wide popularity of Baron Cohen's work means that he is harder to marginalise than, say, Leo Bassi and his effect is very widespread if only temporary. One of the signifiers of popularity is imitation. Ali G was widely imitated on television; costume hire shops even stocked Ali G outfits. Borat was also imitated: the *New Hero of Comedy* programme, dedicated to him, includes a clip of Baron Cohen arriving at a film premiere where he was greeted with a line of Borat imitators. Bruno appears to have been less imitated, perhaps partly because the character was less endearing and was seen by many as too deviant. However, as an example of how far-reaching the effects of such a film are, I witnessed a display of Bruno imitators soon after it was released. At Combe Martin, a small town on the coast of North Devon in the summer of 2009, a fancy-dress wheelbarrow race was held as part of the town's summer festival. One of the entries was a group of Bruno lookalikes, young men from the local rural community, likely to have been fairly conventional in attitude and lifestyle, who posed and strutted, seemingly enjoying the opportunity to explore being outside the heterosexual norms. This play with 'otherness' is not insignificant; the potential for mocking the stereotype had already been accomplished by Baron Cohen. The young men clearly enjoyed making fun within the role rather than mocking it, therefore, identifying with it rather than denigrating it. Furthermore, the somewhat hysterical excitement of their performing indicated that they felt themselves to be taking a risk by behaving in this way and that this could only be sustained by the mutual reinforcement of the group. By popularising outsider perspectives Baron Cohen, through Bruno, had shifted the limits of public acceptability. As Fiske points out: 'The politics of popular culture is that of everyday life. This means that it works on the micro-political level, not on the macro-level, and it is progressive, not radical'.[86] As suggested above, there is an inter-relation between the three forms of communitas demonstrated in this example. The 'existential communitas' of the imitators provided them with mutual support as they transgressed the norms of their own behaviour. The positive, playful public display of this transgression had the potential to soften any homophobic attitudes in the observers. If this was the case, it suggested a wider shift in ideology as well as norms. However minimal, an element of fluidity had been introduced, releasing the men to reveal a hidden aspect of themselves. This demonstrates the effect of the blade strategy occurring at considerable distance from the provocateur's actions.

Conclusion

Baron Cohen's popularity is derived from an appeal both to the constructed cultural values of the mainstream and also to an identification with more universal and permanent human traits. Because of this combination, he can both celebrate and challenge contemporary mores. The challenge to mainstream centres and public levels of acceptability provides a cathartic thrill that is attractive to many of the public, as part of universal popularity. The appeal to mainstream popularity prevents this challenge from seeming oppositional. So the two forms of popularity work together symbiotically. For the public, he occupies a position as both insider and outsider, and this may be derived from him being part of the conventional mainstream, but also separate from it, as a member of a religious minority. Despite the imitation by fans, Baron Cohen does not foster a community, in the way Bassi does through his website, and deliberately confuses the border delineation between 'us' and 'them'. However, as the Combe Martin example demonstrates, his popularity does enable him to shift attitudes of others and to activate them in surprising ways.

In terms of power negotiations, mainstream popularity has provided him with the financial and organisational confidence, power and resources to mount more ambitious projects. His employment of a range of game tactics makes a variety of centres vulnerable because they are forced to operate under unfamiliar rules, which can change or switch into another game mid-play. His ability to change the rules of a game and fundamentally to confuse realities can be seen to be effective, both in the detail of live interactions and as part of a wider strategy. So, it is more possible to make a tentative connection between two theoretical concepts: liminality and 'the edge of chaos'. The questionable ethics of some of Baron Cohen's tactics can be seen as both open-playing, 'infinite' amorality and Machiavellian pawn manipulation in his aim for success.

What Baron Cohen's work demonstrates is the linkage between risk and popularity, and between popularity and commercial value. The latter may require a loosening of the application of ideology in the practice, if not in the over-arching intention. In the case of Baron Cohen's career, this linkage can be observed as sequential progression, of which the example of Ali G at Harvard University is a significant part. I have suggested that the effectiveness of the combination of risky play and structure, the blade analogy, if carefully targeted, can lead to revelation or release of suppressed behaviour and ideology. Baron Cohen's progression from the fluidity of improvisation to the security of controlled production was, arguably, caused by the riskiness of his early game-playing. The abandonment of risk and the accompanying move towards prioritising fame and fortune over ethical aims may be seen as the inevitable result of advancing middle age, but it can also be seen as the release and revelation of conventional norms and ideology that had been suppressed. Thus this process could be viewed as the blade effect rebounding on the perpetrator: he could release by 'permitting' himself to be conventional. Whether this can be accepted or not, it is clear that the duality of structure and fluidity in Baron Cohen's case is both a strength and a weakness. The fluidity of play can destabilise structure, but it can also dissipate the effectiveness of destabilisation because of its inconsistency.

Notes

1　Klein, Naomi (2007) *The Shock Doctrine*. London: Allen Lane.
2　Jacob, Francois (1982) *The Possible and the Actual*. London: Penguin (1989). Prigogine, Ilya and Stengers, Isabelle (1984) *Order out of Chaos*. Portsmouth: Heinemann.
3　Bakhtin, Mikhail, (1969) *Rabelais and His World*. Bloomington: Indiana University Press (1984): 90.
4　Gaulier, Philippe (2007) *The Tormentor*. Paris: Editions Filmiko: 312.

5 Critchley, Simon (2004) *On Humour*. London and New York: Routledge.

6 *Ali G Indahouse* (2002) Film; directed by Mark Mylod. 85 mins. London: Working Title Films, Talkback Productions, Kalima Productions, WT2 Productions for Channel 4 and Studio Canal.

7 *Borat, Cultural Learnings of America for Make Benefit Glorious Nation of Kazakhstan* (2007) Film; directed by Larry Charles. 80 mins. Four by Two Productions for Twentieth Century Fox.

8 *Bruno* (2009) Film; directed by Larry Charles. 81 mins. Four by Two Productions, Everyman Pictures for Universal Pictures and Media Rights Capital.

9 *Borat* cost US$18,000,000 and made US$261,572,744 at the box office plus US $62,689,415 in DVD sales. *Bruno* cost US$50,000,000 and made US$130,788,243 at the box office plus US$11,874,990 in DVD sales (www.the-numbers.com. Accessed 28/03/2012).

10 In the UK, the number of eligible voters turning out in general elections fell by 11 per cent between 1997 and 2005. In the USA, the number of eligible voters turning out in the presidential election of 2000 was 51 per cent, the lowest it has been before or since. (www.idea.int/vt/countryview.cfm?CountryCode=US. Accessed 06/09/2012). Between 2000 and 2004 viewers for *Da Ali G Show* were approximately 5 million per show (www.theguardian.com/film/2001/mar/01/news. Accessed 18/10/2014).

11 There are approximately five interviews between 2004 and 2009, but mostly these are in the context of TV chat shows. 'Baron Cohen rarely gives interviews out of character – he says he finds them "terrifying".' (*Sunday Times*, 21/01/2007).

12 *Rolling Stone* (11/11/2006).

13 *New Hero of Comedy*: Season 1, Episode 3 (07/03/2008) North One Television for Channel 4 (www.channel4.com/programmes/sacha-baron-cohen-new-hero-of-comedy).

14 Gaulier (2007).

15 Lecoq, Jacques (2000) *The Moving Body*. London: Methuen: 124.

16 Ibid.: 125–6.

17 Gaulier (2007): 215.

18 Ibid.: 193, 196.

19 *New Hero of Comedy* (2009).

20 Two examples of his slapstick are Borat repeatedly falling off a running machine (*Ali G in da USA*, 2003), and Borat clumsily knocking over most of the merchandise in a china shop (*Borat*, 2006).

21 Gaulier (2007): 292.

22 *Rolling Stone* (2006).

23 *F2F* Granada Talk TV (1996).

24 *New Hero of Comedy* (2009).

25 Larry Charles, director of *Borat* (ibid.).

26 Turner, Victor (1969) *The Ritual Process*. New York: Aldine De Gruyter (1995): 111.

27 Ibid.: 154.

28 Ken Daviditian (co-actor): 'I don't think there was anything he was not prepared to do' (*New Hero of Comedy*, 2009).
       Richard Curtis (film director): 'Physically and mentally very courageous' (ibid.).
       Andrew Newman (producer, *Ali G, The 11 O'Clock Show*): 'He can push things further than any right-minded person would be able to' (ibid.).
       David Baddiel (comedian): 'big yiddisha balls' (ibid.).
       Paul Kaye (comedian): 'He keeps pushing and pushing, he's an incredibly dangerous and fearless comedian' (ibid.).

29 Ibid.

30 Ibid.

31 Ibid.
32 Csikszentmihalyi, M. (1975) *Beyond Boredom and Anxiety*. San Francisco: Jossey-Bass: 80.
33 When interviewed later by *Time Magazine* (28/07/2009), Ayman Abu Aita stated that signs of alarm by the film crew ('Get out, get out!') had been added later.
34 Robertson, Ian (2012) *The Winner Effect, How Power Affects Your Brain*. London, Berlin, New York, Sydney: Bloomsbury.
35 *New Hero of Comedy* (2009).
36 Ibid.
37 *Da Ali G Show* (2000)
38 Lewin, Roger (1993) *Complexity*. London: Phoenix: 186.
39 Richard Curtis (film director): 'His profligacy is amazing'. *New Hero of Comedy*, 2009).
    Dan Mazer (producer *Ali G, The 11 O'Clock Show*): 'He was eager, tenacious, ambitious, driven, and not through a need for fame but for this vision that he has and this ideology of comedy' (ibid.).
40 *Sunday Times* (21/01/2007).
41 Gleick, James (1988) *Chaos*. London: Cardinal Sphere Books: 261.
42 Ibid.: 61
43 Ibid.: 153.
44 Jacob (1982): 6.
45 Turner (1969): 132.
46 Gleick (1988): 299.
47 Lewin (1993): 59
48 'It wouldn't take very much time for him to become Americanised', says a member of the Magnolia Mansion Dining Society in *Borat*.
49 *Rolling Stone* (16/11/2006).
50 Bakhtin (1969): 212–13.
51 Douglas, Mary (1975) *Implicit Meanings*. London and New York: Routledge: 96.
52 *Unseen Shit, Ali G in da USA* (2002) DVD; directed by James Bobin. Disc One 149 mins. Disc Two 71 mins. London: talkback THAMES for Channel 4.
53 Turner (1969): 95, 96.
54 Ibid.: 109.
55 Huizinga, J. (1938) *Homo Ludens*. London: Temple Smith (1970).
56 Turner (1969): 97.
57 Lewin (1993): 51.
58 Ibid.: 50.
59 Ibid.: 51.
60 Carse, James P. (1987) *Finite and Infinite Games*. New York: Ballantine Books: 9, 19.
61 *Sunday Times* (2007).
62 'I don't know what it means, Thierry's huge success … maybe he's a genius, maybe he got lucky, maybe it means art is a bit of a joke. I don't think Thierry played by the rules but then there aren't supposed to be any rules, so I don't really know what the moral is … I always used to encourage everyone I met to make art, I used to think everyone should do it. I don't really do that so much anymore.' *Exit through the Gift Shop, A Banksy Film* (2010). Film; edited by Chris King and Tom Fulford. 86 minutes. Paranoid Pictures Film Company Ltd.
63 *Sunday Times* (2007).
64 The well-educated sections of society are also selective in the features that they identify with. Ali G accomplishes subversion by means of journalistic interviews that have a supposedly educational purpose (aimed at urban youth culture) and is thus employing a validated method of liberal democracy to subvert what is official and validated. As Kershaw has pointed out artists are 'likely to have more success in securing an effective transaction with the audience if the rhetorical conventions of performance are consonant with – confirm the boundaries of – the ideology of the

community'. Kershaw, Baz (1992) *The Politics of Performance*. London and New York: Routledge: 32

65 Fiske, John (1989) *Understanding Popular Culture*. London and New York: Routledge.
66 Bakhtin (1969): 12, 92, 123, 256.
67 Ibid.: 255.
68 Fiske, John (1989) *Reading the Popular*. London: Unwin Hyman: 64, 65.
69 Bakhtin (1969): 167.
70 Turner (1969): 202.
71 The late Queen Mother was reported to have done Ali G impressions in her nineties for her great-grandsons (www.dailymail.co.uk/news/article-108494/Grandma-did-impression-Ali-G.html. Accessed 10/10/2014).
72 Bassi's liberating feathers-and-honey finale and his alliance with eco-urbanists (pp. 46, 74). Banksy's images of children, escape, and 'idyllic' landscapes.
73 *The Guardian* (31/07/2009).
74 http://news.bbc.co.uk/1/mobile/world/europe/7686885.stm. Accessed 25/07/2011.
75 *Ali G in da USA* (2004).
76 Ibid.
77 *New Hero of Comedy* (2009).
78 *Borat's Guide to the USA* (Part 2).
79 *Da Ali G Show* (2004).
80 Marre, Oliver, *The Observer* (10/09/2006).
81 *The Daily Telegraph* (17/11/2006).
82 www.hollyscoop.com/galleries/celeb-cameos-you-forgot-about/231985. Accessed 22/03/2012.
83 *New Hero of Comedy* (2009).
84 Lecoq (2000): 124.
85 Bakhtin (1969): 255.
86 Fiske (1989): 56.

4   Order out of chaos

An incident in Exeter

In 1986 I was engaged to take part in the opening and promotion of a narrow, recently pedestrianised, side street in Exeter, on which was situated the newly refurbished Arts Centre. One of the solo walkabout pieces, that I performed at that time, had a costume with padded belly, extravagant headwear and appendages strapped to my body, mainly in white, but with pink and blue ribbons wrapped around and streaming off, which could be animated with bird-like shimmering movements. This costume had been created for the *bouffon* genre at Lecoq's school where I had played a kind of grotesque baby-king. It was deliberately unclassifiable in order to be open to all kinds of interpretations and interactions. I was creating difference to see how people responded to hints of the 'other': foreign, gay, mad, vulnerable and foolish people. It strongly suggested a subversion of 'sensible adult' behaviour and also of conventional images of masculinity. The idea (tried and tested in a few other contexts) was to encourage non-adult behaviour by naively promoting play, fun and joy in movement, testing how far people would be prepared to enter into this spirit. I also wanted to surprise and mystify, simply asking passers-by: 'Do you want to play?' with a light, naïf tone of voice. Although making an offer, I did not make clear whether this was a rhetorical character question or a real offer. If a real offer, it was not clear *what* I was offering to play, inviting infinite playing in one way making it easier for the invitee to propose a theme, but in another making it harder because it required them to initiate. It was an invitation to step into the unknown and the level of risk was high because of the possibility of making a fool of themselves in a very public area. By mirroring and developing their actions it was possible to enlarge their movements and convert the stress of the first encounter into a laughing spirit of play. I noticed that the carnival principle of inversion becomes apparent in these situations: the more prepared I was to lower my status by being foolish, the more I raised it relative to those who were more fearful. As with most walkabout performance, the encounters were fairly brief, with people disengaging as soon as the question of the duration of the encounter appeared to distract them from engagement in the game. After perhaps half an hour of interacting with passers-by, I had become used to the situation and began to feel the power that a performer can have in a one-to-one interaction in a narrow street.

It was Saturday afternoon and the local football match had just finished. The adrenalin of the match was evident as a group of lads and their girlfriends confronted me aggressively with shouts of 'Poofter!', 'Tosser!', trying to intimidate me. However, my adrenalin level had already been raised by the vulnerability of parading in such a costume alone, with no 'script' to follow. This adrenalin converted into a refusal to be intimidated and I danced in front of them making fun of their 'tough' attitude and their need to impress. 'So you want to play the tough, macho game? OK, I'll be scared and run away and you shout at me'. They seem confused that I would not back down and kept reinforcing each other with expressions of support and agreement. The situation escalated. They cornered me in a disused shop doorway, with one throttling me and another threatening to punch me. Fortunately, the girls discouraged them and I was left shaken, but feeling as if some threshold had been crossed.

Immediately afterwards I was, of course, shocked by the violence, but also confused as to what had occurred. Years later I remain intrigued by the questions it raised. How is the incident to be perceived from the different perspectives of power negotiations, complexity theory, structure and play? Why did the two sides react so strongly and so quickly? Clearly, there was a clash of culture. I was challenged by their homophobic attitude, they may have been challenged by my transgressive behaviour. It must have taught us to be more wary of each other's culture: perhaps for them the fear of being made a fool of and for me the fear of suffering physical harm. This aversive reaction (backlash) could increase

Plate 4.1 Author in *bouffon* costume (author's collection)

difference in the future by increasing avoidance. However, this negativity may have been balanced by what we had learned from being on the edge of our two cultures. For me, it questioned my right to impose attitudes and actions on others from a position of supposed superior knowledge. Because of the proximity of the Arts Centre and a general awareness of street theatre as a local cultural phenomenon, they probably realised that I was only simulating eccentricity, and therefore, that I was part of the hegemonic arts establishment, despite the lowering of my status with the baby/idiot costume. In common with the majority of the population, they may well have had a fear of being shown to be ignorant in the face of 'art' and/or resentful of its privilege. In terms of physical power, a vulnerable individual was assaulted by an aggressive group. In terms of cultural power, top-down, privileged culture met bottom-up culture. In terms of play, my open-play approach was met with closed-playing contestation and, although I tried to maintain rule-breaking game-play my emotions took me into a structural battle of wills. In terms of complexity theory, my 'chaotic' behaviour was pulled towards the structure of a symmetrical contest, arguably, their solidarity as a group and their closed mentality was destabilised by the confusion caused by what they had encountered. The apparent division in reaction between the men and women would suggest that some subsequent discussion may have taken place, leading, perhaps, to questioning of the assumptions in play. So, clearly, there were many complex processes at work within the event, but the over-riding feature was that the meeting had raised our defences, reinforcing our sense of difference: we had encountered an 'edge'. In this case the 'us and them' type of edge was like a border between us. Only by coming into contact with an 'other' does identity become apparent. This 'other' might be a single individual or a whole environment.

Entity and environment: the border analogy

Systems in the natural world may have a clearly defined edge such as a cell wall, a skin or a shore-line, or they may be less clearly defined, as in the case of a micro-ecological system operating within a larger ecological system. Similarly, in human culture, 'edges' may or may not be clearly defined. Turner suggested the existence of an edge (or edges) to 'normal' or 'everyday' behaviour by identifying instances of transgression and liminality.[1] Beyond the edges, across the 'border', is the unknown, which for conscious beings, may be a potentially terrifying zone of isolation, confusion or danger. However, as McKenzie points out,[2] a liminal position can become normalised. These liminal centres are separate from, but under the influence of, established norms. The establishment of new centres is the third and final stage of the provocative process – the order that can emerge out of a state of chaos. Complexity theory suggests that order may 'naturally' emerge out of the innumerable moments of contact between insentient entities. Or, as in Klein's examples,[3] it occurs as a result of humans' (and other sentient beings') preference for any kind of order over disorder. Or it may be a defensive strategy, reinforcing or restating the demarcation of identity, as in the Exeter incident and the way that the Catholic Church responded to Bassi's provocation. Is there any correspondence between these three kinds of configuration? As I suggested in the chapter on Bassi, in relation to the Catholic Church, the defensive strengthening of the border may create a situation like a Galapagos island, cut off from wider trends and vulnerable to extinctions. Even the risk-taking provocateur may feel the need to protect themselves from adverse consequences, but how do their protective barriers affect their freedom to act? Do they become prison walls? The work of Banksy provides many examples in which these issues are raised. On the one hand he works within a structural frame of contest, mainly with dominant institutions; and on the other he refuses to adhere to anyone else's structure. As an artist whose work is partially illegal, he consequently conceals his legal identity and thus can be thought of as an outlaw. He neither seeks legal protection for his work (copyright) nor submits to operating within legal limitations. His actions suggest that he is acutely aware of the limits of what he can control and what the state and corporate media can control, and thus he can maintain his separateness. So, through an examination of his work, it may be possible to widen understanding of an edge as a border, particularly with the notion that an increased awareness of difference from an other, defines, and therefore, strengthens identity and internal coherence.

Banksy: the outlaw

'Objects are reborn in the light of the use made of them ... the object plays an unusual part and, thus shown, comes alive in a new light ... The object or the person is assigned an unusual, even paradoxical role ... this situation provokes laughter and renewal in the sphere of extraordinary reactions.' – Mikhail Bakhtin[4]

'Can artists who attempt to make strong political statements, even against the art world itself, keep from becoming the darlings of the world they seek to critique?' – Carol Becker[5]

At first glance the inclusion of Banksy in a study of performance provocateurs would seem anomalous. He works in an entirely different medium and carefully avoids any identifiable public appearance. The aspect of his practice that sets him apart and for which he is most well-known is, paradoxically, his anonymity. However, if we can draw significant parallels between his provocative practice and those within live performance, it may be possible to expand the scope of this book in order to widen the application of principles, precisely because he works in a different medium. Therefore, it is not relevant to this study to assess his work in terms of visual art – composition, use of materials or as part of a Warhol-inspired movement of Pop Art. That said, his relationship with other contemporary artists, the galleries and the art market is relevant because, to him, they represent centres that he seeks to provoke from a position that he perceives is on the edge of them. Their response to his work can expand our comprehension of how centres react to provocation. His work can also expand our perception of cultural provocateurs because, like many other visual artists and in contrast to most performing artists, he has created hundreds of artworks. In his case they cover a wide range of intentions, locations and media, even to the extent of producing a feature film. For a variety of reasons that will be explored below, he has become known to much greater numbers of people than live provocative performers, such as Bassi and, therefore, the effects of cultural provocation in a wider public sphere can be examined. His popularity ranges from celebrities, such as the singer Christina Aguilera, and film stars, such as Tom Cruise and Angelina Jolie, who have bought canvases for hundreds of thousands of dollars, to underground activists across the world. His far-reaching influence is evidenced by the work of subversive Russian artist P183[6] and, in Egypt, paintings by local activist-artists on newly constructed walls in Cairo's Tahrir Square 'are homages to Banksy and what he has done in Palestine'.[7] The *Banksy versus Bristol Museum* exhibition (2009) attracted a record-breaking 300,000 visitors in twelve weeks, who waited up to six hours in order to gain entry: 'It has claims to have been the most attended regional art exhibition [in the UK] since 1945'.[8] He was invited to create an opening sequence for *The Simpsons*, and his film *Exit through the Gift Shop* (2010) was nominated for an Academy Award. Banksy is uncomfortable about talking about his work: 'You don't want to explain yourself too well, I guess. If I could explain it in words I wouldn't need to do the picture'[9] and, because of concerns about revealing his identity, he is reluctant to give interviews. Despite this, there has been a gradual accumulation of interview material which is augmented by his writings. Most significantly these are in *Wall and Piece* [10] and *Home Sweet Home*.[11] Some of this writing had already appeared in his early self-published books (*Banging Your Head against a Brick Wall* (2001), *Existencilism* (2002) and *Cut It Out* (2004)). He also made a few significant statements in *Exit through the Gift Shop*.[12] Although there have been a few books written about his career, most notably *Banksy, the Man behind the Wall*, by Will Ellsworth-Jones,[13] there is very little information that has been confirmed by him so I have had to rely on sources that may not be entirely accurate.

Although Banksy's work cannot be formally classified as live performance, his work can be viewed from a performance perspective in various ways. At its simplest, because much of Banksy's outdoor work is executed in locations which are forbidden by public authorities and private ownership, elements of performance are required to mask his actions from authorities. 'The easiest way to become invisible is to wear a day-glo vest and carry a tiny transistor radio playing Heart FM very loudly. If questioned about legitimacy of your painting simply complain about the hourly rate'.[14] At times, his interventions into museums and art galleries required costuming and face-masking in order to remain undetected during installation. At other times, such as the installation of the Guantanamo Bay prisoner dummy at Disneyland, he is required to perform as a 'normal' visitor. Similarly while working in semi-public spaces and at public events, such as the 2003 demonstration against the Iraq war, he must act inconspicuously, playing at being 'not Banksy'. He regards his work not just as items of visual art, but also as performance feats: 'People look at an oil painting and admire the use of brushstrokes to convey meaning. People look at a graffiti painting and admire the use of a drainpipe to gain access'.[15] Moreover, his frequent use of particular spaces and contexts for the inspiration and framing of his work is very similar to site-specific performance work: the images 'perform' with their surroundings. I have suggested elsewhere[16] that outdoor performance works well when it either 'fits' with its surroundings, enhancing one aspect of it, or is in clear opposition. Banksy often uses the shape of an existing crack in a wall as a key feature or, by contrast, places sharks' fins sticking out of a municipal lake. Because his artworks are removed or defaced rapidly after execution and only 'exist' in photos taken by the artist or his crew, they have a similar ephemerality as site-specific performance, so can be treated primarily as temporary interventions in a particular site. Moreover, some of his work is like other forms of mobile street performance; his *Sirens of the Lambs* (New York 10/10/2013) used puppeteers to animate distressed animal toys protruding out of an abattoir truck.

In this chapter I look at three areas of Banksy's work. I begin by examining the subject of his anonymity in order to consider what the implications are of maintaining a position on an edge. This provides an entry point into the central subject of this chapter, which considers Banksy in terms of incorporation into dominant culture and resistance to it. In the second section I consider these issues in relation to his influence over the 'Tesco riots' in Bristol (2011) to suggest that, compared with Baron Cohen, he employs a more moral, pro-gressive perspective. Using the same example, I counter-argue that Banksy simultaneously undermines the structure of contest implied by a progressive perspective. This opens up the question of the nature of power negotiations in this area of practice. In the final section I demonstrate the effectiveness of this dual approach in practice, using the example of Banksy's 2009 exhibition in Bristol. This exhibition and his nearby *Hanging Man* mural (2006) had a trans-formative effect on two centres that, unusually, did not suppress or marginalise his work. Because of his anonymity, he has two identities: the elusive, as the mysterious, renegade artist, and the invisible, as his own, private self, and this duality is a type of ambivalence, different to that of Bassi or Baron Cohen, who are relatively more accessible to the public. Because of the imperative to maintain this separation, Banksy has had to create his own system of organisation. This provides a good example of a 'liminal norm' coming into being. In addition, he has encouraged (street art) collaborations and networks (e.g. within the Stokes Croft area of Bristol) that have coalesced disparate elements, providing some coherence where none had existed before. From the perspective of complexity theory, these examples can be seen as order emerging from chaos.

Banksy works on the same kind of risk edge used by Bassi and Baron Cohen. His early work in particular was concerned with the concrete edge of pulling off a successful coup. In his case, these were not hoaxes, but hit-and-run 'bombing' (a rapid covert spray-painting of all available walls in a specific area) and escaping undetected. One theory of the origin of his professional name was that his real first name (Robin) was used to arrive at 'Robin Banks'.[17] This identification with a bank robber seems plausible not only as a crude anti-capitalist strategy, but also in terms of pulling off a heist, such as his planting of work in famous museums and galleries. 'Tagging' and other street art has the somewhat male characteristic of marking territory, claiming it as one's own and enjoying the ripples that this 'splash' creates. This aspect gives an insight into the invasive strategies of Bassi and Baron Cohen. Like them, he carefully pin-points a particular target for his intervention; for them it is an individual or an institution whereas, for him, it is a physical location (which may include prohibitive notices and other physical methods of control placed by institutions). In stark contrast to Bassi and Baron Cohen, he does not seek a face-to-face edge, but instead has impact through the content and location of his work. Like Bassi he makes some work for the wider public and other work for a narrower range of paying afficionados. The gallery work for the committed observer can afford to be more complex and serious. The street work, for a non-committed public, has to attract attention, and, therefore, he uses simple combinations of two or more elements to create surprise, curiosity and the humour of juxtaposition.

The invisible man

One of the most distinctive features of Banksy's work is his maintenance of anonymity. Unsurprisingly, this extraordinary strategy was originally formed as a practical solution to avoid arrest. When Banksy was fifteen and beginning to get involved with street art, seventy-six of the local graffitti artists were arrested in Operation Anderson (1989) and most were fined. Up to the time of writing Banksy has managed to avoid such a fate, but has had to adopt a permanent role of fugitive in order to do so. The limited extent of the anonymity is, perhaps, generally overlooked. In the collection of essays, *Banksy, The Bristol Legacy*, edited by Paul Gough,[18] John Hudson provides a name, a date of birth and other personal information about Banksy, all unconfirmed but 'beyond reasonable doubt'.[19] Photographs of him, obtained and published by the *Mail on Sunday*,[20] are easily available on the internet, their veracity seemingly confirmed by the subsequent purchase of the photo copyright for an allegedly substantial sum.[21] There are copious amounts of information about him in the Ellsworth-Jones book[22] and in Marc Leverton's *Banksy Myths and Legends*.[23] He can be contacted indirectly through his website[24] or his PR agent. He occasionally lets his thoughts and feelings be known through these and other intermediaries and he talks to camera in his own film, albeit with his face hidden and his voice disguised. Therefore, there is arguably as much freely available information about him as there is for any other camera-shy person who does not want to reveal their address.

That said, being unable to use one's own name is a cost usually associated with criminality, espionage or political prisoners. Being forced to lead a double life requires the constant stress of maintaining a fiction and dealing with the border between the real and not-real on an on-going basis. The original purpose of the anonymity is understandable, but Banksy's wealth, public acceptance and the time elapsed since his early 'crimes' will have mitigated the potential effects of prosecution for that work. Later work, such as his month-long residency in New York, *Better Out Than In* (October 2013), brought headlines around the world that the NYPD were on the hunt for him[25] but this was flatly denied by them[26] so it is conceivable that the story may have been 'planted' for publicity purposes. Prosecution might hamper his free movement across the Atlantic but, as was evident, his popularity and the increased value that his work brings to property resulted in a complete absence of complaints, so this threat is not high. Why has his anonymity been sustained when other provocateurs, who are similarly culturally transgressive, adopt an alternative response, continuing their activities despite repeated arrest?[27] Like members of Pussy Riot, who I will discuss in the next chapter, these provocateurs refuse to acknowledge the right of authorities to restrict their behaviour.

It is clear from many of his statements that Banksy derives great pleasure from the sense of achievement and the adrenalin experience of his clandestine coups. Particularly in his early work, audacity was his primary source of satisfaction:

> The art to it is not getting picked up for it, and that's the biggest buzz at the end of the day because you could stick all my shit in Tate Modern and have an opening with Tony Blair and Kate Moss on roller blades handing out vol-au-vents and it wouldn't be as exciting as it is when you go out and you paint something big where you shouldn't do. The feeling you get when you sit home on the sofa at the end of that, having a fag and thinking there's no way they're going to rumble me, it's amazing ... better than sex, better than drugs, the buzz.[28]

His evasion of arrest is as much a demonstration of prowess as is the scale of the coup and the ripples it creates. The painting of the Palestine separation wall provided both the risk experience and a notoriety that became worldwide. His publicist, Jo Brooks, indicated the sense of threat he was under: 'The Israeli security forces did shoot in the air threateningly and there were quite a few guns pointed at him'.[29] His film provides an example of his ability to cope with pressure and his enthusiasm to embrace risk: on the eve of his first major exhibition in Los Angeles, he decided to insert the Guantanamo Bay figure at Disneyland, narrowly avoiding arrest. Apart from these extreme situations, he also took risks with his exhibitions, particularly the controversial painting of the skin of a live elephant for his *Barely Legal* exhibition (2006). Arguably, as his reputation grew, the risks taken were greater because he had more to lose.

His risk-taking may also have contributed to an 'evolution' moment which has parallels with the seminal incident of Leo Bassi's career involving a bicycle accident (p. 43) and the moment when Sacha Baron Cohen realised that Ali G was credible on the street (p. 98). Banksy recounts the moment when he realised the potential of stencil work, when he was hiding from security guards: 'As I lay there listening to the cops on the tracks I realised I had to cut my painting time in half or give up altogether. I was staring straight up at the stencilled plate on the bottom of a fuel tank when I realised I could just copy that style and make each letter three feet high'.[30] Once he began to use stencils and pictorial images, his style departed from the surprisingly strict conventions of graffiti artists who insisted on simply 'tagging' (writing one's chosen name) with freehand spraying. Because of his middle-class education and home, he did not easily fit in with the Bristol graffiti scene, centred in the working-class district of Barton Hill.[31] This early experience of being an outsider wanting inclusion, an experience comparable to those of Bassi and Baron Cohen, may have contributed to his long-term adoption of the role of fugitive.

Banksy's early street art involved practical challenges of gaining access, avoiding detection and working with the location. Although patterns of practice would have emerged, each action required solutions that had no precedent. While it is clear that Banksy must have experienced what Csikszentmihalyi terms 'flow',[32] it is also clear that he derived as much pleasure from the achievement as from the process. In terms of the mountain climbers that Csikszentmihalyi cites, Banksy is as much interested in arriving at a summit as he is in matching his skills to the challenges of a rock face. Although there may be a reduction of ego within the 'flow' of the activity there is an enhancement of ego in the ability to dominate by imposing his presence where it is forbidden to do so. His obvious interest in seeking out these adrenalin-filled experiences suggests that he may be subject to the 'Winner Effect', outlined in Chapter One, in which ever higher risks are taken. As I have suggested, the consequent high level of self-esteem can lead to arrogant independence. In Banksy's case it is not only physical challenges he surmounts, but also the contest with dominant power. This sense of himself being in such a contest is suggested by many of his recurring images (such as that of surveillance cameras). If the game is to win a contest over dominant powers then a perpetuation of the 'hit-and-run' fugitive role provides the opportunity for further pleasurable victories. Moreover, the longer that it is sustained, the greater is the 'victory'.

Presence and absence

Having adopted the clandestine image, its usefulness for publicity purposes must have become apparent. At the time of writing, the quest for his identity remains a popular story in the international press after two decades. The story has a wide appeal as it resonates with a tradition of wrong-righting maverick folk heroes who hide their identity or their presence. In mask work, the less that is defined in the shape of the mask, the more the audience is able to project emotions and thoughts onto the *tabula rasa*. His sense of injustice, his defiant hit-and-run tactics, his band of confederates and his escape from authorities into invisibility are reminiscent of the Robin Hood legend. Spartacus, Zorro, the Lone Ranger and the Scarlet Pimpernel are other examples. Many commentators have remarked on the attractive power of his mystique as a key factor in his success. So the anonymity can be seen as a public relations exercise as much as a strategy to protect his private life. More significantly, as an invisible celebrity, he is better able to avoid the focus being on his personal life rather than his work. He has often referred to his concern that the reality behind the tantalising mask cannot match the excitement of speculation: 'the reality of me would be a crushing disappointment to a couple of 15-year-old kids out there';[33] 'I wish you were talking to an imposter. I don't have much of a personality, so it's difficult to "be" one'.[34] However, as with much of Banksy's work this self-deprecation is double-sided:[35] the presentation of low status is useful to gain status, in this case by seeming more open and honest than most interviewees and careless of the self-promotion norms. His 'absence' means that there are fewer, potentially constrictive, expectations and interpretations. Some viewers of *Exit through the Gift Shop* noted how Banksy had substituted himself for the main character, so that he could self-reflect on his work and its reception without being present.

> Banksy traded roles with Thyerri when he asked for the tapes to remake the documentary. Thyerri then took on Banksy's role of artist, at a time when the public was looking for a way to express that they related with this artistic medium. Switching roles with Thyerri allowed Banksy and the rest of the street artists to remain detached from their audience. Brilliantly setting the stage for the real show. The public's reaction to Thyerri unwittingly playing his role as the mainstreamer. ART MIMICS LIFE MIMICS ART ... copy of a copy![36]

This substitution is another form of his absenting himself from public gaze beneath layers of filters and mis-information, so that the 'real' disappears.

Banksy's anonymity can also be viewed in relation to the 'History of Nemo', cited by Bakhtin,[37] which was popular in the fourteenth and fifteenth centuries. By using 'nemo' ('nobody') as a name of a character, the meaning of prohibitions is transformed into its opposite, a negative becomes a positive, as in 'Nobody is allowed to ...'. This was a play with negation as part of the carnivalesque play with the inside-out, upside-down reversals that inverted validations and prohibitions in order to reveal truth by means of paradox. Similarly Banksy plays with absence and presence. This relates to him performing as 'not Banksy', referred to above. His street work reveals his presence in the neighbourhood, but he himself is not present. The imperative, placed on celebrities by the norms of the commercial media, that 'No celebrity must miss an opportunity to promote themselves' is turned into a positive if Banksy says he is 'no-celebrity'. From this perspective, Banksy's absence can be seen as a denial of the acceptance of the subject being transformed into a commercial object. Despite the incorporation of his work into capitalist structures he has partially avoided his personal life being owned by them.

So, Banksy was both imposing his increasing presence and absenting himself. This established a pattern of duality which has had a number of consequences. Firstly, his popularity gives him power to gain access to sites and opportunities, but his secretiveness means that his work can pop up in a wide variety of locations, legal or illegal. 'In these combatants' stratagems, there is a certain art in placing one's blows, a pleasure in getting around the rules of a constraining space'.[38] Thus he can create surprises, such as the painting of a public wall or the unexpected exhibition in Bristol. This was announced only days before its opening, which thus became a news story rather than an arts story in the press and media. He can use his popularity, not be used by it. Because his face is not well known, he can mix with the public on level terms. For example, a friend of mine was employed at the Glastonbury Festival to take care of the litter bins. He noticed a man spray-painting the bins and chased him away. Eventually they got into a playful scrum in the mud. Afterwards he was informed that he had been wrestling with Banksy. Therefore, Banksy can have two identities. Bakhtin suggested that, through the use of costume and mask, carnival revellers in the Middle Ages could temporarily abandon their professional roles and personal identities. For Banksy, ironically, his professional role can be abandoned by having an unremarkable appearance, allowing him to merge with the mass.

Secondly, the maintenance of the fugitive role perpetuates a sense of fear. Using Bateson's notion of complementary relationships,[39] the fugitive role implies the presence of a pursuer, thereby reinforcing and perpetuating the existence of an invisible oppressor. Not many other UK artists maintained the kind of a strident oppression–resistance model that had been created in the polarised 1980s, during a relatively liberal period of domestic UK government policies (1997–2008). Although Banksy uses humour throughout his work, it is not the laugh of the free as Bakhtin describes it: 'Laughter liberates not only from external censorship but first of all the great interior censor; it liberates from the fear that developed in man during thousands of years; fear of the sacred, of prohibitions, of the past, of power'.[40] So, by projecting the fearful persona beyond the period of its relevance, Banksy is actually reinforcing and sustaining a notion of a powerful, oppressive system. His promotion of himself as needing to create a space in which he can be more free, also promotes the notion of him being confined. Sacha Baron Cohen refuses to be intimidated and plays with threat for his own ends. He diminishes a sense of oppression by not accepting its power. There is a suggestion of concealment behind his extreme characterisation and he is concerned to keep his private life private, but he does not demonstrate a need to go to the more extreme duality adopted by Banksy. Bassi is happy to appear in public and talk to journalists, refusing to limit his freedom of open expression; the threats to him have been severe, yet he does not allow them to restrict his movements or actions.

Thirdly, straddling an edge in this way requires creating a defensive structure. The strategy of anonymity requires tight security and, despite his casual demeanour, Banksy maintains a rigid control over his team, members of which have been excluded after unwittingly revealing information to the press. His tight circle of friends and colleagues are fearful of even expressing an opinion in relation to his work. They are aware of the responsibility that his trust in them confers. Even those of comparative status, such as his friend Damien Hirst, must operate according to his rules in their relations with him. The organisational structure around Banksy, even if it has an alternative ideology and norms, is nevertheless a controlling, hierarchical one. Within the structure there are all three forms of Turner's communitas – norms, ideology and a shared experience (of conspiracy). The development of this structure out of the communitas of his early collaborations within an equal community of street artists is a good example of Turner's suggestion that all spontaneous communitas inevitably suffers a 'decline and fall' into structure.[41] Paul Gough, in the concluding summary to the 2012 collection of essays refers to the difficulties of 'authorisation' of the writing by Banksy's office and also to the conditions attached to the contract for the 2009 exhibition.

> Regional galleries and museums ... don't relish ... the challenge of working with an artist, his crew and his PR machine, notorious for insisting that things are done strictly on their terms. One phrase that I heard over and over again during the creation of this book was that everything had to be done 'by the rules'.[42]

The vehemence with which the 'rules' are applied by his office suggests that there is an atmosphere of fear, not only with friends and colleagues, but in the person who is at the centre of it. The anonymity appears to have accelerated the process of him establishing his own closed system. The system has very clearly delineated boundaries in the sense of who is included/excluded. For those outside the structure, the imagined experience of communitas of conspiracy seems attractive, the more tantalising because of its inaccessibility, but the anonymity acts as a barrier to any possible experience of communitas with him. Although he can wrestle in the mud with strangers he cannot be open and honest with them: the protective walls have become a prison. This, along with his renown and financial success, has made him remote from his communities (e.g. that of emerging street artists). The resentment, at what is seen as betrayal in his denial of community, has led to defacement of his most iconic work.[43] His power and influence are seen as dominating and exclusive. This might in part explain the destructive conflict with the street artist Robbo and his team.

His preference for stencil work over tagging was one of the exacerbating factors in the conflict with Robbo. This, rather tribal, conflict has led to a sad over-painting of each other's work by Robbo's supporters or, allegedly, by Banksy himself.[44] According to Robbo, this conflict began with Banksy showing disrespect and Robbo punching him.[45] Banksy was threatened by the status of this older, well-established artist, and Robbo was threatened by the growing renown and commercial success of Banksy. It can be seen as the conflict between two centres of influence and is reminiscent of the vehement and destructive conflict that tends to emerge between the sub-divisions of marginal political parties. Their contest over territory is unsurprising within a practice that uses the imposition of one's identity ('bombing') as a key strategy. Here the edge-as-border is, appropriately, negotiated on a wall, with Banksy demarcating his own space within which to operate. This territorialisation is another example of the connection between centre formation and empowerment from successful risk-taking.

Finally, this separation along with the acquisition of fame and fortune gave him a different perspective. Although in many ways he is a modern representative of the carnivalesque, he does not fit within Bakhtin's model in many significant ways. The rigidly controlled, hierarchical structure, that he needed to create, means he can ignore feedback from within it and he is protected from feedback from without.

> But it's part of the job to shut the fuck up and not meet people. I never go to the openings of my shows, and I don't read chat rooms or go on MySpace. All I know about what people think of my gear is what a couple of my friends tell me, and one of them always wants to borrow money, so I'm not sure how reliable he is.[46]

He is, therefore, liable to be less challenged than he would have been if he had been operating alone. This enabled him to sustain a perception of power negotiations in a simple oppression–resistance binary, rather than engaging with complexities. As I shall argue below, this outlook affected his perspective on the Tesco riots and his choice of action in response to them. Because of this higher status, he sees himself as leading by example: 'I paint hard for Easton and if every area had someone painting hard for it, the country would be a far more colourful place'.[47] Using Bateson's notion of complementary relationships, the more he becomes the active leader, the more he encourages passive following. Particularly in a developed Western society, it is easy for members of sub-cultures to reaffirm their shared sense of identity with emblematic gestures, the superficiality of which may encourage the apathy of its constituents: they delegate their indignation. As Eugene Byrne put it: 'What a lot of graduates want, especially as they get older, is the appearance of rebellion with none of the inconvenient or expensive actuality'.[48] In this sense, Banksy has stimulated imitation, a radical chic, rather than autonomy, a substitution of norms rather than an independence of thought. Thus attempting to activate others by leading through example, in this case, is self-defeating.

How can he avoid becoming a new leader, who is passively and unthinkingly followed? There are signs that he has attempted to avoid this position – by staying out of the limelight, by self-deprecation, by avoiding claiming copyright. As he put it: 'If you've built a reputation on having a casual attitude towards property ownership, it seems a bit bad-mannered to kick off about copyright law'.[49] Particularly in his later work, many of his images are unsigned which suggests a decreasing need to claim credit and boost his own profile. Many of his street pieces are small and discreet, located in temporary or marginal spaces; this does not suggest a sensationalist flamboyance. Like Bassi, he is accused of being a self-publicist, but unlike the performer he remains invisible.

> There's a problem with being in the public eye – you have to become very tough, to grow a thick skin and ignore other people's opinions. It's unfortunate because those are the traits you actually least want in your public figures or artists.[50]

However, there are strong suggestions that, as compared with Bassi and Baron Cohen, Banksy privileges lone activism over being a team player. There are some instances of him taking on a leadership role but this is more in terms of strident individualism than organising a campaign. He has a small team of assistants but he does not share control with them and may dismiss their feedback:

> I have a great little team, but I tell you what – they all hate this fucking film. They don't care if it's effective, they feel very strongly that Mr Brainwash is undeserving of all the attention. Most street artists feel the same. This film has made me extremely unpopular in my community.[51]

He devotes a whole page of his *Wall and Piece* to tell the story of the man who sparked the downfall of Romanian dictator, Ceausescu, as an example of the independent thinker who, with the right action at the right time, can cause a political avalanche.[52] He also cites the lone figure who faced the tanks at Tiananmen Square and, on the front page of his website (in 2011), he carried a photo tribute to Brian Haw, who held a solo vigil outside the Houses of Parliament for over ten years as a protest against the Iraq war.

Finally, his organisation has provided him with the support to operate an alternative means of production. Unlike Bassi or Baron Cohen, who must rely on established means of production and are thus subject to incorporation or suppression, Banksy is not so vulnerable to reactions of the central cluster. His dual identity means that the product, that is Banksy, can be viewed with more detachment by the man himself. This may explain his ability to maintain an ambivalent attitude to fame and fortune. 'I tell myself I use art to promote dissent, but maybe I am just using dissent to promote my art. I plead not guilty to selling out. But I plead it from a bigger house than I used to live in'.[53] Despite his scorn for advertising and the capitalist system, it is clear from his entrepreneurial and marketing strategies that he is prepared to operate within it. The Banksy brand, like any other, is promoted to increase sales, yet the artist is cynical about the market. He has nurtured the suggestion that fame and fortune have been thrust upon him but Ellsworth-Jones has indicated that, in fact, he worked hard for several years to sell his paintings to influential London galleries.[54] Similarly, despite having an appearance of free happenings, the main purpose of his exhibitions and annual *Santas Ghetto* installations is to promote and sell his paintings.[55] Much of his street work can be seen as ongoing self-promotion as much as art that is for, and on behalf of, the people. As will be outlined in the final section, the Banksy product can become partially incorporated, but the artist remains elusive and uncontrollable.

However, Banksy appears to be very conscious of how fame and fortune have separated him from even his close community, many of whom had changed the nature of their relationship with him by selling artefacts that had been exchanged in a friendly barter.

> When the paintings suddenly started going for, like, really big money it definitely weirded me out, and I kind of went away to the middle of nowhere and I stopped making any more paintings. But … the whole time the auction houses were just selling paintings that I'd done years before and sold for not much money. Or paintings that I traded for a haircut or, yer know, an ounce of weed and they were going for like 50 grand.[56]

There is a similar ambivalence amongst other street artists and supporters in the debate over whether his fame and fortune should be viewed as a 'sell-out' or as the admirable result of a 'heroic' career, which provides an empowering example and, as I have argued above, is thus popular.

Using the border analogy in a very literal way, Banksy's continued refusal to reveal his official identity can be viewed as that of a political exile who refuses to return to a home country despite a change of regime. By means of this self-exclusion, he places himself beyond reach, outside of the system. Other provocateurs such as Bassi and Baron Cohen seek to affect the centre and its system from a position within the structure, albeit from a position close to the edge. As such they remain in a weak position, subject to suppression, marginalisation and incorporation. By placing his true identity beyond reach of authorities and corporate media, Banksy uses the edge as a protective barrier, a mask, to prevent central authorities reaching the person. By having a dual identity, Banksy can be both within and without. The mask of his public persona is within the system, a product, subject to incorporation, which can thus be regarded as a commercial franchise of the real person. Many shy celebrities have this duality of persona but with Banksy the separation is more acute. So the location of the edge, in this case, is precisely between the mask and the real person.

Banksy and the Tesco riots

In this section I examine Banksy's relationship with the Tesco riots in Bristol (2011), in order to tease out the relationship between the border analogy and the fulcrum analogy. The Tesco riots provide an unusual instance of an artist having a direct influence over political events while maintaining personal distance. In this sense, it is a good point of comparison with Bassi, who does become personally involved, and Baron Cohen, who does not have such a clear direct influence. The example demonstrates an interplay between the real and the not-real, the serious and the playful, structure and communitas. In both theoretical and practical senses, the situation was 'on the edge of chaos'. As such it provides an opportunity to bring together ideas from different theoretical areas with Banksy's artistic practice and apply them to power negotiations in cultural provocations of this sort.

Banksy had two points of influence over the Tesco riots, one direct and the other indirect. One of his most famous (and still surviving) murals, *The Mild Mild West* (1999) (Plate 4.2), is located right in the heart of the small area, Stokes Croft, where the riots took place. The mural depicts a teddy-bear in the act of hurling a petrol bomb towards riot police.[57] Since the time it was painted, the area had gradually transformed from a seedy, run-down offshoot of the city centre to a hub for counter-cultural activities, including an explosion of street art, community enterprises, alternative galleries, rehearsal rooms, music venues and contemporary circus companies. This development was partly as a result of a significant expansion of student accommodation in the vicinity which in turn made it an opportunity for entrepreneurial small businesses such as independent cafés, restaurants, temporary exhibition spaces and performance venues. The rising economic prospects of the area brought with them an element of gentrification that attracted multi-nationals such as Costa and Tesco. The opening of a small

Plate 4.2 The Mild Mild West, Banksy, 1999 (photo: Bim Mason 2014)

Tesco store was, therefore, viewed by the counter-cultural community as an unwanted imposition. It was said by them to be a threat to the survival of locally owned stores,[58] but since there was no comparable store in the immediate vicinity, located between two extensive shopping areas, it would appear that objections were partly influenced by political considerations. Although there had been demonstrations and some vandalism around the store, the riot was sparked by an attempted eviction of a graffiti-covered squat, located almost opposite the newly opened Tesco store. There was a perception by some in the counter-cultural community that the eviction was part of an attempt to move them out of the area, which they felt they had revived, and that the Tesco store was part of the same process. Because one drunken man on the roof of the squat acted as if he was preparing a petrol bomb, the police 'decided to raid the squat and found a "volatile organic compound" in a bottle, although it was not flammable. A green container had traces of petrol and there were four disposable lighters'.[59] The significance of the possible petrol bomb as a key factor in the eviction does raise the question as to whether the man and the police were influenced by the Banksy mural. Although it is hard to evidence such an influence, the sentiment expressed in the painting probably helped sustain a notion of opposition to the police over the twelve years between its painting and the riots, during which time community relations with the police had otherwise generally improved. During this period the status of Banksy had transformed from little-known local artist to one of international fame, and his status in Bristol had been enhanced by the museum exhibition two years earlier. It can be inferred that, because Banksy had demonstrated the positive impact that outsider art could have on the local economy,[60] he had influenced the municipal policies that had enabled the flourishing of the Stokes Croft area. Because of his local-hero status, it is not unreasonable to assume that, for some individuals, the mural normalised violent posturing towards the police. As well as the long-established multi-racial community, the area attracts transient people who identify with the counter-cultural ideology and may wish to prove their ideological identification in order to be included in the community. Banksy's anti-consumerist stance and his advocation of direct action would also have been widely known. So, for those (mainly young) people who were seeking an experience of belonging, the mural provided a model of action that could be enacted by participating in the riot. The simplicity of the binary opposition with dominant forces could be easily grasped and the contest with the police generated partisanship and a sense of community where none had existed before. This process can be observed in very different contexts: for example in an environmental dispute in Russia.

> Yegevenia Chirkava was upset when a forest she walked in, with her daughters, was cut down to make way for a motorway into Moscow funded by one of Putin's associates. They protected the trees after a long battle and have to maintain a vigil over the forest. She said 'I didn't come to politics, politics came to me' ... Can a woman who spends so much of her time looking after her daughters in this tiny flat really scare the Kremlin so much? 'Of course they are afraid of me but it's the same as when they tried to discredit the dissidents in Soviet times, it has the opposite effect. People want to know why they are abusing us, then they get interested. Then they join us ... The most important thing is to change the way people think – we are not struggling for power; as Chekhov said "We are struggling to drive the slave mentality out of ourselves".'[61]

Contest can serve to stimulate a greater sense of community and to draw others into becoming active. As Turner says: 'we very often do find that the concept of threat or danger to the group ... is importantly present. And this danger is one of the chief ingredients in the production of existential communitas'.[62]

The other, more direct, influence that Banksy had on the riot was his donation of two thousand posters to help pay for the legal costs of those arrested and to assist two key community arts enterprises: Coexist, which ran the building where the mural is sited, and the Peoples Republic of Stokes Croft (PRSC). The two companies had, up to this point, maintained a neutral stance to the riots, condoning neither side and showing solidarity with other enterprises that had been damaged in the general mayhem. However, the image on the poster was of a smouldering petrol bomb in a Tesco labelled bottle (Plate 4.3) and, because of the donation, these companies were implicated by the local press in the violence and even blamed for it.[63] These events can be looked at from two theoretical perspectives. The first is to consider the power negotiations in terms of oppositional resistance, with serious intentions and real consequences, and the

Plate 4.3 Tesco firebomb poster, Banksy, 2011 (photo: Bim Mason 2014)

second considers them in terms of the ludic quality of Banksy's work. By examining these two angles together the relationship between play and various kinds of edge can bring together Turner's communitas–structure dialectic and complexity theory.

One of the recurring themes of Banksy's work is that of controls, both in terms of authoritarian restrictions and also cultural manipulation through advertising. In his writings he refers to public spaces being bombarded with advertising messages and the need to respond with counter-messages.

> The people who truly deface our neighbourhoods are the companies that scrawl giant slogans across buildings and buses trying to make us feel inadequate unless we buy their stuff. They expect to be able to shout their message in your face from every available surface but you're never allowed to answer back. Well, they started the fight and the wall is the weapon of choice to hit them back.[64]
>
> I always felt it was all right to answer back a little bit, I suppose. That the city shouldn't be a one-way conversation.[65]

Banksy's art suggests a narrative of oppression; his images propose a narrative of an artist living in a totalitarian state. The clandestine nature of his activities and the tight control he places on his associates would be appropriate to the situation experienced by Pussy Riot in Russia. This narrative challenges the notion that the UK is a liberal democracy and the promotion of this oppression–resistance paradigm, by means of the *Mild Mild West* mural, may well have contributed to the conditions for its manifestation. By engaging in resistance to a perceived opponent, the contest is validated and thus enhanced; by ignoring the opposition the contest is nullified. Abercrombie and Longhurst have pointed out there are two strands of resistance.

> While many writers within the IRP [Incorporation–Resistance Paradigm] are deploying theories of power which are at least recognizably Marxist, or have been developed out of a debate with Marx's ghost, others are using models that derive from Foucault, Bakhtin or de Certeau. Although these are all theories of power, they can have different theoretical effects. Most importantly they produce different understandings of the notion of opposition and resistance. For the former, the oppositional readings that might be developed by audiences are *relatively* codified and almost politicised accounts directed at a uniform form of power that can be identified by audience members. For the latter, opposition is rather more evasion, a kind of determined unseriousness, a form of play that refuses to take power seriously and is thus undermining.[66]

However, in order to prepare for this discussion it is necessary to define the nature of his resistance, particularly with regard to how structured it is. In some ways his work can be seen as a battle over public opinion. His evasion from legal retribution can be seen as a 'victory', his opponents and goals are defined. As such his contests are, in Carse's terms, 'closed play'. However, in his strategies he uses 'open play'. He ignores the rules by continuing to paint illegally, and changes the rules, for example, by inverting the market in art. As he says in *Banging Your Head against a Brick Wall* (2001): 'The quickest way to the top of your business is to turn it upside down'. Some of his work has serious political intention with limited possibilities of interpretation and other work is much more open-ended, playful and uses humour. Most of it combines these two aspects.

At face value, Banksy's poster intervention was using his potency, derived from his popularity and income-generating capabilities, to partially redress the imbalance of power in the contest between the authorities and the Stokes Croft community. By sharing the income between the three groups, he suggested that there was common cause between them and with him. His gift implied that there was an alliance of interest in the resistant struggle against the onward march of the multi-nationals and their guardians and that this resistance is important for society.

> The interests of those with power are best served by maintaining the status quo. The motor for social change can come only from a sense of social difference that is based on a conflict of interest, not a liberal pluralism in which differences are finally subordinated to a consensus whose function is to maintain those differences essentially as they are.[67]

As suggested by his individualistic path, Banksy would also have viewed this contest in terms of preserving an identity that had been self-developed rather than 'manufactured' by the forces of advertising and media hype. Banksy might well have felt some pride and affection for the way the area had developed its own aesthetic and lifestyle in a similar way to that he had developed his own. However, by 'hoisting his flag in [the PRSC's] camp', as Katy Bauer put it[68] he took on a leadership role after the main event had occurred. He brought the disparate elements together through the sharing of income from the posters and, because of his financial power and local status, was able to suggest to the outside world, through his poster image, how the riot events were to be best perceived. He was unwilling or unable to accommodate the fact that the PRSC did not want to be 'lumped together' with the rioters, to have their identity hijacked. In effect he had incorporated them into his more powerful centre, adding a layer of structure to the model of action provided by the mural. In Turner's terms he had crystallised the structure onto the existential communitas. In complexity terms he had moved the situation out of chaos towards a more ordered state. I will return to this analysis, but will first consider the situation in terms of play, in order to better approach the counter movements of ordering and disordering in this example.

What is the function of a riot? On one level it is simply an expression of anger and, therefore, there is usually an inciting incident. At this level it is not trying to achieve anything specific. It may emerge out of a demonstration with specific political aims, but at the point where rioting breaks out, the aims are superseded by emotions, the effects of which may well be counterproductive to the persuasive potential of a demonstration.

> the volcanic view of protest ... usually posits that disruptive events are the irrepressible blow-out of a vast and usually invisible mass of turbulent socio-political material ... [It] suggests that protest is somehow always *within itself* out of control. The sources of radicalism in the performance of protest consequently are always by implication then associated with the irrational, the uncontrollable, the dark side of the human.[69]

The emergence of rioting out of a demonstration marks the shift from the closed rules of finite play to the open-endedness of infinite play. Riots are also open-ended play in the sense that they are experiments; they test the will of the authorities and the tactics of the police; they test the degree of public sympathy and test the respect given to particular laws, particularly around limits to freedom of expression. Finally, the rioting individuals test their own limits in terms of risk and transgressive behaviour, which, along with the focus of anger, has the effect of creating a community of what may previously have been disparate elements. Huizinga contends that one of the higher forms of play is 'as a contest for something', that 'until quite recently war was conceived as the sport of kings' and that 'war and everything to do with it remain fast in the daemonic and magical bonds of play'.[70] Viewed from this perspective certain aspects of the Tesco riots were ludic. Certainly, from what I personally witnessed, many of those involved treated it simply as playful contest with the police, advancing and retreating, seeing what they could get away with. The first serious outbreak occurred after the pubs had closed and, therefore, the initial trouble had a social and almost light-hearted quality. A consignment of police riot gear was seized upon and the items taken away as trophies. The fact that the police tried to disperse people down alleys that were dead ends or that led straight back to the riot area was treated 'as a joke'.

However, these riots were different from the riots that occurred later that summer in other English cities, in that there was very little consumer-driven looting. The opening of the Tesco store and the eviction at the squat provoked responses that had an ethical dimension and thus there was a more serious intention behind the riot. As Huizinga says: 'It is the moral content of an action that makes it serious. When the combat has an ethical value it ceases to be play … [play] has no moral function. The valuations of vice and virtue do not apply here'.[71] Additionally, the consequent injuries and the threat to fragile livelihoods made it a serious matter for some. Violence is not a game for those who suffer real consequences as a result: 'play is not "ordinary" or "real" life'.[72] However, both Banksy's mural image and the poster image, like all his work, are ludic. He may play with 'real' issues but he is constantly reframing and inverting them. The mural and poster images entail comic and fanciful juxtaposition. However, the *Daily Mail* ignored the ludic aspect with the headline 'Banksy fans the flames of Tesco row'.[73] The *Daily Mail* owns the *Bristol Evening Post* which made clear that it was on the side of Tesco and against the PRSC.[74] Their website quoted local politicians who condemned Banksy for the poster.

> Bristol West MP Stephen Williams condemned the piece as 'completely outrageous … It's all very well being provocative but this is incitement. I think it's grossly irresponsible.' … City council leader Barbara Janke said: '… the decent citizens of Bristol who have been disgusted with the violence and intimidatory tactics of the recent rioters will be rightly appalled by Banksy's apparent willingness not only to identify himself with their cause but to aid them in their cowardly attempts to evade justice'.[75]

The PRSC also recognised this possibility when they first saw the poster: 'it was not fun, it was too hard … a local graffitti artist came in ranting about the image, saying how he found it thoughtless and inflammatory and how he would have to distance himself from the PRSC if we accepted it'.[76] Like the Palestinians who commented on his paintings on the Separation Wall,[77] those who are faced with the real consequences of the issues that he deals with do not appreciate his playful attitude, which may seem inconsiderate, particularly because, in both these cases, his intervention was brief, un-asked-for, and because he can disappear into remote non-involvement as soon as he has made his statement. It may appear that he is using the conflict for his own ends, in much the same way as Bassi has described 'piggy-backing' on matters of popular interest.

> Banksy's gift might leave us wading through mud while he floated off to fresher pastures … Of course he'd ascend whether we drowned or not. It didn't take long for us to know two things for sure: 1. Banksy decides how

things are going to go. 2. He's not too concerned about how that might affect how anybody else's things go.[78]

So on both sides of the argument, Banksy's poster was perceived as being seriously oppositional. The dual nature of his intervention was not recognised by these representatives of the opposing side even though others recognised it. 'Geoff Gardiner works at Fred Baker Cycles, which was damaged during the attack on the Tesco Express store next door on April 22. He said: "It's all a bit tongue in cheek so it doesn't offend me"'.[79] The conclusion can be drawn that, by associating the PRSC with the violence, Banksy's poster aided the inaccurate perception promoted by the *Evening Post* and thus aided the cause of Tesco and the apologists for multi-nationals. Therefore, in terms of the local power negotiations his intervention appears to be ill-considered. However, this apparent lack of concern for how his intervention might rebound on his public image and that of the PRSC can also be seen as a deliberate tactic of undermining the seriousness of both sides, of subverting the oppositional structures. He appears to ignore concerns about being 'right' or 'wrong', or of his recently won acceptance by the Bristol central cluster, or being rejected by the Stokes Croft artist community. It can be imagined that he was more concerned with a wider opposition to multi-nationals and, therefore, less concerned with the details of a particular situation. However, given his apparent long-standing familiarity with the area, it is more likely that his ludic images reflect a ludic attitude to the politics. Instead of the closed play of political contest, with its defined, if unwritten, rules about expressing clear unequivocal messages, he favours the tactic of open-playing freedom and self-expression. His actions, in this case, suggested that he is not fearful of being misunderstood or controversial, but is presenting a humorous image that can be read in different ways.[80] This is play on a specific edge. Had the poster presented a more direct political resistance, it would have strengthened the coherence of the reaction of the central cluster, alienated more sections of the general population and thus marginalised the Stokes Croft community further. Had it been more playful, the image would have been ignored, dismissed or marginalised in other ways. Despite a clear statement as to which side of the oppositional contest he favours, he undermined a structural approach. In terms of the fulcrum analogy, his ideology and intention were clear and consistent over the years between the painting of the mural and the poster donation, yet he retains fluidity, by using confusing humour and ambivalent meanings in both images. Provocateurs can be seen as the disturbers of structure. This strategy can be more effective than the chaotic rioters, because their actions simply strengthen structure. Play, on the other hand, inhibits the reinforcement of structure. In terms of Turner's theory that existential communitas tends to crystallise into norms and structure, Banksy's insistence on play inhibits the inevitability of this process.

So, his emphasis on play is de-structuring and moves in the direction of the chaotic. However, his alignment with political standpoints is progressive, Modernist and structural. By engaging in both structuring and de-structuring he attempts to locate society, including himself, on 'the edge of chaos'. Seen in these terms, he is part of a cyclical process of structural breakdown and recon-figuration. The awareness of difference that is at the heart of the border analogy, particularly the simple 'us and them' binary that Banksy uses, attracts disparate elements and creates a sense of community. This move towards structure is simultaneously and paradoxically undermined by his refusal to 'play by the rules'. This duality of approach inherent to Banksy's intervention in the events of 2011 contains some parallels with the duality between challenge and play in much of his work and, in particular, his exhibition at the Bristol Museum (2009).

The border of acceptability

In this section, I consider the border in terms of limits of acceptability, in order to approach the question about the relationship between popularity and challenge. I examine Banksy's work on the border of acceptability with three inter-related entities in Bristol: the individual attendees at the 2009 exhibition, the museum and the wider Bristol community. These three examples can be seen as widening ripples of scale. I suggest that, like Bassi and Baron Cohen, he uses game-play confusion. In his case, it is through playing with the boundaries of genres and conventions and, in one example, literally 'breaking the frame'. However, I begin by discussing the particular nature of his challenge as distinct from that of Bassi and Baron Cohen.

In the previous chapters, I outlined the context in which the challenge to authorities and centres of cultural hegemony takes place. In Bassi's case, the spectators are led, by him, to a place where they witness his challenge to the authorities. In Baron Cohen's case, there are two levels of spectatorship – those who are confronted by his provocation within the films and those who witness the discomfiture of these 'targets' from the safety of the cinema seat. These latter can be said to be the intended audience. As with Bassi's spectators, they have entered into a contract with the artist by, for example, buying a ticket. With street art, as with street theatre, there is not the same kind of pre-planned commitment: the work is imposed on the public environment. Members of the public can choose to devote time to spectate the work or they can ignore it. However, whether they are attracted or averse to it, they may not be able to avoid it. As such, spectators may be challenged by this, unasked for, imposition. Banksy has referred to street advertising as 'Brandalism'[81] in response to street art being framed as vandalism. Although he proposes an equivalence between the two, the difference, in terms of the spectator experience, is that his work appears in un-designated, and, therefore, unexpected places. It is intended, at least partly, to cause reactions of surprise and wonder. As with much site-specific work, the spectator may be induced to see the physical surroundings in a new light. This might be by framing a hole in a wall (Bethnal Green, London 2002) or suggesting a park lake contains sharks (Victoria Park, London 2005) or, at the Bristol Museum exhibition, inser-ting a dummy Guantanamo Bay prisoner into a historic biplane (2009). These images use odd juxtapositions which create humour as well as curiosity. Humour attracts and lightens, whereas curiosity activates. As I will discuss below, the

Edwardian-era museum offered a site with a strong character that he worked both with and against. Unlike the spectators of his street work, the attendees at the Bristol Museum exhibition were clearly committed because they had to spend up to six hours queuing to enter. This was a challenge in itself, and, because of the commitment, he was able to present more complex pieces.

Popularity and challenge at the Bristol exhibition

I have indicated that there are two kinds of provocation, one to an absent authority or institution, the other to the spectator who is present. The first kind generates communitas by establishing partisanship, the other may be exciting if it is acceptable within its context but that this conditionality implies risk. In this section I focus on these elements of excitement, context, acceptability and risk, to gauge how, and how much, spectators were challenged by his work. The Bristol exhibition offered an opportunity to observe the reactions of large numbers of people and to ascertain the profile of those who were attracted to it. In addition, my impressions can be put into sharper focus because the exhibition has been documented from a range of angles in *Banksy, The Bristol Legacy*.[82]

The high visitor numbers and the length of time that visitors were prepared to queue indicates the popularity of the exhibition. The majority of the attendees were white[83] middle-class, and at least comfortably off.[84] The experience of waiting in the queue for some hours provided an experience of communitas, as it combined sharing discomfort as well as positive expectations. The familiarity with Banksy's previous work and the oppositional title of the exhibition, *Banksy **versus** Bristol Museum*, suggested contest and thus promoted partisanship. The controversy surrounding the artist was as much a part of the attraction as the artefacts. For example, one of the first installations on the visitor route was a mock-up of his studio, which was accompanied by an audio recording of a real radio phone-in about the vandalism/art controversy surrounding Banksy. This cleverly developed the experiential communitas into a communitas of ideology. One aspect of this ideology was his attitude to art. Banksy's street work and its countless reproductions will have disseminated his belief that visual art should not be exclusive to those who have received higher education in the subject. As Fiske says: 'Aesthetics is naked cultural hegemony and popular discrimination properly rejects it ... unlike aesthetics, relevance is time and place bound'.[85] Banksy's promotion of accessible art must have been reassuring to visitors but it was only one aspect of his ideology. He would also have been known for his counter-cultural views: anti-establishment, anti-war, anti-globalisation, pro-women and pro-underdog. These attitudes must have been at least tolerable to those attracted to the exhibition. It is likely that many would have attended, or been sympathetic to, the protests against the Iraq war that Banksy had attended.

The large numbers suggest that the exhibition attracted types of visitors beyond those who might normally attend visual art exhibitions. Statistics show that there were more people over forty attending than those under twenty-five and that the vast majority were first-time visitors to the museum from outside

Bristol.[86] These two factors suggest that for many there may have been a frisson of excitement at the unknown because of Banksy's association with urban youth culture. The format and conventions of the exhibition were expected to be unfamiliar (i.e. there was not a pre-existing communitas of norms) but the public felt sufficiently confident to stand in line for several hours. This example suggests that the edge-as-border is not simply a matter of that which is culturally acceptable, but is more nuanced; that shared ideology may be more important than shared norms. This relates to the distinction between what Baz Kershaw defines as rhetorical conventions and authenticating conventions. Kershaw suggests that audiences are more able to engage with ideological difference if the norms of presentation are familiar to them.[87] These two perspectives may be complementary rather than conflicting. It is not that one form of communitas is more important than the other but that the pre-existence of one facilitates the nurturing of the other.

So, if the norms and form are challenging, providing a sense of a shared ideology is reassuring. The sense of communitas can be confirmed by means of a shared joke[88] often at the expense of symbols of power and dominance, thus providing a sense of partisanship with the artist. If the joke is at the expense of the artist or art in general then spectators are further reassured. In the exhibition Banksy appeared to be aware of potential concerns of non-specialists faced with the challenge of attending an art exhibition. As well as providing wonder at the exotic assortment of images, he demystified his process and the role of the artist. The mock-up of his studio exposed his methods and included notices disparaging his art, claiming he was 'not a good artist' and was 'crap at drawing flowers'. This self-deprecation extended to art in general. One image was of two crudely drawn figures with speech bubbles. One says: 'Does anyone actually take this kind of art seriously?', the other replies: 'Never underestimate the power of a big gold frame'. Other visual jokes suggest he is 'making fun of everything'.

The playful quality of these images allowed some kinds of challenge to be engaged with. In particular Banksy highlighted the gap between ideology and practice. For example, as well as critiquing power and authority, he also targets apathy and self-satisfaction. One example in the exhibition was the painting of two overweight Western tourists photographing themselves while sitting in a rickshaw pulled by a small child. The image may be uncomfortably resonant with all those who have felt awkward with the difference in living standards when travelling to poorer countries. Another example, from the exhibition, is the painting of a punk protester fussing over his counter-cultural appearance. This highlighted the display of tokens and emblems of resistance, which some attendees may recognise in themselves, or others, as part of their motivation for attending the exhibition. The final piece developed this idea: it was a Constable-esque landscape in a gold frame over which was crudely daubed an arrow with the instruction: 'Exit through the gift shop'. This was not only a reference to his film, but a comment on the consumerism of the event. (The gift shop did, indeed, sell a souvenir book of the exhibition). From conversations I heard around Bristol at the time, I became aware that there was a 'must-see' hysteria around the exhibition similar to that around some music events and festivals where attendances are 'collected' to enhance the status of the owner as much as for the sake of the experiences themselves.

The nature of Banksy's challenge to the dominant forces is different to that of Bassi and Baron Cohen because he is less concerned with pulling down those that are privileged; for example, by exposing hypocrisy, corruption and prejudice. He makes fun of representatives of authority, but not particular individuals. For example, at the exhibition, an animated sculpture depicted a riot policeman on a child's rocking horse and a painting of the House of Commons depicted it as populated by apes. Because the superior laugh is not personal this mitigates any sense of vindictive negativity and this makes it more widely acceptable. Although he uses the downward movement, he is also interested in giving value to what has been overlooked or accepted. In his street work, he considers overlooked locations for their unique qualities and gives them value, in contrast to the insensitive placement of public advertisements. He also gives value to those whose low status has been overlooked or accepted: children, monkeys, rats and other animals. Thus, in terms of carnivalesque inversions, as described by Bakhtin, his emphasis is as much on the positive upward movement, empowerment, which I have identified as one of the three aspects of popularity.

Play and open-ended meanings are a mild form of risk-taking because they engage spectators in an exploration of the unknown. The exhibition offered a problem to solve: as well as specific areas that were filled with his work, other artworks and assorted items were 'hidden' alongside items of the permanent museum collection. So, for example, a briefcase full of fake money was placed amongst the gold and silver collection and a dildo was placed next to similarly shaped stalagmites. The quest for these items was both 'solving a mathematical problem' and 'exploring a strange place', which Csikszentmihalyi identifies as two of the four main pleasure activities. He states: 'discovery and exploration imply transcendence, a going beyond the known, a stretching of one's self toward new dimensions of skills and experience'.[89] The journey into the unknown was transformed into a pleasurable treasure hunt (which at the same time encouraged spectators to appreciate other artefacts in the museum). Unlike with the work of Bassi and Baron Cohen, in which the spectator is relatively passive, Banksy's exhibition and street work allow for more spectator options in the order that they observe images, the length of time they spend with them, and the literal angle of their perception.

As well as this physical quest, Banksy offered a quest for interpretation. Much of his work is ambiguous, complex, or is open to misinterpretation. For example, his £10 notes, with the image of the Queen replaced by that of Lady Diana, can propose that the princess would have made a better queen, or it can be viewed as a lament to a future denied or it can be seen as linking Diana with money, a comment on the commercial exploitation of her life and death. It is also possible that the use of her image was simply a practical way to avoid accusations of forgery when producing money for a performance event. Open meanings prevent the image being classifiable. During my street theatre research project (2008), we found that as soon as behaviours were classifiable – for example as pre-planned performances or marketing strategies or 'student pranks' – they lost interest with the general public. Our aim was to maintain active curiosity as long as possible. Like the Dada-ists, Banksy is an infinite-player in the sense that he changes or breaks the rules. This can be seen in terms of literally breaking the limits of the frame: one landscape picture in the exhibition was tilted and showed water and a boat flowing out of the golden picture frame. In another, figures have been cut out of the canvas to have a cigarette break outside the image. In his previous work, the escapist images on the Gaza wall can be seen as frame-breaking, both in a figurative sense and also in the illegitimacy of painting them. Similarly his street work breaks the privileging norms associated with fine art, particularly in terms of location, permanence and respect. However, this opening up to rule-breaking can also be seen as a message in itself:

> Its presence [Banksy's work] in its context communicates not only his message but his dedication to effecting the change he promotes in that message, whether he's defying Israeli hegemony by painting the separation wall in Palestine or bypassing the elitist review board of a museum by hanging his work himself.[90]

Banksy also plays with blurring the differentiation between the real and the not-real, introducing an element of the unpredictable. His disguises, deceptions and trompe l'oeils visually confuse, especially when manifested in the everyday reality of public spaces. In the exhibition, a leopard-skin coat seen from one side is an animatronic leopard seen from the other. He often denies responsibility for work that he has done. He validates cheating, for example, a sculpture in the exhibition appropriated the famous quote, attributed to Picasso: 'The bad artists imitate, the good artists steal' with Picasso's name crossed out and Banksy's inserted. He continually questions the validity of appearances: the 'sweetness' of children and animals is often shown to be a performative, concealing some form of threat, a bomb or a club. His inversions question why one item is honoured and another is despised. Reactions to his hazing of perception are evidenced by responses to *Exit through the Gift Shop*; many viewers could not believe that it was not a scripted fiction.

> Yeah I don't buy it for a second. Banksy has literally elevated pranksterism to high art. MBW [Mr BrainWash], the movie, this interview, very likely Banksy himself are all grand pranks within pranks within pranks. It's turtles all the way down .[91]

However, Banksy asserts the opposite.

> Ordinarily I wouldn't mind if people believe me or not, but the film's power comes from the fact it's all 100% true. This is from the frontline, this is watching an art form self-combust in front of you. Told by the people involved. In real time. This is a very real film about what it means to 'keep it real'.[92]

If this is true, it suggests that, like the boy who cried wolf, when he does want to present real facts as such, he is not believed. Spectators, trying to interpret his work, understandably apply his usual (consistent) approach of ambiguity and, therefore, conclude that the work is another example of open game-playing. This is another example of de-structuring open play reducing the effectiveness of challenge.

As discussed above, he favours an oppositional binary and this leads him into a simplification of difference, emphasising a validation of one side (his own position) and the negation of the other. As Bakhtin says: 'The satirist whose laughter is negative places himself above the object of his mockery'.[93] In the carnivalesque, as outlined by Bakhtin, negation and affirmation can be played with, in order to create ambivalence, for example, by confusing/inverting the use of abuse and praise. He suggests that this is an aspect of the death–rebirth nature of the carnivalesque and that it is its double-sided, inter-dependent, two-way nature that gives it such depth. In Banksy's work there is little ambivalence between what is validated and what is denigrated, even though there is often ambiva-lence over the meaning of his images.[94] The exhibition included a painting of a woman wearing a hijab, over which was worn a plastic apron with a trompe l'oeil image of a lingerie clad body. She held a frying pan with eggs and the piece was entitled *How Do You Like Your Eggs?* This surreal combination of signs of female servitude provided an anti-sexist message that was politically correct and serious, confirming the ideology of the spectators rather than challenging it.

So Banksy is popular because he achieves the right balance. The ideology of the visitors is generally confirmed and they share a communitas of conspiracy against absent, un-personalised authority figures. There is a slight element of challenge to the spectator, but this is mainly in terms of deciphering and exploring an unknown (but safe) territory. The unknown and unclassifiable norms were enjoyable because they were accompanied by humour of juxtaposition and the superior laugh. He emphasises the positive upward movement of empowerment. Spectators may be able to recognise something of themselves within some of the figures of fun, but they are not singled-out in public. A slight hint of dis-comfort will enhance the notion of exciting transgression without it being difficult to accept. The playful tone and self-deprecation removes any sense that the spectator is being heavily critiqued. Although there are playful contra-dictions, paradox and ambivalence, there is a strong ethical thread through all his work. Despite the iconoclasm there is no sense of nihilism: he makes fun of pretension and power, but never of the powerless, providing a picture of how ethics can be promoted within a fractured Post-Modern context.

Museum as centre

In the chapter on Bassi I examined his interactions with centres that are national/ multi-national organisations. In the chapter on Baron Cohen I examined centres at their smallest human scale of two people. Banksy's work in Bristol provides examples of two scales in between the macro and the micro: a museum and a city. These provide further examples of reactions to provocation, including an unusual instance of a centre adapting to changes within its system that has occurred as a result of provocative challenge.

As stated above, the title he gave to the exhibition, suggested a contest: 'the public witnessed at first hand the clash of two utterly opposing archetypes, the bastion of culture, the authoritative institution versus the other, the outsider, the individual, the anonymous prankster'.[95] The perception of subversion of 'the establishment' was heightened by the contrast between the irreverence of his images and the traditional appearance of the museum, with its Edwardian stained glass, brass rails and marble columns. However, it is clear from accounts of this relationship as outlined in *Banksy, The Bristol Legacy*, that the attitudes behind the facade of the museum were not traditional, opposition did not exist; the authorities were delighted by his offer to exhibit his work, if somewhat overwhelmed by the logistical implications. In fact, this was a form of take-over, with Banksy's team insisting on the way it was to be done, inverting the conventional imbalance of power between curators and artists. This suggests a temporary replacement of one hierarchical structure with another, rather than a more fundamental reconfiguration of power relationships within its system. However, in the same book, the anonymous contributor describes the changes that had occurred within the culture of the Museum service that enabled it to accept the takeover of the building in the face of resistance from some of its staff.[96] This provides a rare example of a centre that opens itself to provocative influence from beyond an edge which, in this case, is the limit of its total control. The conservation function of a museum can lead to a culture of pro-tection of artefacts that can only be fully appreciated by the initiated few. Its other function, to display and educate, has become more prominent since the 1990s, in an attempt to widen visitor profiles and change the relationship from top-down informative education to more participatory activities. This was because 'we tend to work with the same people, create the same projects and attract the same visitors'.[97] We can see in this statement implications regarding the closed circularity of a culture, sufficient to itself and receiving positive feed-back from within its own sphere, but isolated from the wider culture. The 2009 exhibition challenged the position of the curator as the arbiter of value by allowing the artist to set the priorities. As Anna Farthing put it: 'This reintro-duction of personal passion introduces activism to the museological mix'.[98]) She argues that museums should be a site of cultural contention: they 'need to be initiated, programmed and facilitated on a regular basis by those on the inside, who feel sufficiently supported to respond to events on the outside'.[99]

However, the public perception of museums' continuing role in conferring value and status to artefacts will take longer to transform. For example, there were concerns over the inclusion of Banksy's Tesco fire-bomb poster in the display at the newly opened M Shed Museum of Bristol,[100] because the poster appeared to support violence and the museum could be seen as condoning that support. The inclusion can be seen as the centre (both the central cluster and its sub-centre, the museum) engaged in an act of mature democratisation, an embrace of all perspectives within the city. The museum was able to side-step controversy by framing it as an artefact within the city's history of dissent, denying any sense of automatic validation. Treating it with this dispassionate objectivity, as a fact of history, neutralises it, diminishing its potential for activating partisanship. It was also an acknowledgement of the lack of power of the image to seriously threaten either the museum or civil society and, therefore, can be seen as an act of patronising marginalisation reducing Banksy to a merely cheeky local hero. Similarly the exhibition can be seen as an act of incorporation: his work was allowed inclusion and consequently some validation from the centre that is distinct from the validation of popularity. The endorsement of the *Evening Post* neutralised the exhibition: his work was shown to be within the acceptable boundaries of a central institution and thus removed any possibility of a cultural transgression. He was deemed to be safe.

City as centre

The changing relationship between Banksy and Bristol provides a good case study of the provocative process. Despite the growing local interest in and popularity of his work, the local authorities employed suppression and marginalisation strategies against his street work in the years up to 2006, erasing it, seeking prosecution and framing the work as worthless vandalism. His *Hanging Man* mural (Frogmore Street, Bristol 2006) was placed right opposite the city's Council House, taunting the authority. The controversy around this painting proved a turning point because the Council was becoming aware of the untenability of its previous strategies.[101] The local newspaper, the *Evening Post*, had softened its hard-line dismissal of his work under new editorship from 2005. The public became actively involved in this controversy because the authorities needed to refer to the public in order to not lose credibility as a democratic institution. The Council canvassed local opinion via its website: the majority of whom favoured retention.[102] Despite this, calls for its removal were led by a Conservative Councillor, Albert 'Spud' Murphy, in an interview for the *Evening Post*. However, three years later, when the mural was defaced, this same Councillor rushed in his own equipment to restore the painting. 'I'll do it myself ...' he told the BBC.[103] This example indicates how two centres (the City Council and the *Evening Post*) were catching up with cultural changes within the entity (the city) brought about by the outsider activating debate. On a wider, more complex level it was a contest over image: Banksy portrays authorities, connected to the central cluster, as repressive, but in Western countries they must still maintain control without seeming repressive. These contests are closely observed by the wider public who may enjoy the tactical ingenuity of the single figure outwitting the wide-reaching systems of control because it represents a resistance to a top-down flow of norms and ideology.

In Bristol, this change of official attitudes was confirmed during the 2009 City Museum exhibition, with the formerly hostile newspaper offering thanks to the artist in its front page headlines, primarily for the economic benefits that the exhibition had brought to the city. The exhibition marked an acceptance in the cultural centre towards bringing about changes to that centre. For Banksy, this inclusion separated him further from those remaining on the edge of public acceptability, such as unrecognised 'taggers', evoking their hostility. It is unlikely to be coincidental that a defacement of the *Hanging Man* coincided with the media brouhaha surrounding the opening of the exhibition. Following the 2009 exhibition, Banksy was increasingly seen as an economic and cultural asset; for example, his association with the city adds to its attraction for prospective students. 'The economic value of Banksy's artwork and of Banksy himself as a productive asset have been spectacularly revealed … [The city] is possibly seen as more vibrant and might be perceived as a city that embraces the unconventional and edgy'.[104] Andrew Kelly, the Director of the Bristol Cultural Development Partnership, hinted that this acceptance by the centre was conditional and that he was doubtful whether Banksy will play by the rules: 'That Banksy is associated with Bristol is generally a good thing *(when he behaves himself)*' (my emphasis).[105]

If this example is treated in terms of complexity theory, the process can be simplified into the interaction of three components: the centre (or cluster of centres), the system surrounding it and the environment surrounding that. Referring to biological evolution, Jacob states that: 'What is called "progress" or "adaption" is only the necessary result of the inevitable interplay between the system and its surroundings'.[106] Banksy's work can be seen as an integral part of changes in the surroundings – the graffitti movement that had originated in New York and was brought to Bristol by the artist 3D, in the early 1980s. As early as 1985 the Arnolfini gallery, the city's centre for contemporary arts, presented an exhibition of graffiti artists, partly organised by 3D and included artists from New York.[107] This movement can be seen as part of the much larger cultural shift towards, what Eric Hobsbawm describes as, a democratisation of art that occurred in the second half of the twentieth century.[108] The controversy over graffiti and other unofficial street art can be seen as society catching up with shifting attitudes emanating from artistic circles. However, unlike avant-garde work that is presented in contemporary art galleries, which has a less immediately perceptible impact on wider society, graffiti had representatives who were less dependent on critical and commercial validation and, therefore, had less to lose. Thus they were more prepared to take greater risks to impose their work on the public space in a way that was too transgressive to those whose norms have been formed by official art institutions. Not only was there a rapid impact on the public consciousness by this means, but also the public reaction to it was fed back to the centre relatively rapidly and accurately via internet technology. The canvassing of opinion in relation to the *Hanging Man* has close similarities with Jacob's observations based on biological evolution. He states that 'No matter how an organism investigates its environment the perception it gets must necessarily reflect so called "reality" and more specifically those aspects of reality directly related to its own behaviour'.[109] Arguably, the gathering of information and openness to the change of behaviour it proposed led to the city's evolution into a more attractive and dynamic cultural centre. 'The increase in performance that accompanies evolution requires a refinement of perception, an enrichment of the information received concerning the environment'.[110]

Since 2008 Bristol City Council has opened two official graffiti sites and has authorised retention of 'good' street art whilst eradicating 'poor' street art. Banksy's work, of course, has the stamp of approval. The Council has also supported two festivals of street artists, both through financial support and also by providing an entire street to paint. This street and others nearby, similarly adorned, have become a significant tourist attraction. It is evident that street art in Bristol has created its own 'niche'.

> In ecology, as in human societies, many innovations are successful without such a pre-existing 'niche'. Such innovations transform the environment in which they appear, and as they spread, they create the conditions necessary for their own multiplication, their 'niche'.[111]

This notion of the 'niche' is similar to the liminal norm, which as I have suggested, can be seen as a sub-centre of the main central cluster. As such, it is tolerated because it is seen as useful to the central cluster but is also circumscribed; the tolerance is conditional on behaving acceptably. On the other hand the niche/liminal norm can be seen as 'a foot in the door': establishing a secure, if limited, base from which future advances can be made. Once the base is established the transition phase of provocation can be said to have been completed. The location of the border has shifted.

The three examples that I have explored – museum, city and exhibition visitor – represent three different scales of centres that do not use defensive strategies of suppression or blocking. Nor does Banksy abandon ideological challenge in the way that occurred with Baron Cohen. Instead there has been a complex meeting of two perspectives. The centres have accepted and adapted to propositions of the provocateur, but in so doing the thrust of the provocation has been neutralised. The niche/liminal norm might be able to expand its influence, capitalising on initial advance but this phase is not within the scope of the open-playing, destabilisers of structure that are the main subject of this book.

Conclusion

The examination of Banksy's work confirms a number of significant features of provocation. The observation by the public of a contest between a powerful cluster of centres (e.g. police, local authorities, local press) and a smaller, weaker centre (an individual or sub-culture) stimulates partisanship and thence an activation of the wider social environment. His edge-play with other centres: the art market, the graffiti sub-culture, the Bristol Museum and also himself, suggests similarities of the processes involved, despite differences of scale and context. It also appears possible to separate the inevitable commodification of popular work from incorporation of the person who produces that work, but that this is achieved only by the exceptional strategy of self-imposed public anonymity. This self-defensive strategy can take on a life of its own, perpetuating itself beyond the original cause and causing friction at the borders because of the perceived necessity to rigorously enforce them. The person at the centre may become increasingly powerful and potentially autocratic the more that their position is unchallenged within the demarcated entity. In this unusual case, this tendency is mitigated by the ability of the central person to operate as a 'nobody' in the wider society.

Additional to Banksy's opposition to the dominant centres were oppositions with other, more liminal, centres: the contemporary art market and the Robbo supporters. His individualistic approach is accompanied by expressions of solidarity, not only with those with whom he is directly connected, but also with distant communities without powerful voices. This suggests not only a sense of ethical responsibility, but also that self-imposed isolation generated an interest in communitas with unknown others. In complexity terms this could be interpreted as a single particle operating independently, and thus chaotically in relation to other particles, becoming aware of a whole environment, making connections, which ultimately would lead to order. However, despite this move towards configuration, Banksy is adamant about retaining independence of action. This dialectic is mirrored in the dialectic between ideology and norms, discussed in relation to the Bristol exhibition: if ideology is shared, a difference in norms can be more readily explored. It can be inferred from this that a sense of ideological communitas does not necessarily inhibit relative freedom of action (allowing for internalised constrictive norms[112]). This is backed up by the way that, in liberal societies, very different lifestyles are tolerated if they do not conflict with basic principles, such as not harming others, fairness and so on. A second conclusion is that a phase of separation and isolation led into a phase of configuration, as he built his network. This can be related to the provocative process outlined in Chapter One: after the initial provocative action the parts of the entity are in turbulence and seek order and stabilisation.

This tension between independence and communitas, 'freedom' and order, fluidity and structure, is reflected in other aspects of his work. One outcome of the adoption of anonymity is that his organisational structure became tighter. He also attempted to pull together the disparate counter-cultural elements involved in the riots. Yet these attempts were more concerned with solidarity and an experience of communitas rather than structure. He not only avoids creating structures that might inhibit the independence of his actions, but actually destabilises them. This confirms the suggestion in the chapter on Bassi that ambivalence between pulling together and de-structuring is both a strength and a weakness. The open meanings of the Tesco poster denied the clear un-equivocality required in a political context and led to confusion and misinterpretation that harmed his allies. However, his ideology was clear and did offer a counter-flow of messages. His ideology has gained more weight through its consistency over the years, despite the turbulence caused to his life by the acquisition of fame and fortune. Because of this consistency, and because of his dual identity, he has succeeded in avoiding becoming incorporated. His apparent understanding of the major aspects of popularity and the border of public acceptability has led to fame and fortune which has prevented him becoming suppressed or marginalised. Within the context of British society he can be seen to have stimulated a process of cultural change. The employment of a dual approach as a strategy can be seen as effective in transforming centres as long as they have a pre-existing disposition to receive feedback from the provocateur about changes in the external environment. What does Banksy's work tell us about the edge-as-border? It can be concluded that the border as 'us and them' creates partisanship which generates community, but in the case of the Tesco riots, that shared ideology and an experience of communitas does not necessarily lead to sharing of norms and structure formation. It can also be concluded that this resolves an opposition between independence and a sense of communitas, creating solidarity without limiting individual actions. An acute awareness of the border of public acceptability, and how to use it, can produce power, and the use of the border can allow ideology to be consistent, leaving the provocateur relatively uncompromised in his practice, enabling the gained power to be used effectively in the service of the ideology.

Notes

1   Turner, Victor (1969) *The Ritual Process*. New York: Aldine De Gruyter (1995).
2   McKenzie, Jon (2001) *Perform or Else*. London and New York: Routledge.
3   Klein, Naomi (2007) *The Shock Doctrine*. London: Allen Lane.
4   Bakhtin, Mikhail (1969) *Rabelais and His World*. Bloomington: Indiana University Press (1984): 374.
5   Becker, Carol ed. (1994) *The Subversive Imagination*. London and New York: Routledge: xviii.
6   *The Guardian* (26/02/2012).
7   Ahdef Soueif (14/04/2012) *The Guardian* (www.theguardian.com/commentisfree/video/2012/apr/13/ahdaf-soueif-art-arab-spring. Accessed 28/04/2012).
8   Lee, David, Endearing enough, but it's not art. In: Gough, Paul (ed.) (2012) *Banksy, The Bristol Legacy*. Bristol: Redcliffe Press: 128.
9   www.briansewell.com/artist/b-artist/banksy/banksy-metaphysical.html. Accessed 16/06/2011.
10 Banksy (2006) *Wall and Piece*. London: Century.
11 Wright, Steve (2007) *Home Sweet Home*. Bristol: Tangent Books.
12 *Exit through the Gift Shop, A Banksy Film* (2010) edited by Chris King and Tom Fulford. 86 minutes. Paranoid Pictures Film Company Ltd.
13 Ellsworth-Jones, Will (2012) *Banksy, the Man behind the Wall*. London: Aurum Press.
14 Banksy (2006): 237.
15 Ibid.
16 Mason, Bim (1992) *Street Theatre and Other Outdoor Performance*. London and New York: Routledge: 139.
17 Clarke, Robert (2012) *Seven Years with Banksy*. London: Michael O'Mara Books: 57.
18 Gough, Paul ed. (2012) *Banksy, The Bristol Legacy*. Bristol: Redcliffe Press.
19 Ibid.: 21.
20 *Mail on Sunday* (12/07/2008).

21   Ellsworth-Jones (2012): 107.
22   Ellsworth-Jones (2012).
23   Leverton, Mark (2011) *Banksy Myths and Legends*. Hamburg, Germany and Berkeley, California: Carpet Bombing Culture, Gingko Press.
24   http://banksy.co.uk/faq.asp.
25   *New York Post* (16/10/2013). (http://nypost.com/2013/10/16/banksy-clowns-a round-in-new-work/).
26   *New York Daily News* (18/10/2013). (www.nydailynews.com/news/crime/nypd -searching-banksy-source-article-1.1488808).
27   'Stephen Gough, AKA "The Naked Rambler", has been convicted 17 times since 2003, including being imprisoned for insisting on walking naked the length of the British Isles' (Forsyth, Neil, *The Guardian*, 18/07/2012). Since the 1970s, the French street theatre company, Turbo Cacahouete, have repeatedly been in trouble with the police because of their insistent use of nudity and irreverence for religious and sexual norms. Alexander Brener (see Chapter Six) spent several years in gaol for spraying a dollar sign on Kazimir Malevich's painting *Suprematisme* as well as being fined for various other provocations.
28   *The Guardian* (17/07/2003).
29   Wright (2007): 60.
30   Banksy (2006): 13.
31   Ellsworth-Jones (2012): 32.
32   Csikszentmihalyi, M. (1975) *Beyond Boredom and Anxiety*. San Francisco: Jossey-Bass.
33   *Swindle Magazine*, 8 Banksy the Naked Truth by Shepard Fairey and Roger Gastman (Bk 8) (30/11/2006) (www.swindlemagazine.com/issue08/Banksy.php. Accessed 16/06/2011).
34   *Time Out* (01/03/2010).
35   He makes fun of artists in general, graffiti artists in particular, revolutionaries, hedonists and didactic messengers: 'People who should be shot: Fascist thugs, Religious fundamentalists, People who write lists telling you who should be shot' (Banksy, 2006: 110).
36   Posted by Stanley Kachuik (15/02/2011) (edendale.typepad.com. Accessed 16/ 06/2011).
37   Bakhtin (1969): 413.
38   de Certeau. M. (1984) *The Practice of Everyday Life*. Berkeley, Los Angeles: University of California Press: 18
39   Bateson, Gregory (1972) *Steps to an Ecology of Mind*. St Albans: Granada.
40   Bakhtin (1969): 94.
41   Turner (1969): 132.
42   Gough (2012): 144.
43   Bauer, Katy, The view from Stokes Croft. In: Gough (2012): 75.
44   www.juxtapoz.com/current/exclusive-interview-with-robbo-on-banksy-graffiti-and-more. Accessed 16/06/2011.
45   Ellsworth-Jones (2012): 50–1.
46   *Swindle Magazine* (2006).
47   Wright (2007): 36.
48   Byrne, Eugene, Hanging out down the council house: street art's outlaws and the Bristol establishment. In: Gough (2012): 89.
49   *Sunday Times* (28/02/2010).
50   Ibid.
51   http://edendale.typepad.com/weblog/2010/12/banksy-yes-banksy-on-thierry-exit-skepticism-documentary-filmmaking-as-punk.html. Accessed 16/06/2011.
52   Banksy (2006): 23.
53   *Time Out* (2010).
54   Ellsworth-Jones (2012): 168–72.

55 Ibid.: 125–9.
56 *The Sun* (2010).
57 The content of the image derived from police raids on free parties: 'I said that, as far as social expression went, we felt pretty oppressed. We were pretty ordinary, fluffy, party people, and we were being bullied by police with riot shields and truncheons. The teddy bear was his [Banksy's] idea.' Jim Paine (quoted in Wright, 2007 : 24).
58 https://notesco.wordpress.com. Accessed 25/10/2012.
59 www.bristolpost.co.uk/Bristol-Tesco-riots-Brothers-heart-trouble-jailed/story-13806378-detail/story.html. Accessed 25/10/2012.
60 Plumridge, Anthony and Mearman, Andrew, Banksy: the economic impact. In: Gough (2012): 110–17.
61 Hewell, Tim, *Newsnight*, BBC (02/03/2012).
62 Turner (1969): 154.
63 Bauer. In: Gough (2012): 72.
64 Banksy (2006): 8.
65 *The Sun* (2010).
66 Abercrombie, Nicholas and Longhurst, Brian (1998) *Audiences*. London: Sage: 28.
67 Fiske, John (1989) *Understanding Popular Culture*. London and New York: Routledge: 19.
68 Bauer. In: Gough (2012): 76.
69 Kershaw, Baz (1999) *The Radical in Performance*. London and New York: Routledge: 120.
70 Huizinga, J. (1938) *Homo Ludens*. London: Temple Smith (1970): 16.
71 Ibid.: 6.
72 Ibid.: 8.
73 *Daily Mail* (05/05/2011).
74 Citing only one trader, the next door neighbour of Tesco, the *Bristol Evening Post* website (7/04/2012) claimed that 'local traders and residents now believe Tesco has sparked the regeneration of Stokes Croft, not aided its demise' (www.bristolpost.co.uk/year-riots-Tesco-praised-Stokes-Croft-Bristol/story-15746826-detail/story.html. Accessed 25/11/2012).
75 www.bristolpost.co.uk/Banksy-s-petrol-bomb-art-aid-community/story-11283091-detail/story.html (07/05/2011). Accessed 25/11/2012.
76 Bauer. In: Gough (2012): 72.
77 'Old Man: You paint the wall, you make it look beautiful
    Me: Thanks
    Old Man: We don't want it to be beautiful, we hate this wall, go home'
    (Banksy, 2006: 142)
78 Bauer. In: Gough (2012): 73, 74.
79 www.bristolpost.co.uk/Banksy-s-petrol-bomb-art-aid-community/story-11283091-detail/story.html. Accessed 25/11/2012.
80 'It said that Tesco was the danger, the threat to peace, ecology, diversity, stability and common decency. It said Tesco would sell anything. It said Tesco and its ilk were the bomb, not a couple of pissed off blokes with jumpers tied round their noses' (Bauer. In: Gough, 2012: 72).
81 Banksy (2006): 196.
82 Gough (2012).
83 See photos: Gough (2012): 87, 110.
84 Plumridge and Mearman. In: Gough (2012): 116.
85 Fiske (1989): 130.
86 Plumridge and Mearman. In: Gough (2012): 116.
87 The recent history of British 'political' theatre seems to bear this out, from Joan Littlewood's Theatre Workshop use of music-hall in *Oh What a Lovely War!*

(1963), for a working-class audience, to Nicholas Kent targeting a more literary audience with his verbatim re-enactments of judicial inquiries, including those into the murder of Stephen Lawrence (1999) and Bloody Sunday (2005). By contrast, my own play, *The Joy Society* (2001) was more heavily criticised by a traditionalist theatre reviewer (*Venue*, 04/10/2001) for delivering a non-linear narrative 'presented as theatre' than for some of the very provocative material.

88   Critchley, Simon (2004) *On Humour*. London and New York: Routledge: 65–75.
89   Csikszentmihalyi (1975): 33.
90   Fairey, Shepard (30/11/2006) http://thejailbreak.com/2009/07/31/shepard-fairey-interviews-banksy-for-swindle-magazine. Accessed 16/06/2011.
91   'Kesey' (21/12/2010) http://edendale.typepad.com/weblog/2010/12/banksy-yes-banksy-on-thierry-exit-skepticism-documentary-filmmaking-as-punk.html. Accessed 16/06/2011.
92   Banksy, ibid.
93   Bakhtin (1969): 12.
94   One of his most famous images was misread when placed in a particular context. 'I did this piece in Soho, with a masked man throwing a bunch of flowers over a giant barcode. I put "Pest Control" on it, meaning "the pests control the city", as opposed to the pests being controlled. This mate of mine rings me up and says: "Are you homophobic?" I'm like, no not at all. But coz it was in Soho, and had a geezer throwing flowers, that's what they thought.' (www.briansewell.com/artist/b-artist/banksy/banksy-metaphysical.html. Accessed 16/6/2011).
95   Anonymous, on behalf of Bristol Museums and Art Galleries. In: Gough (2012): 61–2.
96   Ibid.: 59–67.
97   Ibid.: 62.
98   Farthing, Anna, Banksy vs Bristol Museum: Bristol Museum vs Banksy: who won? In: Gough (2012): 106.
99   Ibid: 108.
100   Ibid.: 107.
101   Byrne. In: Gough (2012): 81–85.
102   Bristol Council canvassed public opinion on the retention of the painting through its ask bristol website. Over 90 per cent of respondents voted in favour of retention (Wright, 2007: 93; Byrne. In: Gough, 2012: 82).
103   Ibid.
104   Plumridge and Mearman. In: Gough (2012): 110, 113.
105   Kelly, Andrew, Banksy and Bristol's cultural development. In: Gough (2012): 93.
106   Jacob, Francois (1982) *The Possible and the Actual*. London: Penguin (1989): 176.
107   Wright (2008): 8.
108   '"Art" (if that was the right word) was seen to come from the soil rather than from exceptional flowers growing out of it. Moreover, as the populism shared by both the market and anti-elitist radicalism held, the important thing about it was not to distinguish between good and bad, elaborate and simple, but at most between what appealed to more and fewer people.' (Hobsbawm, Eric, 1994, *Age of Extremes*. London: Michael Joseph: 514).
109   Jacob (1989): 411.
110   Ibid.: 410.
111   Prigogine, Ilya and Stengers, Isabelle (1984) *Order out of Chaos*. Portsmouth: Heinemann: 196.
112   Bassi's honey-and-feathers finale was both a demonstration of his relative freedom from internalised constrictive norms and a promotion of anarchist principles.

5 Comparisons

This chapter provides an interlude, reflecting on the three key artists in the previous chapters and preparing the ground for the final chapter on circus. The chapter structure that I formed in Chapter One, and solidified in the three subsequent chapters, will now become more fluid, thus mirroring the formation and breakdown within the subject matter.

Comparing the key artists

Leo Bassi is different from Banksy and Sacha Baron Cohen in that he has retained an open interactivity with various communities, including face-to-face contact with local activists as well as online contact with cultural associates. As compared with the other two, he has been less interested in personal wealth and more interested in developing a personal philosophy and maintaining relatively normal social relationships. Banksy and Baron Cohen have arrived at a position of fame and fortune because of a provocative stance early in their career but, in contrast, Bassi has moved in the opposite direction becoming more profoundly provocative as his career progressed. Although he has targeted both left-wing and right-wing institutions he does not 'make fun of all' as much as Banksy and Baron Cohen. Like the other two he is playful in his work but he is prepared to be clearer with his messages and unafraid of expounding his political and cultural views in public, for example on chat shows. Banksy is also unafraid of making unequivocal statements but these tend to be more dis-sembling or couched in irony. Bassi has shown that he is prepared for direct confrontation (with TV companies and religious groups) in a way that Banksy and Baron Cohen avoid. This has resulted in two consequences; the first is that he has been prevented from reaching a wider audience because of being excluded by commercial TV. This has meant that he has become more mar-ginalised than the other two because his potential to mount actions has been limited by his relative lack of acquired capital. The second is that he has been at greater personal risk (of his life) and this has been exacerbated because he is more accessible. Both Bassi and Baron Cohen use improvised confrontations with real-life persons but Bassi rarely uses permanent hoaxes and he is often not masked by a character or hidden behind a wall of anonymity.

By comparison, Baron Cohen is less connected to an oppositional community. Over the period in question, he has not demonstrated any acts of solidarity with any community as he had done with anti-Nazi groups in his youth. His messages are less overt; he tends to pinpoint weaknesses, contradictions and is more interested in the 'psychology' of societies and, unlike Bassi and Banksy, does not provide any suggestion of utopian aspirations. His aim to reveal prejudice in Western society, that he pursued from 2002 to 2009, seems to have been abandoned in favour of targeting a bogey-man of the American mainstream, the Arab dictator, suggesting that he has become substantially incorporated. Although he has taken life-threatening risks in some of his acts of incitement, the highly sophisticated and complex operation that surrounded these actions provided a certain level of control that mitigated the risks.

The most obvious distinguishing feature of Banksy is his anonymity. This allows him to operate relatively normally in public but his financial success has separated him from the community he still feels himself to be a part of. So that, although he retains an oppositional stance, he is not an interactive part of an opposition in the way that Bassi is. Indeed he (or his success) has stimulated a sadly destructive conflict with parts of that community (the 'war' with Robbo) even while attempting to promote the work of other artists. He uses both clear unequivocal messages as well as more confusing or playful ones. Through an original and clever use of public relations he has managed to both achieve financial success and to avoid becoming incorporated into the norms of the art market, but this has been achieved at the cost of maintaining an iron grip on colleagues, associates and friends. However, the centre that he was originally in contest with – the civic authorities – have shifted their position in response to his provocation whereas the much larger targets of Bassi and Baron Cohen have remained closed or even stiffened resistance to openness.

Despite these differences between them the similarities are significant because of the different media in which they work. All three have described a key moment when they were full of adrenalin, when a chance occurrence resulted in a major breakthrough in their practice.[1] To begin with they all experienced some degree of errancy, splitting off from a particular community that had been important to them. In Bassi's case it was because of the decline of traditional circus, for Baron Cohen it was both the comfortable middle-class English society of his education and also the Jewish cultural groups. For Banksy it was, firstly, his private school and secondly the graffitti culture. All three engaged in a David and Goliath contest with the wider system and were keen to demonstrate their prowess in this asymmetric struggle, arguably as an attempt to reclaim status within the rejected community by championing its values. These binary contests involved events that were aimed at inciting a counter-reaction which would reveal contradictions, hypocrisy and repressive tendencies. The various contests were one way to engage the public as a way to become actively involved even if only (as with Baron Cohen) in order to become more able to identify prejudice. The other way they all engaged the public was through popular comedy, deftly improvising to confuse and destabilise. All three use the carnivalesque modes of parody and inversion.[2]

The relationship with their community groups is significant because it provided a sense of them as outsiders to it or to the wider society or both; all three identified with communities that already had a sense of being outside mainstream society. In terms of complexity theory, this difficulty of 'fitting in' to their community or mainstream society can be seen as the turbulence that leads to the laminar phase. The errancy is equivalent to a bifurcation. For a few years they remained in a culturally fluid state, arguably their most creative. This exploratory state provided the right (adrenalin-filled) conditions for minor occurrences to make a significant impact on their work.

> A system far from equilibrium may be described as organized not because it realises a plan alien to the elementary activities, or transcending them, but on the contrary, because the microscopic fluctuation occurring 'at the right moment' resulted in favoring one reaction path over a number of equally possible paths. Under certain circumstances therefore, the role played by individual behaviour can be decisive … Self-organization processes in far-from-equilibrium conditions correspond to a delicate interplay between chance and necessity; between fluctuations and deterministic laws. We expect that near bifurcation, fluctuations or random elements would play an important role, while between bifurcations the deterministic aspects would become dominant.[3]

This appears to confirm that edge-playing may be linked to an 'aptitude to evolve'. These moments of inspiration provided the innovation which they employed successfully over the subsequent years. As their work became more widely recognised, their sense of their own identity became more established as they 'rewrote the rule book' of their particular medium. They began to be able to have greater control over the conditions of their work, including their personnel, to the point that autocratic tendencies began to become apparent (Banksy, but also Baron Cohen). They had become the centre of a system that they had brought into being. As a consequence the relationship with their originating communities shifted. In Bassi's case the traditional circus had changed so fundamentally during the forty years of his career that he could be treated both as the returning prodigal son and also as a representative of the central tradition. In Baron Cohen's case he appears to have reaffirmed his Jewish identity and fully embraced celebrity culture. Despite his popularity with the wider populace, Banksy seems to have remained detached both from the street art scene, within parts of which he is regarded disparagingly as a 'sell-out', and also from large parts of the contemporary art scene who find his work too simplistic. Despite becoming accepted, or at least tolerated, as part of the cultural landscape, all three still retain varying degrees of a sense of themselves as outsiders. They appear to wish to sustain this (self) image and are facilitated in this by the slowness of large-scale centres to respond to shifts in public attitudes. Although it appears that this outsider status is not as important to them as it once was, certainly both Bassi and Banksy have become locked into sustaining the opposition to central institutions that they had at the outset of their careers.

Comparing Pussy Riot and Burlesque

Up until this point I have written exclusively about male provocateurs. Whilst this area of work is predominantly a male one because it involves bravado, territorial domination, power negotiations and, as I have suggested, may be connected to increased levels of testosterone, it is not exclusively so. Therefore examples of female provocation can expand an understanding of the nature of provocation: women may also have to claim a space in which to begin to provoke. I write from a male perspective, just as I write from the perspective of someone formed by experiences of street theatre, and although it is clearly better to write about what you are most familiar with it may also be the case, following the premise of this book, that an outsider perspective may be useful to navigate the complexities of the two types of female provocation that follow. These offer very different ways of overcoming an initially weak position in two very different contexts – Pussy Riot in Putin's Russia and Neo-Burlesque performance in the UK and USA. The different contexts have different issues of power and challenge and thus carry different senses of the word 'provocation'. One follows the confrontational model and is thus liable to suppression and marginalisation, and the other is more subtle and insidious but is liable to incorporation via commercial pressures. Because the types of provocation they use are appropriate to their context, they reflect the nature of their respective cultural and political systems. For example, unlike in Putin's Russia, Burlesque performers in the UK and USA feel safer to be sexually provocative because they can be relatively confident of remaining in control of situations they create.

In discussing these two examples, it is not my intention to make an argu-ment for a particular position within the vast and complex field of the many different strands of feminism and post-feminism but I will refer to these as a way to inform the respective ideological contexts. Just as I am aware of the problems of comparing artists in different media, I am also conscious of the dangers of comparing a very specific example with a much more generalised field. How-ever, although Pussy Riot have become famous because of just a few events, the earlier work of two key members with art-activist group, Voina, covers a wide spectrum of actions, from the serious and didactic to the more playful, just as the Burlesque performance covers a range of work from highly provocative to conventional. Indeed it is common for a single Burlesque performer to have a range of different acts with different levels of challenge, from the wholly com-mercial to the unmarketable. Arguably, the two examples stretch the definition of popular culture that I have outlined above: Burlesque because the nature of its 'mainstream' popularity is so commercially driven, and Pussy Riot because they are not concerned with wide appeal or using popular humour to shift attitudes 'from the inside'. By comparing these two areas of female provocation, this section can make a bridge between the work of Banksy in the previous chapter and the world of circus in the final one. Many of the issues of transgression and/or incorporation that Burlesque deals with are highly comparable to those in circus. The Pussy Riot context also informs an understanding of the perspective of the Russian provocateur described at the beginning of the next chapter.

Pussy Riot

Pussy Riot sprang to worldwide renown with the video dissemination of their *Punk Prayer* intervention in the Cathedral Church of Christ the Saviour, Moscow (21/02/2012), and the subsequent arrest and trial of three members. Although described as a punk band they never played for money and their membership was undefined. The 'band' itself had been in existence for only about six months before the cathedral event and only ever performed in public five times, usually for only a few minutes. Two members had participated in events by the performance art collective, Voina, which was formed in 2007, centred around philosophy graduate, Oleg Vorotnikov, who led others from university and artistic backgrounds to perform a range of one-off actions in public. These included jettisoning live cats at sales-counter staff in McDonalds (01/05/2007), a pop-up feast/wake inside a Moscow metro carriage for the recently deceased writer, Dmitry Prigov (24/08/2007), group sex in front of political texts at the Timiryazev State Biology Museum (29/02/2008), a mock-hanging of two gay men and three central Asian guest-workers in a supermarket (07/09/2008), painting a phallus on a drawbridge leading to the Federal Security Service in St Petersburg (14/06/2010) and overturning a police car (20/09/2010). This last action led to the arrest of Vorotnikov and Leonid Nikolayev who Banksy helped, by paying £80,000 for their bail.

When discussing the Pussy Riot phenomenon it is not easy to be definitive. Statements by members may be intended as only of temporary relevance, later superseded as fluid ideas and situations move on. Also it may not be clear who can speak on behalf of the group or even who is considered a member. Some statements suggest the group is all-inclusive – 'Anyone can be Pussy Riot'[4] – and at other times it appears as highly exclusive. The members who are most familiar in the West, Nadia Tolokonnikova and Maria Ayokhina were declared not to be members by anonymous other members of the group.[5] In this way the loose association mirrors the kind of sub-divisions and in-fighting amongst graffiti artists. As with Banksy, fame is regarded by some previous colleagues as 'selling out', a betrayal of original principles. For those enjoying the fame it can be seen as a vehicle for disseminating ideas. Like Banksy, Pussy Riot members conceal their identity (behind their colourful balaclavas) and, in their cathedral protest, made a hit-and-run 'splash' in a public space.[6] However, instead of the street, their more significant intervention into the public domain is via social media. Like many of Banksy's pieces the artefact itself can only have a brief life because of its location but the dissemination of the image and its effects are the more substantial part of the artistic work. Indeed, in narrow artistic terms, the Pussy Riot artefacts themselves are unsophisticated: in their punk band incarnation they did not claim any high level of musical expertise. However, this is clearly not the point, the music is simply used as a cultural vehicle for activist texts, just as the works of Voina used different media (the hanging of shop-workers was a 'theatre' event, the graffittied bridge was street art, the 'orgy' in the Biology Museum was like a Live Art action, and the feast on the Metro was a temporary installation).

The first question raised by the Pussy Riot phenomenon is about the relationship between the suppressive context and the nature of the provocative action: how one defines the other. The *Punk Prayer* action was an attempt to expose the links between state power and the affluent upper hierarchy of the Russian Orthodox Church and, although this is comparable to Bassi's *Revelacion*, the context is very different. Bassi could rely on a relatively free press and an independent judiciary whereas, in Russia, TV channels are controlled by the state and, with very few independent newspapers available in such a huge country, it is possible for the state to limit knowledge of current affairs and encourage aspects of popular prejudice that are favourable to the government. In addition Putin took steps in 2014 towards controlling social media specifically and the internet in general. Small actions of dissent can be easily suppressed through a range of tactics. For example, the intended Pussy Riot demonstration/performance at the Sochi Olympics (2014) was hindered by hours of questioning in police custody in relation to a supposed theft at their hotel. Similarly, in a documentary film after their release from prison, there is footage of a railway guard trying to stop the interviews by insisting that (any?) filming is prohibited on public transportation.[7]

In a 2013 Levada Centre poll[8] a majority of Russians said they prioritised the maintenance of law and order over issues of freedom and human rights. Given this context, the opposition tried to build a broad support base for a mild agenda. In order to seem like a more moderate but viable alternative to Putin's rule, they had to compromise to the point of excluding a visible LGBT presence at opposition rallies. As well as having to reduce their ambition and being marginalised through Putin's media control, the opposition was also physically suppressed, with peaceful demonstrators imprisoned for many months before trial. In addition to the muting of the political opposition, artists must also be careful to be uncritical. As veteran music critic and art historian, Artemy Trointsky, put it: '[Russian] popular artists humiliating, slavish dependence on the corrupt government and criminal business is common knowledge'.[9] As a result there is an 'absence of a daring political message on the musical and art scenes'.[10] Artists must therefore make a clear decision whether to accept the consequences of challenge or accept their situation; there is a division into 'with' or 'against', characteristic of the border analogy. In this suppressive context, statements need to be bold so that they cannot be ignored; as an anonymous member of Voina put it: 'Contemporary art is used as actionism often verging on political provocation … disruptive activism is the only kind of politically engaged art still possible'.[11] 'Voina' translates as 'war' and, despite Pussy Riot's colourful and playful medium, this background of confrontation produces a strategy of shock tactics that appear to invite retribution. 'We need to destroy the whole system. It's rotten from head to tail. Only radical revolutionary action can change anything. Talk and compromise get you nowhere'.[12] Indeed attracting a strong reaction seems to be as much a part of the contest as the nature of the initiating action. As with Bassi's *Revelacion* (pp. 61–6), this authoritarian reaction stimulates a much wider libertarian reaction, in this case worldwide, and these waves of debate, fed by members' statements, are an integral part of the work. As defence lawyers at the trial pointed out, the event itself was of no great consequence and church officials had stated that hardly anyone had been offended. It would have been ignored if the video recording of it (inter-spliced with excerpts from a similar event) had not been posted on Facebook. The context defines the nature of the provocation. However, is this bold approach counter-productive?

The *Punk Prayer* and other visible examples of what must appear as chaotic behaviour to the majority of the population serve the government. This is a good example of order emerging out of chaos, building systems and borders in order to reduce unpredictability. As well as the video footage of the 'sacrilege' at the cathedral, the image of Nadia Tolokonnikova participating in Voina's public group sex, while nine months pregnant, was also used by conservative newspapers to confirm the alien character of the group[13] and build support for the government. 'If you're against Putin, that means that you're against the Orthodox Church ... this formulation makes Putin's power more stable. The hatred [for Pussy Riot] being cultivated in Russian society will become a source of legitimacy for Putin'.[14] So the approach of Pussy Riot can be seen as actually causing a divisive hardening of attitudes, arguably creating more division and polarisation than had existed before.

> Opposition activist Vladimir Milor writing on his website gazeta.ru warned that the Pussy Riot trial could serve to deepen the chasm between the liberal opposition and the rest of the Russian society. 'It is practically impossible to explain the girls' action in a positive light, this is extremely beneficial to the authorities' ... The Kremlin has used it to divert attention from the opposition's true cause – to end what it sees as a corrupt and illegitimate regime ... Pussy Riot has put people like [opposition politicians] Milor and Navalny in a tough spot. They have to stand up for liberal values and against a new inquisition ... but they cannot be seen as enemies of the Orthodox faith and traditional values. Otherwise they have no hope of turning people who hold these values against Putin, and that is crucial if they are ever to win power.[15]

Because of Putin's power and control, democracy cannot function well, so the only possibility for change may seem to be pressure from outside the country. From this perspective a spectacular 'splash' can be seen as effective in attracting outside attention, making active use of internet media outside of state control. Just as the Ukrainian-originated feminist activist group, Femen, have gained wide media attention by the simple but effective tactic of revealing their bare chests at their protests, Pussy Riot have also provided powerful images that attract the media, both in terms of their 'outrageous' actions and their 'telegenic' appearances behind courtroom bars. Having gained attention, their carefully crafted arguments are thus provided with a platform for articulation that was denied in any other public domestic forum.

So, in this context, the provocation needs to be spectacular rather than subtle in order to avoid being easily suppressed or marginalised. In one sense this can be seen as providing a sharp edge necessary in terms of the blade analogy, so as to reveal that which is hidden. An activist supporter of the group, Petr Pavlensky,[16] said: 'Activism is the struggle to shake up society; political art is aimed at the destruction and exposure of the apparatus of power. Under certain circumstances, it is a catalyst to the political process'.[17] In the case of the Pussy Riot trial many problems were revealed: 'the problem of the court system, the problem of the prison system, problems of defending yourself in such cases. A lot of their problems emerged, including the problem of the cultural politics in our society, in our governments'.[18] In turn, these problems, internal to Russia, were 'revealed' to the world. However, the almost negligible effect on international participation in the 2014 Sochi Winter Olympics questions whether their appeal to the global community can produce actual results. Despite this, the Pussy Riot trial, together with the more general repression of LGBT minorities, can be said to have contributed to an adjusted view of Russia, in the rest of the world, as authoritarian and anti-progressive. 'The "propaganda of the deed" strategy is appearing to pay off ... The image of Russia as "a European Iran" was strengthened'.[19] Although such an image may strengthen Putin internally, his attempt to place legal restrictions on internet providers suggests he is not comfortable with the lack of control over messages coming out of Russia and rebounding back into it. By both shoring up the borders, limiting the outsider perspective, as well as reinforcing the sense of a threatened 'us-and-them' outlook of the Russian traditionalists,[20] he can bind his cluster of oligarchs, state, church, business and media centres to the rest of the entity strengthening its cohesion at the expense of adaptability to global developments.

The second point of interest in Pussy Riot is why did they become so popular in the West and what assumptions did that reveal? The three aspects of popularity that I have outlined (p. 25) are useful to answer this question. Firstly, they appealed as risk-takers, and provided widely accessible images of their risk-taking, such as being arrested and assaulted by whip-wielding Cossacks at the Sochi Olympics (19/02/2014). The fact that they have been prepared to risk suffering the consequences to their personal and family lives, and have elected to go on hunger strike, has an impressive power for the more comfortable artistic and feminist progressives in the West. Secondly, they are empowering, not only as strong women but also, because they were referred to as a 'punk band', they may be incorrectly thought of as underdog populist entertainers triumphing over stern censors. Thirdly, their identification with the West through their English name, artistic methods and anti-Putin sentiments signalled communitas with various groupings. The tour of the West undertaken by Nadia Tolokonni-kova and Maria Ayokhina has included public discussions with Judith Butler and Rosi Braidotti[21] who appeared to be glad to be able to welcome them into their circle. In Oslo they were embraced by groupings of both musicians[22] and the visual art world[23] (despite those centres having to stretch their definitions in order to be able to include them). Similarly, in the USA, politicians appeared to be enthusiastic to be associated with them; they were privileged to have photo opportunities with Hillary Clinton and at the Senate (April 2014), mainly because of their anti-Putin stance but also for their stance on freedom of expression and human rights.

This incorporation created an assumption that they supported other Western values such as capitalism. However, it is clear from their work and their lifestyle that this is not the case. The early action of Voina, propelling live cats at staff in McDonalds was stated to be an anti-capitalist action. Their lifestyle at that time was anti-consumerist, living simply on waste food, in clothes that had been obtained from bins or friends and avoiding paying for train tickets. Like Banksy, they believed that art should be free or unmarketable, refusing to play music for money, and like him, with their balaclava concealment, they attempted to avoid both arrest and a personality cult. More profoundly, like him they favour wider societal concerns over and above the fashion for self-reflective or introverted art that can be seen as an aspect of the West's preoccupation with the individual. An example of their discomfort with the conventional focus on the individual is when they appeared on an Irish chat show[24] and were asked how it felt to be so famous. They reorientated the conversation by replying: 'People who sit on [chat-show] couches have little relation to reforming something, they don't have any relation to reform at all'. So through their astute recognition of the subtle signs of the initial inducements of capitalism they have managed to play on the edge of incorporation without succumbing to its flattery and rewards.

The third observation about the Pussy Riot phenomenon relates to the fulcrum analogy: structure, 'wildness' and the ambivalence between the two. The diffi-culties that Pussy Riot have created for the political opposition in being associated with blasphemy and scandal are comparable with Leo Bassi's difficult relation-ship with the main Spanish Socialist party. In their actions and statements the group clearly suggest that they are not interested in compromise or transactional politics but in direct actions as a means to overthrow Putin. Their commitment to freedom of expression and disinterest in democratic process suggest that they are not interested in cultural relativism. Their punk anarchism has been perceived as not only politically irresponsible but also socially irresponsible, in the sense of lack of care about consequences to others. The *Punk Prayer* event can be seen as similar to Voina's action in McDonalds. In this earlier event the intended target was multi-nationals and by extension the capitalist system. However, in the moment of the action, the recipients of provocation were the counter staff who were unlikely to have had much choice where they worked. By contrast, Pussy Riot's action in Red Square, *Putin Zassal* (20/01/2012), had no inter-mediary because it was directed straight at the Kremlin. If there is an intermediary the action becomes personalised. Terrorists may target politicians or serving soldiers but increasingly the tactic has been used whereby individuals far from the conflict, either geographically or ideologically, are also targeted as a means to attack their government's policy. Observers of this action will perceive it as unjust and oppressive, focussing on the personal tragedy rather than wider political issues. In much the same way provocative stand-up comedians or street performers need to be careful to avoid picking on just one member of the audience in order to make fun of what they can be seen to represent. By emphasising the personal offence caused to Orthodox believers, Putin was able to mask the real object of the provocation. As in such cases as the Beshti affair[25] and Salman Rushdie's *The Satanic Verses*,[26] democratic institutions have to balance freedom of expression with causing 'offence'. Whilst the severity of their sentence was an issue, Putin could portray himself as a dispassionate moderator.

However, just like Bassi and also Banksy, particularly in his dealings with the Bristol Tesco riots, Pussy Riot combine ideological contest with an unstructured approach: 'We intend to carry out a wild action, with an emphasis on wildness, rather than illustrating an ideology'.[27] The carnivalesque, 'lower-body' sensationalism of *Fuck for the Baby Bear's Heir* created a notoriety that provided a platform to disseminate their 'upper-body' message. Similarly, their attitude to legality is ambivalent: they are careless of breaking laws on chosen occasions but are very careful to remind individual guards, prison authorities and prosecuting lawyers as to the precise letters of laws, rules and regulations. This can be seen as hypocrisy but, using the fulcrum analogy, they are simply being adeptly adaptable to different games being played, employing a more procedural, systematic game when it is forced upon them, denying a loose arbitrary approach by law enforcers when their own fluid approach has been denied. Again, this is similar to Banksy's ambivalent approach to commerce: he indicates his disdain for the commercial art market but is extremely adept at working within it.

In discussing the image presented by the group it would be wrong to omit that key members have often been described as 'telegenic'.[28] This quality is as much to do with their naturalness as their physical appearance. Unlike Sacha Baron Cohen's interviewees, they do not appear to be intimidated or interested to play by the rules, often looking uninterested or sharing a private joke during interviews. This absence of intimidation is partly as a result of the number of interviews they have undertaken and partly because, as they say, 'We are free people, and free people feel no fear'.[29] Repeated experiences of placing themselves in such vulnerable situations have increased their freedom of action. Despite the adverse consequences, the risk-taking has not led to a reduction in their provocative stance. Arguably, neither has it led to the kind of increasing level of risk characteristic of those described by Robertson in *The Winner Effect*,[30] who are predominantly male. However, they must be aware of their own physical attractiveness, because it is often referred to, and to be aware that this is a factor, however minor, in the invitations they receive. They must also be aware of the prurient interest in *Fuck for the Baby Bear's Heir* which, as I have suggested, gave them a notoriety that was useful to them. This has parallels with the tactics of Femen. When asked about Femen, members of Pussy Riot made it clear that they are aware of how media interest in the female body can be exploited:

> Our opinion on Femen is a complicated story. On one hand they exploit a very masculine and sexist rhetoric in their protests – men want to see aggressive naked girls attacked by cops. On the other hand, their energy and the ability to keep going no matter what is awesome and inspiring.[31]
>
> Their surprise displays and protests against authoritarianism are similar to us, but we look at feminism differently, especially the form of speech. We wouldn't take our clothes off, and will not.[32]

The exploitation of this kind of interest provides a link to the next section on Neo-Burlesque. Whereas Neo-Burlesque concerns the refinement of the tease, Voina's 'public orgy' de-eroticised sex, treating it as reproductive act, within the context of a museum of Biology. Similarly, in the action entitled *How to Snatch a Chicken* (20/07/2011) the insertion of a supermarket chicken into the performer's vagina treated sexual parts in a manner far from the erotic. The punk attitude of: 'We don't care what others think about us' is a form of carnivalesque release, whereas Neo-Burlesque is very focussed on what others think/feel about the self-image being presented. The next section explores this other sense of 'being provocative'.

Burlesque

Unlike the preceding discussion of Pussy Riot, this section has a much wider focus, referring to a range of artists who include a broad range of work in their portfolio of acts. Neo-Burlesque covers a huge spectrum across the play continuum (p. 40), and from very commercial work to the unmarketable. As with work included under the term 'circus', which I discuss in the next chapter, artist–performers may not share much common ground. So to discuss this form in relationship to other types of provocative performer it is unavoidable to make some generalisations that may not be applicable in all cases. Although some books on the subject have done so, it is difficult to speak about *the* (Neo)-Burlesque performer. There is a confusing mix of opinions and, as with 'New Circus', the qualifying 'Neo' has become less used, not only because of a lessening need to distinguish itself from the 'classic' model as it became more established but also because, increasingly, it has come to resemble it, both aesthetically and in its ambiguous politics. For this reason I will refrain from using the prefix unless it is necessary to distinguish the contemporary from early twentieth-century forms.

The history of the revival and reinterpretation of Burlesque in the 1990s and its relationship with the development of feminism is well documented.[33] Versions of it have become widely popular but it remains controversial, not so much because of older concerns about its salacious quality but more because of what it currently signifies about the position of women (and men) in a modern Western society. The rise in its popularity can be seen as an aspect of 'third wave' feminism and a legacy of the sex-positive tendency. This libertarian tendency was resisted by those who opposed pornography in the so called 'Feminist Sex Wars'. The shift between the two tendencies can be approached through my own brief experience of the Burlesque effect whilst performing a fire-eating act in the late 1970s, in the comic character of a Sidney Singe. He attempted to impress with bravado as he placed fiery torches on his skin and even down his underpants, realising too late the pain he was about to self-inflict and appearing to burn himself repeatedly. To establish the absurd machismo of the character there was a sequence which involved isolated muscles being flexed. In this period, during the second wave of feminism, it was impossible for either myself or the audience to take this narcissistic machismo seriously. However, despite the enjoyment in the parody on both sides, it became clear that the wolf-whistles from women were only half-ironic and I also had to acknowledge that, in performance, I relished my physicality and its public display. Therefore there was an ambiguous mix of playing both within and without the parody. Both were forms of play but one took account of the time-specific ideological context and one did not.

Before considering the subject in terms of different kinds of power relationships, it is useful to approach it through this ambiguity. It can be viewed, in terms of the fulcrum analogy, as an interplay between structure and control (including commercial imperatives) on the one hand, and fantasy, play and release on the other. One of the attractions of Burlesque is its unpredictability: like when going to see circus, audiences expect to be surprised as well as impressed. There is an expectation of being challenged, even though the level of it may vary. In New York the Burlesque scene is more influenced by Live Art, whereas in the UK it tends to be more formulaic and predictable. However, there are some notable exceptions in London, such as the work at The Double R Club, which is inspired by the film and TV director, David Lynch. Ben Chu described one evening there:

> The compere, Benjamin Louche, mimed an abortion operation on stage with a pair of ancient medical tongs. A woman dubbed Traumata pulled needles out from under the skin of her forehead. The blood ran down over her white corset and underwear as she lifted her arms into the cruciform pose, looking like a sexualised female Christ minus the crown of thorns. To round off the night, the Burlesque dancer Fancy Chance gyrated inside a giant cloth vagina. After being 'born' from within, she bit through a thick umbilical cord which squirted a dark fluid down the front of her baby costume. It's twisted. Sick, even. But that's the point.[34]

So Burlesque defies easy definitions, celebrating diversity in form as well as in sexual norms.

In the sense that Burlesque celebrates the 'lower body' and is about enjoying play it is carnivalesque. The use of parody, dressing up and pretending to be a transgressive other is also carnivalesque. This playful fluidity appears to be in contrast to the 'upper body', serious judgement of anti-pornography feminism which, critics argue, sustains a puritan, intellectual disdain for sensuality. As I have indicated in Chapter Two, political correctness is problematic for provocateurs per se because, although they may sympathise with the intention, it implies imposed control. These binary opposites view Burlesque as either exploitation or empowerment; the ambiguous nature of carnivalesque suggests that it can be both simultaneously. Many early Neo-Burlesque performers consciously and overtly made fun of stereotypical and normative images of women such as 'housewife' or Marilyn Monroe. The stripping was often used to demonstrate the hetero-normative assumptions that were concealed within these stereotypes. The comically ironic subversion was aimed at the out-dated ideology of those beyond the immediate audience. However, as the commercial value of this kind of performance became realised the subversion began to disappear. As Jacki Willson says of leading Burlesque performer, Dita Von Teese: 'Without being coupled with an ironical, critical or reflective questioning of sexual power, erotic display risks falling immediately back into unchallenging, stereotypical "off the shelf" readings of female sexuality'.[35]

Like carnival itself, the transgression is temporary; for the majority of Burlesque performers the transgression is acted or enhanced for only short episodes, comparable with the Bruno impersonators at Combe Martin (p. 117). This is in contrast with the Archaos performers, discussed in the next chapter, for whom forms of transgression were a permanent aspect of 'the life'. However, as with other types of provocation, the distinction between the permanent 'real' and the temporary simulation is hard to discern, the interplay between the two is complex. In addition to the performers' real experience of sensual pleasure in their own body and its display, there is likely to be an audience interest in the true identity of the performer: whether the nature of their display is an expression of a 'real' fantasy. This is particularly the case because, in Burlesque, most of the work is created by the performers themselves.

As I have outlined in respect of Bruno, there is a question over whether a parody of a stereotype, rather than undermining it, actually reinforces it. In the case of Burlesque this is particularly pertinent because the level of ironic subversion may be so subtle as to be hardly perceived (if not absent altogether). Whether this short-lived play with stereotypes subverts them or reinforces them has a parallel with the questions that have been asked of Mediaeval carnival: whether it was a 'release valve'[36] in which a temporary period of licentiousness was tolerated in order that tight control could be maintained in the long term, or whether, as Bakhtin suggests,[37] the repeated, if temporary, subversion of the Church and Feudal authorities prepared citizens for the more human-centred sensibility of the Renaissance and Reformation. With such complexity in modern culture it is futile to ask whether Burlesque is a symptom of the interest in body-culture or is contributing to it, it is both. Just the way that pole-dancing has become as normalised as Pilates as a way of keeping fit, so aerial-hoop classes and the Burlesque aesthetic have become normalised.

In terms of power relationships, it can be argued that contemporary Burlesque performers can increase their control through gaining greater financial independence. Figures such as Mae West and Gypsy Rose Lee are admired not only for their aesthetic but because they were strong, independent positive role models, creating a successful and self-controlled business out of just their bodies. Contemporary performers such as Dita Von Teese have successfully emulated these early performers, gaining power through business and marketing, exploiting male desire and creating freedom for themselves by obtaining greater control. For those attempting to emulate this success story, working within a commercial system, a form of target-centred contest is implied in their competition with each other. As described to me by Burlesque performer, Alex Hofgartner, this competition is fierce because of the crowded market, with many performing very similar acts to others. There is pressure to keep creating new acts and costumes and there is competition for territory: '*my* act, *my* costume designer'. Negative comments are harder to bear than, for example, in theatre because the work is more physically exposing and therefore personal.

Additionally the stereotype of the dangerous seducer, preying on hapless men, exploiting their readily accessible interest in sex and drawing them under her control, is a powerful one, and one that is far from that of the exploited prostitute who has little control over the men they interact with. Even though this stereotype reinforces an idea of women as predominantly sexual objects, contemporary Burlesque frames it within a 'retro' style, much in the same way that some circuses recreate a nostalgic, romantic image of an aesthetic that had faded away decades before, that has an attraction precisely because culture has moved on to the new and unfamiliar. The character is unreal, operating within a fantastical spectacle. There may be a few onlookers who confuse fantasy with reality but the context makes it very clear that this is a play. So to a certain extent, much Burlesque is escapist: 'a velvety, decadent cocoon from reality' as Willson describes the work of Von Teese.[38] Magic, masks and other forms of illusion are often employed so that, through fantasy, spectators can play with 'otherness': the exotic, forbidden and deviant, just as in dreams we experiment with different scenarios. The separation between audience norms and the imagined world within the Burlesque act, a border between 'us' and 'them', provides an edge and thus a frisson of excitement. The separation is reinforced because the scale and layout of venues may inhibit direct contact. Dita Von Teese often performs in huge spaces, safely remote from the spectators: it is purely a spectacle with only a distant relationship to the audience. Eye contact is not possible with the audience invisible in the darkness beyond the stage lights.[39]

However, other Burlesque performers do make eye contact and establish a relationship. Alex Hofgartner describes her onstage attitude to the audience in this way: 'Are you with me? Are you following me? Let's do this together. But not in a sexual way, more like taking people on a journey'.[40] As well as contrasting her work with that of Von Teese, she also separated it from those performers who, through design or lack of experience, do suggest real eroticism. 'The more erotic it is the more uncomfortable it makes people. As when you have somebody who is more sensual, people aren't so sure how to react. Acting a character is not real so it's safe. Acting is usually hammed up and caricatured'. In the case of more sensual performers, the relationship is comparable with Baron Cohen's work, where the performer is playing but the spectator is 'really' affected. The play, therefore has real power; Willson refers to the argument put forward by Robert C. Allen: 'that in order to be transgressive the performer *has* to be an object of desire ... otherwise they are perceived as comically grotesque'.[41] In these terms the provocation is comparable to Bassi's *Big Brother* action: the game hooks the dominant power into engagement, so that it cannot be ignored or marginalised.

When discussing power relationships within Burlesque performance, the fact that most of the audience are groups of women (e.g. 'hen' parties) or are couples is critical to understanding the nature of its contemporary form. Rather than stimulating desire, the audience is encouraged to express a sense of community, sharing in the freedom of the performer: 'When you go to a Burlesque show you are encouraged to shout and cheer. It would be weird if just the men were cheering ... It's about daring, rather than to turn people on'.[42] In such a female-dominated context, expressions of lewdness by the few men would unite the rest of the audience against them. The narrative of the performance is more about the attitudes of an individual personality to their own body, rather than about males viewing females. Like Bassi in his baby pigeon sequence, the audience can feel an enlargement of the potential space for their actions, because they witness their representative, the performer, doing so.

Power can also be viewed in terms of its opposite: vulnerability. Some Burlesque performers, such as Luna Rosa in the UK, play high status, intimidating the audience and taking their time. Others, such as Hofgartner, play a vulnerable character but this may be used as another way to gain power over spectators. 'I don't feel vulnerable when I'm not wearing any clothes', she says. This is partly because of her experience of working in a strip club for many years, which provided her with an expertise in how to control different situations. Through one-to-one dancing she learned how to manage client expectations which would vary from sexual availability, through getting drunk together and 'making friends', to the men wanting to confess some inadequacy or needing to be cared for. 'You have to have a tough skin. Some performers exploited male vulnerability or gullibility for money, others tried to help', so there is a wide moral spectrum within the genre, just as individual performers have a wide spectrum of acts. As I have suggested occurs in walkabout performance, appearing to make oneself vulnerable can convey a sense of power because it suggests that the performer is unconcerned with what spectators think.

The tease in Burlesque is a power–risk relationship that is inherently ambivalent. Audiences are attracted by the unpredictability: the opening up of fantastical possibilities and potential deviancy draws them into the unknown, with the performer carefully manipulating the development of their expectations. As Katherine Liepe-Levinson points out,[43] seduction is an alternation between exposure and concealment, surrender and control, being chased and leading on. The sophisticated construction and careful nuancing of this play with power relationships seems far from the crude one-off, hit-and-run performances of Pussy Riot, even though their political awareness may be more developed. So Burlesque provocation may be empowering in the moment, both as a release from internalised norms and in the relationship with the immediate spectators. However, in the wider frame of the position of women in society, what effects do the images presented in Burlesque produce? Does the commercialisation of the sexual body, inherent in most Burlesque, have parallels with contemporary sex slavery? Is the power relationship in the room a fractal of the bigger picture or of an altogether different kind?

Of course, Burlesque performers have some degree of choice and control over how they present themselves but, to a certain extent, this is like the notion of consumer 'choice' within modern capitalist society: the choices presented concern what items to purchase not whether the act of purchasing is in the best interest. To take a much more extreme example, in the early stages of sexual grooming a victim is often led to feel they have, or have already made, a choice; the wider, long-term situation is not recognised by them. In the other examples of incorporation that I have already discussed, the artist is offered a choice whether to accept official validation, in various forms, as well as financial reward, in return for sacrificing some independence of control. So, is Burlesque the same? It can be argued that stripping is inherently demeaning because whoever it is for, however it is perceived and whatever the position of the performer, the person is being presented primarily as just a body rather than as a whole person. Whether, or how, they strip, Burlesque performers care deeply about their appearance and Willson argues[44] that this is as much about the male gaze as the hijab or niqab, because they are both about controlling the way women are seen in public. In this model all women are encouraged to be concerned about how they appear to others (looking good/respectable/stylish) and to avoid being seen in clothing that they might choose to wear in the private space (i.e. what is comfortable for them). Therefore the hijab and sexy underwear can both be viewed as versions of same thing: being defined primarily through the eyes of another.

Many Burlesque performers would argue that, because they create their own style of performing and choose where to play it, the work is an expression of their full personality and that, if they avoided sensual physical expression, they would be privileging the intellect over the physical. In this sense, the subject of their provocation is the classical hierarchy of the mind over body, in yet another form of Bakhtin's 'upper body'–'lower-body' Carnivalesque inversion. The so-called 'Feminist Sex Wars'[45] can be seen as a manifestation of this duality. This aspect may be more significant than the ambiguity around subverting or acquiescing in male domination. Because of the existence of Boylesque (male Burlesque performance) and all the various LGBT based versions of Burlesque, the assumption that the style is essentially a manifestation of hetero-male dominance would appear to be too simplistic. The contemporary fashion for males to relish in their own bodies from pop videos, gym fitness and male stripping suggests that Burlesque may be a single aspect of a wider development in narcissistic body love. It also could be seen as part of the shift to the predominance of the image over that of the word.

Conclusion

In contrast to Burlesque performers, Pussy Riot members appear to care very little how they appear to others in their performances, they are concerned with the statement rather than the reception. They are unconcerned about being accepted whereas Burlesque performers want to be publicly accepted in all their sensual fullness, drawing observers into their game and engaging with them. Pussy Riot members refuse to compromise whereas Burlesque is about balancing individual expression with the expectations and desires of the audience. These two attitudes produce two different outcomes: the confrontational attitude of Pussy Riot creates divisions, even amongst the opposition, and one result is a reinforcement of norms in the wider public. Despite their iconoclastic and anarchic artistic forms, ironically they produce a sub-division of centres and greater structure, which are all aspects of the border analogy. Or, in terms of the fulcrum analogy, they tip the balance towards chaotic fluidity so far that they cause a reaction back towards structure. In contrast, Burlesque can be viewed as an insidious subversion of norms from the inside, subtly challenging hetero-male assumptions and entertainment norms and thus the commercial product within a capitalist system. However, because it operates within a largely commercial system, 'difficult' work can be marginalised and the rest is encouraged to be more about style than substance and is thus vulnerable to incorporation.

Despite their lack of concern for winning over the middle ground of the Russian electorate, Pussy Riot ostensibly operates for the benefit of others whereas Burlesque is concerned with the self. This may be partly as a result of the different background, one in a (former) socialist system and the other in a capitalist system. The latter encourages self-desire and self-indulgence whereas the former provides a validation of self-sacrifice and experiences of physical hardship in the interest of others. It is interesting to consider the potential fate of each example in the context of the other. In the macho culture of Putin's Russia, Burlesque would be unable to flourish as it does in the West, likely to be either suppressed or incorporated into 'girlie' shows. If Pussy Riot, in their original incarnation, were somehow transposed into the West they would likely to be tolerated (if patronised) but would probably need to adopt some of Banksy's concealment tactics in order to maintain a separation of themselves so that they can use, but not be used by, the market.

Notes

1 For Bassi, the bicycle accident during his street show (p. 43). For Baron Cohen, the moment after a film shoot when he realised his Ali G character was being received as a real person (p. 98). For Banksy, the revelation of the potential of stencilling while hiding from pursuing police (p. 129).

2 Bassi raises up the clown and the rubber duck, pulling down the Pope and politicians. Banksy raises up rats and chimps, pulling down police and the military. Baron Cohen uses a rapid inversion, switching praise to abuse in his rodeo speech.

3 Prigogine, Ilya and Stengers, Isabelle (1984) *Order out of Chaos*. Portsmouth: Heinemann: 176.

4 *The Guardian* (30/08/2014).

5 Pelly, Jenn, *Pitchfork* (06/02/2014) http://pitchfork.com/news/53860-nadia-tolokonnikova-and-masha-alyokhina-no-longer-members-of-pussy-riot/. Accessed 12/08/2014.

6 A band member made clear their opinion that only vivid illegal actions can bring media attention (interview with Steve Rosenberg for the BBC Russian Service, 22/02/2012).

7 Vice News (05/02/2014) www.vice.com/vice-news/pussy-riot-goes-back-to-jail. Accessed 25/07/2014.

8 www.levada.ru/sites/default/files/2012_eng.pdf. Accessed 28/07/2014.

9 Bershidsky, Leonid (21/08/2012) 'What Madonna doesn't get about Russia's punk protest'. http://www.bloombergview.com/articles/2012-08-21/what-madonna-doesn-t-get-about-russia-s-punk-protest. Accessed 08/08/2014.

10 'Serafima' (23/08/2012) 'Serafima' is one of the aliases used by Pussy Riot members when they are interviewed anonymously. www.cupblog.org/?p=7663. Accessed 21/07/2014.

11 http://thenewheroesandpioneers.com/magazine/2014/07/pussy-riot-voina/. Accessed 10/08/2014.

12 Member in *Pussy Riot: A Punk Prayer* (2013) Documentary film; Directed by Mike Lerner and Maksim Pozdorovkin. 88 mins. Roast Beef Productions for HBO.

13 This alien character is further exacerbated by their English name; 'Pussy Riot' is not a translation from Russian.

14 Kasin, Oleg, *The Guardian* (17/8/2012).

15 Bershidsky, Leonid (2012).

16 Pavlensky achieved notoriety for sewing his lips together to protest about the treatment of Pussy Riot members (23/09/2012) and on another occasion nailing his scrotum to the street surface (10/11/2013).

17 www.vice.com/en_uk/read/petr-pavlensky-testicles-red-square-police-day-russia-puttin.

18 Pussy Riot's Yekaterina Samutsevic 'I am here, free' – video (27/12/2012) www.theguardian.com/music/video/2012/dec/27/pussy-riot-free-speak-group-video. Accessed 04/08/2014.

19 *The Guardian* (17/08/2012).

20 The respected Levada pollsters concluded in 2013 that a majority of Russians (39 per cent to 37 per cent) said several years imprisonment would be a just punishment for the Pussy Riot trio. Only 7 per cent felt either respect or sympathy for the women as compared with 31 per cent who felt irritation or enmity. In a 2010 poll they concluded that 74 per cent of Russians view homosexuality as a 'moral perversion' or a 'mental illness'.

21 www.youtube.com/watch?v=BXbx_P7UVtE. Accessed 23/07/2014.

22 www.youtube.com/watch?v=1a9k8T5xgeo. Accessed 23/07/2014.

23 www.youtube.com/watch?v=TlJ6ioRVzew. Accessed 23/07/2014.

24 Brendan O'Connor on *The Saturday Night Show* (01/02/2014).

25 Sikh protests at a controversial theatre play (18/12/2004). http://news.bbc.co.uk/1/hi/england/west_midlands/4107437.stm. Accessed 13/03/2014.

26 www.theguardian.com/books/2012/sep/14/looking-at-salman-rushdies-satanic-verses. Accessed 26/02/2014.

27 Oleg Vorotnikov quoted by Rozanov, Danila, Voina: artists at war (18/02/2011) www.opendemocracy.net/od-russia/danila-rozanov/voina-artists-at-war. Accessed 04/08/2014.

28 Hale, Mike (09/06/2013) www.nytimes.com/2013/06/10/arts/television/pussy-riot-a-punk-prayer-in-hbo-documentary-series.html. Accessed 02/08/2014.
    Kampfner, John, The Pussy Riot trial won't bring down Vladimir Putin, *Independent* (14/08/2012) Accessed 04/08/2014.
    Shoard, Catherine (13/06/2013) www.theguardian.com/film/2013/jun/pussy-riot-a-punk-prayer-review. Accessed 04/08/2014.
    Karlin, Anatoly (23/08/2012) m.aljazeera.com/story/2012823795897200. Accessed 27/07/2014.
29 http://liberalvideo.com/2014/02/06/pussy-riot-tells-amanpour-we-are-free-people-and-free-people-feel-no-fear/. Accessed 04/08/2014.
30 Robertson, Ian (2012) *The Winner Effect, How Power Affects Your Brain*. London, Berlin, New York, Sydney: Bloomsbury.
31 'Serafima' (11/03/2012) www.vice.com/en_uk/read/A-Russian-Pussy-Riot. Accessed 04/08/2014.
32 Maria Ayokhina (02/11/2012) RegioNews. Archived from the original on 02/11/2012. Retrieved from Wikipedia 25/09/2014.
33 e.g. Willson, Jacki (2008) *The Happy Stripper*. London and New York: I.B. Tauris.
34 *The Independent* (01/08/2011).
35 Willson (2008): 148.
36 As proposed by Victor Turner and Max Gluckman (Gluckman, Max, 1963, *Order and Rebellion in Tribal Africa*. London: Cohen and West; Turner, Victor, 1974, *Dramas, Fields, and Metaphors: Symbolic Action in Human Society*. New York: Cornell University Press; Eagleton, Terry, 1981, *Walter Benjamin or Towards a Revolutionary Criticism*. London: Verso and NLB).
37 Bakhtin, Mikhail (1969) *Rabelais and His World*. Bloomington: Indiana University Press (1984): 465–74.
38 Willson (2008): 156.
39 Hofgartner, Alex (2014). Interview with Bim Mason (23/06/2014).
40 Ibid.
41 Willson (2008): 164.
42 Hofgartner (2014)
43 Liepe-Levinson, Katherine (2002) *Strip Show: Performances of Gender and Desire*. London and New York: Routledge: 171.
44 Willson (2008): 168–70.
45 An ongoing controversy between feminists who are against pornography and those who consider this attitude prudish, censorial and a denial of the sexual.

6 Provocateurs provoked

In this final chapter I will use the language and notions that I have established in the previous chapters to examine examples of practice that are initially provocative because of their radical innovation and subsequently become familiar, established and thus, in turn, a target for provocation themselves. As such they follow on from the processes suggested in the examination of Bassi, Baron Cohen and Banksy, in which the structures they have found it necessary to establish and the recognition they have attained begin to reduce their outsider status. With the three artists already discussed, although there are minor suggestions of their new liminal centres being challenged (Banksy by Robbo, and Bassi in the *Radical Hits* project), the process is less visible than in the following examples. The first example is a single event within one theatrical performance and this serves as an introduction to the second, much wider example, involving the evolution of contemporary circus. These examples aim to demonstrate a fractal link between individuals working within a sector of performing arts and the entire sector (a cluster of centres) working within wider society. The introductory example of practice is not from my own practice and the main body of the chapter is not about the work of an individual artist but about many different companies.

Contest or collusion

A provocative event occurred at a performance of *Spectacular* by the company, Forced Entertainment, at the Arnolfini, Bristol (06/03/2009). The show involved two actors. One, dressed in a skeleton outfit, described how the performance normally unfolded with a warm-up comic, a band and dancers. He gradually expanded on the idea of the breakdown and failure of the intended performance. The other actor entered later and began a sequence of theatricalised dying. During the performance someone in the audience started laughing loudly at slightly inappropriate places but this did not seem particularly odd because, due to the nature of the show, many people were laughing at different places. Gradually the laughs of this particular man became very evident and he began to make comments or imitate some of the onstage sounds. The actors looked at him, with increasing directness, in order to signal that he should stop. The programmer of the Arnolfini left her seat and went to tell him to leave, which he refused to do, saying he would laugh more quietly, which he did for the next twenty minutes. He seemed to be intelligent, not particularly drunk or mentally disturbed, just eccentric. He gradually began to get noisier again until one of the actors asked him to leave. This led to a dialogue until the man stood up, addressing the audience: 'Don't you find this boring?' The audience was uncertain whether this was all part of the piece so there were murmurs of agreement when he asked: 'Don't you want to see something extraordinary? I show you something extraordinary' He undid his trousers, squatted down, and, with a big effort, defecated into his hand. 'There!' he said, showing his handful. 'And more?' He smeared it on his face. A member of the front-of-house staff tried to remove him but she did not know how to. In response to her inaudible requests he laughed loudly, saying 'No, no, Stanislavski would absolutely approve of what I have done. Don't you know that?' She could not find a reply. Nobody knew what to do. A cameraman, videoing the show, switched his camera off, and tried to encourage the audience to boo him off: 'Do you want him to go?'. However, they were still not sure whether this was a set-up because of the theme of the show and its direct contact with the audience. Gradually there was enough of a collective 'Yes' in the audience and he allowed himself to be led out to the exit. Soon after the man's departure, his companion left, saying 'They are going to give him hell out there', leading us to imagine the drama continuing elsewhere, just as, within the play, we had been asked to imagine another performance. After the departures, the actors recovered their script and continued well up to the scripted line: 'Well, things haven't gone exactly according to plan tonight', which received a big laugh because we could not see it only in terms of the 'official' play.

The play came to an end and everyone went out to the bar to get a drink before the after-show talk. Everyone excitedly discussed the intervention – was it real or a set-up? Who was he? If it was not a set-up how had it fitted so perfectly with the theme of the piece? How was it so perfectly timed, creating growing discomfort throughout the piece and then interrupting the piece only towards the end? Back in the theatre the after-show talk began, with the two actors and the programmer of the Arnolfini making it clear that it had indeed been an unexpected intervention and that the man was known for doing this at other people's events. They described it as an act of vandalism not dissimilar from attacking a painting in a gallery. They said his mentality was childish, that the (idea behind?) the intervention was boring and that he was clearly a self-indulgent ego-centric. They said they needed control over the event, a sealed space, and that although the intended piece looked improvised it was, in fact, tightly fixed.

As a spectator the event generated great pleasure; being unprepared, it was hard to believe what was being seen, we were taken into a liminal zone. The pleasure mainly derived from the level of risk being taken by others and experienced as a spectator: not only the raising of stakes by such an extreme act but also the high levels of unpredictability, which was partly due to the real/not real confusion. Were the 'theatre staff' real? If so, the acting was well done, and we, the audience were being duped into booing the man out of the auditorium. Would we be exposed as fearful, conventional kill-joys? If, on the other hand, the act was not faked we were watching a real struggle for power with an open-ended outcome. By showing what he was capable of the man had become powerful. What else was he capable of? This power matched, for a short time, dominant power, represented by the theatre, leaving him un-removeable. This wider dimension of the power struggle made it all the more fascinating. There was also pleasure in the discomfiture of the actors; the status shift from rehearsed pretendings to real actions: the collapsing stage-set and other such ruptures have been a source of comedy throughout the history of theatre. Like most real-life comedy we can laugh even whilst empathising with the suffering. Despite the stress and discomfiture, everyone present, the spectators, instigator, actors and theatre management would have experienced all four of the sources of pleasure, as identified by Csikszentmihalyi; friendship from the communitas derived from sharing the liminal experience; risk; solving the riddle of confusing signals; and creatively from entering an unknown place.[1]

The man is Alexander Brener, a Russian performance artist, and his companion is his artistic collaborator, Barbara Schurz. The event raised many issues. The act of Brener could be seen as an extension, even an enhancement, of the show's theme of failure, discomfort and the breakdown of formal theatre conventions. In the after-show talk it was stated that the death gasps and groans were meant to discomfort the audience and be a counterpoint to the light banter of the skeleton character. The company director, Tim Etchells,[2] says he is interested in creating events in which:

> the witness struggles to find new modes of understanding in the wake of activity that break pre-existing rules and the principles that shore them up. The result is a radical form of anxiety that interrupts those thought processes that normalise experience, that renders events knowable. 'The artwork that turns us into witnesses,' he writes, 'leaves us, above all, unable to stop thinking and reporting what we have seen'.[3]

Although uninvited, Brener appeared to be trying to achieve the same aims as the company, which Etchells outlines thus:

> We wanted the unstable. The trembling. The thrill of live decisions of different materials, different … theatre that placed you in a situation rather than describing one to you. A theatre in which your agency as a watcher was an acknowledged and known part of the performance from the outset. A theatre that felt more like an event. A theatre that made demands. A theatre that was ugly, awkward. A theatre that liked its ambiguities, its undecidedness, its disconnections. A theatre that was very very funny, ridiculous, absurd … A theatre that divided audiences.[4]

In terms of wider culture, the event can be seen as a bifurcation of a bifurcation; contemporary theatre is already a marginal sub-genre; this event marked a further division. If experimental theatre is seen as a centre in itself, with Forced Entertainment a sub-centre, then Brener can be seen as a fractal of that system, replicating in miniature, and shorter time-span, features of the larger entity. Or the event can be seen as an example of the way that liminal activity has become normalised into a new centre and thus attracting provocation. The company, originally known for its challenges to form and its refusal to compromise for the sake of the market, has nevertheless become validated because of the interest they have generated in academic circles. The inherent tension between the two attractors of validation and norm-challenging, promoting the image of deviancy while adhering to safe practice, suggests contradictions that may become a target.

Brener was desecrating the high-art sanctity of the Arnolfini with a most basic bodily function, raising up excrement and casting down the cerebral, in a carnivalesque celebration of Bakhtin's 'lower-body stratum'. He had performed a similar action at the ICA, London (2008), during a panel discussion on *Violence to Endurance: Extreme Curating* between leading performance artists, writers and a curator of the Frankfurt Museum of Modern Art. At that event he is quoted as saying: 'I am not here as an artist. I am here as a spectator who wishes to participate', echoing Etchell's interest when 'the spectator is a part of the event, existing within the same space and time. Active presence in a common situation'.[5] The art critic Tom Jeffreys, who witnessed this event, had some sympathy with Brener's position:

> The point that Brener and Schurz may be attempting to make is this: for all this talk of violence, endurance and strategies of shock, all that is really taking place here is that six more or less well known art world figures are talking about themselves, their work, and their thoughts. Brener – to some extent understandably – objects. Early on Brill cites Roland Barthes and how he argued that shock can be employed as a means to disorganize, that destruction can be a constructive option. Brener is simply enacting these ideas, here and now in this little room in the ICA.[6]

In terms of maintaining a position on an edge, there is not only the problem of the company becoming incorporated into the centre, but also the problems Brener has in maintaining his position as a way of life. He spent several years in jail for spraying a dollar sign on Kazimir Malevich's painting *Suprematisme* as well as paying fines for various other provocations. As alluded to in 'A Letter in Defence of Alexander Brener',[7] he lives with a high level of financial insecurity and instability, having been charged on one occasion with vagrancy. In addition he is attacked by most of the established contemporary art world that might otherwise defend him. This is because of his didactic opinions of that world, which are outlined by his supporters:

> For Brener, the majority of Russian art is not democratic because it derives from a very narrow circle of Russian intelligentsia ... He distinguishes avant-garde art from Modernism by the difference in their impact. Avant-garde art has an ethical impact, which is completely different from the formal impact of Modernism.[8]

The reactions expressed in the after-show talk, which both dismissed and closed down discussion of his work, are a good example of the marginalisation of such artists. This attitude is mirrored on the internet with entreaties not to give him the benefit of further attention. Again this seems to be a fractal of the way experimental theatre has been criticised. As Andrew Quick says:

> The performers in Forced Entertainment's work are not breaking rules just for the sake of it, in order to pursue a nihilistic assault on meaning (an accusation that is often flung at experimental art practice by those that judge it to have little social or political value). Rather, Etchells is staking a claim for those aesthetic practices that take the risk of negotiating material without relying on an immediate recourse to a rule, to pre-established ways of making sense of everyday occurrences.[9]

This can also be seen in terms of the border analogy: because the performers had felt threatened by Brener's intervention they distanced themselves from him, differentiating his perspective and values from their own. More significantly, seen in terms of the fulcrum analogy, they had reduced their improvisational fluidity and fixed their structural systems, both in the long term, as a result of established reputation, and in the short term, as they moved from the relative security of the rehearsal room to the more stressful public performance.

> If the performer is not exposed, not connected with what is happening now in the room, not entirely engaged with the elemental relation to the people gathered in front of them, then this seems, for the later work, like an act of bad faith or evasion, a step back down from what is required in your theatre.[10]

The company deliberately plays on an edge between inviting a live, unpredictable response and limiting that unpredictability. Using the blade analogy, Brener can be seen to be revealing the contradictions in this approach.

Circus complexity

Having examined processes of centre formation at the scale of individual artists and small groups, it is useful to examine these transition processes in much larger entities over a longer period. A good example is the development of circus over the last 250 years, from its sudden emergence in the mid-eighteenth century, through periods of decadence and renewal. It provides a useful case study because it is has a very distinct set of practices that separates it from other forms of performance. Circus has often (but not always) been regarded as a marginal activity; this is partly due to the itinerant nature of many circus companies which, historically, presented a very visible statement of separation with the temporary structure of the circus tent. Even when the structures are permanent, the extra-ordinary physical practices of the performers create a mystique among the wider population that confirms their ex-centric status.

This discrete artform has been a site of cultural contention, oscillating between challenge (through various forms of danger) and reassurance (through confirming norms). These oscillations have been responsive to, but separate from, shifts in the surrounding cultural and political contexts. Although changes in the wider culture affect it, they are filtered through the necessities of practice. Because, historically, circuses have been fairly fragile commercial enterprises there has been a requirement to retain wide popular acceptance. So, with the notable exception of Archaos, circuses generally do not aim to be provocative in the sense of the artists previously discussed. However, the provision of an experience of danger, both physically and culturally, is core to their identity. The examination of circus and its relationship to society is therefore useful to address questions of the relationship between popularity and challenge. In terms of centres, the relationship between sub-components of a centre (circus specialisms) and the whole entity suggests a connection between the repetitive activities of circus and the cultural attitudes thus formed. This can be seen as an example of fractal self-similarity between the micro scale and the macro. It can also help to differentiate those elements which are at the core of circus practice from the aesthetic and other cultural accretions. This approach is particularly necessary because circus, unlike other artforms, has acquired a specific and fixed norm in the public's imagination, perpetuated by images in children's books, for example. This norm has become so dominant that everyone engaged in the industry must take it into account, positioning themselves in relation to it when using the term 'circus' in any form of publication. Power negotiations are discussed on an individual level, in terms of risk and empowerment, and on a company level, in terms of marginalisation and incorporation, using comparisons between Archaos and Cirque du Soleil. The question of maintaining an existence on an edge can also be examined in these terms.

Circus outside in

As with the previously discussed provocateur work, circus is ambiguous, combining opposite tendencies. In addition to the tension between challenge and reassurance there are other combinations and contradictions between closed play and open play, between structure and release and between fear and laughter. It can be argued (but, for the sake of brevity, I will not attempt this here) that the ambiguity derives from the twin roots of circus: firstly, that of martial arts, which evolved into sporting spectacles, and secondly, ritual practices, that transformed into the presentation of exotic behaviours and exotic bodies. The modern history can be broadly divided into three phases, beginning with a gradual formation of disparate elements into a fixed set of practices which was then followed by the establishment of an orthodoxy that was resistant to change. This resistance led to the breakaway 'new circus' movement. Although the full history is a fascinating one, I have avoided too much detail because other writers have already described it[11] and because it would obscure the main subject of this book. The three phases suggest an oscillation between two tendencies: one is expansive, inclusive and innovative, the other is exclusive, conservative and introvert. These tendencies concern the attitudes within circus culture rather than those in relationship to wider society. The phases roughly correspond to historical periods, but there is much overlap with examples of innovation occurring at the same time that a conservative orthodoxy was being established.

The formation of modern circus

The first phase of modern circus, from the late eighteenth century to the late nineteenth century, can be said to be fluid both in terms of form and content, with disparate elements being added, some of which were discarded within a few decades. Displays of equestrian skills, which were the dominant feature of the original format (1768), were not new but, partly influenced by Astley's military service,[12] the decades of colonial wars and, later on, the Napoleonic Wars, the equestrian arts were placed in a context of battle re-enactments and patriotism. Like their precursors in the Roman Coliseum, these displays of martial skill have similarities with both the ancient Olympic Games and the spectacle of modern sports events. Other features quickly accrued to this new form. Comic knockabout characters, presumably similar to the present-day rodeo clowns, displayed failure as a counterpoint to the displays of prowess. As circus performances began to be presented inside covered arenas and buildings they incorporated the old form of Harlequinades and the new form of Pantomime. However, both of these had begun to disappear from circus programmes by the middle of the nineteenth century, bequeathing a legacy of comic routines and various types of clown.

In this first phase, the burgeoning British Empire was exploring potential areas for development around the world (Cook's first voyage 1768–71), coming into contact with unknown fauna and cultures. These expeditions provided access and infrastructure to enable the transportation of large animals to be displayed for the first time outside the aristocratic houses. These displays manifested to the general public the reach and power of the Empire and providing an image of domination of the wild or 'uncivilised', under the pretext of scientific research. The circus tent was often accompanied by a separate tent which enclosed a menagerie of exotic animals and an exhibition of curios from the natural world and exotic cultures. In addition there were examples of humans with physical abnormalities sometimes with a suggestion of a hybrid of animal and human. As Darwinist ideas spread through the second half of the nineteenth century exotic species and peoples were framed in a hierarchy of evolution and degrees of civilisation, with the educated white male at its apex. Leo Bassi noted that circus entrepreneurs 'piggy-backed' on these new discoveries and new technologies. At a time when newspapers were full of the stories of African exploration, particularly the iconic meeting of Livingstone and Stanley, circuses had responded to the interest with African themes.

> if you look at the [circus] posters from that time you see that the names of the artists were there but the most important attractions were things like 'The Biggest Gorilla in The World' or women with beards. Getting stories from other people in my [circus] family I heard that what we presented were black people in cages presented as cannibals. They were just normal people who had come over from Nigeria to work and there were stories about how, after spending most of the day almost naked, they had to hide at other times so people couldn't see they dressed normally. People thought that when they were seeing 'The Alligator Woman' in a cage they were seeing a new discovery brought back from the latest expedition to Africa. Siamese twins, too, were presented in this way.[13]

Once the public's attention had shifted from African to Arctic exploration, penguins, seals and wild 'Eskimo' dances were presented instead.

This period was one of great change, not only through the impact of revolutionary wars on the continents of Europe and America but also through the effects of the Industrial Revolution. Leo Bassi makes the point that the iconic 'big top' was only possible because the Industrial Revolution had enabled canvas to be mass-produced at a price affordable to the early entrepreneurs. The relatively huge, yet temporary, structures were a source of wonder in themselves. Other technological innovations were embraced: at the time of the first roller-skates Bassi's family temporarily abandoned performances and boarded the floor of the tent to enable skating tuition to take place.

> There were strange, magic things like Professor 'so-and-so', whose picture showed people flying around him and this was a scientific event because he was 'able to suppress gravity' with a little machine with a funnel on it. And this was written up in serious newspapers. Also at this time you could see articles on the Eiffel Tower and the Great Exhibition at the Crystal Palace. I had a wonderful circus poster of The New Edison Invention of an electric bulb, a big thing, probably powered by a dynamo being wound, and it would begin to glow and this would have been the first time that people had seen electricity before, or at least an electric bulb. This was the real attraction of the circus … People were thrilled with the feeling that they were entering a new world, totally revolutionary, that all the aristocracy and the class system would be changed by the arrival of science and education; that the 'anti-gravitational machine' would enable the workers to fly over the aristocracy.[14]

As well as showcasing new technologies and discoveries, the circus could respond to the interest in major world events. The real or imagined terrors of invasion, resulting from the upheavals of the French Revolution, were felt across Europe so that the re-enactment of the battle of Waterloo, which was presented by European circuses for decades after the event, had a very direct resonance with its audiences. At the end of the nineteenth century, Buffalo Bill's re-enactments of the resistance battles of the Native American peoples combined martial arts with exotic dances and animals (bison). Right into the twentieth century American circuses were presenting versions of historical events, such as Columbus and the Discovery of America, the Boxer Rebellion in 1899, the Mahdi's rebellion in Sudan and even the manoeuvres of models of the American Fleet in the Spanish–American War of 1903. 'Spectators could share a cosmopolitan experience of the new empire that offered more than the purely visual sensation of reading about foreign affairs in a newspaper; they could smell the acrid odour of the gunpowder'.[15]

The final element of attraction of nineteenth-century circus was its transgressive attitude to gender roles. In a period when women's clothing was meant to conceal their shape, the female acrobat/wire-walker/trick-rider/aerialist required tight fitting sleeves and leggings in order to be able to perform. The result was perceived as erotic and there were constant fine adjustments, required by authorities. The colour of tights was not allowed to be flesh-coloured, then not white, then not black. Women were not allowed to straddle a horse. In addition, as Peta Tait points out, 'Observers seemed to conflate the dangers of physical risk-taking with those of a seductive sexual identity that was considered socially dangerous'.[16] Circus proprietors were pulled between the commercial potential of erotic edginess and the particular sensitivities and restrictions of each location. More fundamentally, in a period that became more male-dominated, women were often portrayed as physically and morally weak, dependent on men, impractical, irrational and unreliable. The female acrobat presented an image contrary to this notion; strong, independent, daring and unashamed of her body. Restrictions on female performers began to be imposed after the fatal fall of Madame Blondin in 1863, which shocked the British public and prompted the intervention of Queen Victoria, especially because Blondin was eight months pregnant at the time and thus transgressed notions of motherhood. However, from the 1880s, female aerialists gradually became more successful than men.[17] As a result, gracefulness and elegance became as valued as muscular skill for both male and female performers. Partly as a result, some male performers cross-dressed, such as Lulu (1870s), Hodgini (1908–14) and Barbette (1920s), and many others,[18] or were of uncertain gender, such as Lusita Leers (1920s and 1930s), destabilising the erotic and other gender projections that were placed upon performers.

As can be observed in this brief summary of early circus, there are a number of 'edges'. All of them presented the unfamiliar and challenged norms – gender stereotyping, wildness or 'otherness', technical innovation, extraordinary human capabilities, the violence of slapstick, the evocation of real battles and the terrors of invasion. The precarious finances of these new ventures made them highly sensitive to shifts in the cultural environment. As well as the content, the form was fluid, introducing and discarding elements from decade to decade. It was forward-looking, up-to-date, looking outside of itself for new ideas; it was not overtly subversive yet at the same time, in trying to appeal to the mass public by introducing innovations and discoveries, it inevitably introduced a multi-perspective relativity.

> In many cases, an act's wondrous quality and its transgressiveness blurred the boundary between respectability and unrespectabilty, making the circus in turn, a highly contested institution … the topsy-turvydom of the ring extended beyond it, rendering the circus's role in this society far-reaching.[19]

So, although not setting out to be provocative, circus tended to be challenging both because it was introducing the unfamiliar and because the necessities of practice required abnormal costuming. Danger could be presented under the guise of patriotic display, education or sport and these ideological guises could reassure and provide a safe frame for the unusual forms, much in the same way that I have suggested occurred at Banky's Bristol exhibition (p. 146).

The ossification of circus

However, by the end of the nineteenth century, circus had settled into a known format, so much so that royalty felt it was respectable enough for them to come to the circus rather than the circus being invited into the royal courts (Astley had gone to the court of Louis XV in the previous century). Competition for audiences began to shift the emphasis from content to scale: the first two-ring circus was in 1873 (Barnum, Coup and Castello) and the first three-ring circus was in 1881 (Barnum & Bailey). As well as tent size, the entry parade into town provided an opportunity for proprietors to display comparisons of scale with their rivals. In the USA, where ambitions of scale were most advanced, circuses required military-style organisation with precisely prescribed duties, sequences and timetables to manage the vagaries of large numbers of casual labourers. Organisation was strictly hierarchical with extreme wage differentials and the intermingling of different levels minimised by means of a kind of caste system.[20] 'Performers and biographers repeatedly point out that circus life was often highly regulated by conservative values and familial relationships'.[21]

The competition in size demanded maximising audiences to maintain a corresponding level of income, and therefore it made good business sense to attract whole families. Consequently, the visit to the circus as well as the show content was made 'safer' and more predictable. However, just when this circus norm was becoming fixed, technical innovation moved on, providing another form of mass entertainment that could bring many of the same edges as circus had done. Some proprietors embraced the new movies so that many of Europe's public would have had their first experience of cinema in a showman's tent.[22] In the

USA, 1930 saw the pinnacle of the romance with circus, typified by Ringling Brothers and Barnum & Bailey's Circus that year. After that time the Depression 'incited roustabouts to rally for better wages and conditions'.[23] In 1938 there was a strike and finally, in 1956, Ringling Brothers and Barnum & Bailey's Circus was forced to close by unions insisting on a minimum wage. However the 'romance' of circus was being perpetuated even while the institution itself was coming apart. 'Institutional live circus becomes overlaid with twentieth-century artistic representation of an idea of circus. The pattern of making a film from an earlier fictional representation is common'.[24] Films such as Cecil B. DeMille's *The Greatest Show on Earth* (1952) provided an iconic representation of the circus world for decades to come. Circus began to reflect cultural shifts in gender representation; males tended towards the intrepid hero with a body-builder shape and women were relegated to a supporting role, supplying 'glamour'. 'Flying and catching was done by males and females up to the 1930s but by the 1950s and 1960s the "shapely" female aerialist standing on the platform was integral to spectacle but not the important flying action'.[25]

In the USA, the demise of the Entry Parade, the switch from wooden-spoke wheels to metal ones and the abandoning of the railroads as a main means of transport were lamented in circus journals. Similarly, under the later impact of new circus, the shift from the vast three-ring circus format to the more intimate one-ring was seen as radical and was resisted. The insistence on following precedent, that was a distinctive trait of circus in the early part of the twentieth century, can be seen as another way to make the abnormal safe and was partly a result of the lowering of the age of the audience. During a period of great social, technological and cultural change, aficionados tried to recreate childhood experiences of visits to the circus. The shift from fluidity to fixed norms, that this brief outline demonstrates, reoccurs several times in circus history so, before proceeding by outlining more recent instances, it is useful to question why it occurs. I now explore this tendency to conservatism and how it is engendered by the practice.

Conservative tendencies in circus

Although there are significant associated elements, the essence of circus can be defined as the attempt to accomplish difficult or dangerous feats, succeeding or, in the case of clowns, failing. A strong element of risk is implied and although this would suggest that circus practitioners are frequent risk-takers the amount of repetition and controls put in place means that there are only low levels of unpredictability. However, because the spectacle of danger is not entirely simulated, spectators experience it vicariously, identifying with the performer. For example, if the performer's body descends rapidly there may be a visceral 'rush' or, when there is a successful outcome after failed attempts, the relief and triumph of the performer will be partially shared by spectators. They will experience this identification more if a member of the audience is drawn into the action, whether this is real or faked. New circus companies often make use of ordinary clothing and everyday physicality, rather than the styles of unattainable heroes, in traditional circus, in order to enhance this identification. It may be that, through habituation, the performer appears unaffected by the experience of their activities and this is often the case in traditional circuses, where twelve or more performances per week may be demanded. If this is the case, the spectators will have a reduced sense of edge. For this reason, it is common practice in traditional circus for aerialists and jugglers to include two 'failed' attempts before a third successful one, in order to suggest unpredictability. In contrast, some performers play with the audience's expectation of risk by affecting the opposite; a nonchalant ease is a common manner adopted by jugglers.[26]

The history of circus indicates a continuous strand of reassurance and a necessity to apply controls.[27] This 'making safe' is evidence of the disturbance that may be caused by attending circus, whether this is a matter of witnessing physical feats or cultural transgression. This disturbance is potentially transformative, particularly because circus is also a site of play. A more specific example, seen in traditional circus, is the recurrence of clowns between the technical acts. This is an indication of the necessity of easing tension, lightening the mood, often by using a failed imitation or parody of the previous skilled act or, through slapstick, making the appearance of pain seem harmless, in a carnivalesque reversal. The thrill of risk may be pleasurable in itself but the use of play ensures that there is not an aversive reaction to the potentially disturbing. Arguably this 'making safe' has taken on a life of its own so that traditional circus has gradually become a show for children with accompanying adults. 'Making safe' is a form of applying controls, reducing unpredictability, and is therefore one of the factors in generating conservatism in circus.

On a personal level, technical training in circus skills tends to engender what Carse termed 'finite play'.[28] Because of safety considerations, acrobatic and aerial disciplines follow a linear system of increasingly difficult progressions. The achievement of one manoeuvre will signal readiness to begin a subsequent stage. In manipulation disciplines, because there is less risk of personal injury, there is more latitude but at the same time the complicated juggling patterns are systematised into formulae, known as 'site-swaps'. It is not coincidental that many who favour systems, such as computer programmers, engineers and mathematicians are attracted to juggling. Training in all disciplines takes careful consideration of the properties of weight, balance, efficiency of effort and velocity. The controls are intended to limit variation and unpredictability. The construction of routines is usually from a selection of established positions or patterns with the most impressive trick at the end. The huge investment of time devoted to training (over twenty-four hours per week, every week for decades would not be uncommon) means that the level of difficulty of a manoeuvre generally takes precedence over all other (e.g. artistic) criteria in the selection of tricks for a routine. Much of the learning is achieved through auto-feedback on repeated practice rather than through instruction. The repetitions produce an experience of 'flow', an absorption in the activity that reduces awareness of the surrounding environment.[29] This prolonged experience of being 'inside a bubble' engenders a sense of independence and uniqueness, often leading to a slight disdain for those who have acquired other kinds of knowledge through theory rather than practice.

Unlike for theatre and dance, training for circus involves increasing degrees of specialisation to achieve the necessary high levels of competence. The training is thus like sports training with clear targets, methods and a hierarchy of accomplishment. Working within these specialisations creates another kind of 'bubble'. Small formations of specialists share techniques, establishing a micro-hierarchy and a sense of community which distinguishes them from others. So, for example, not only will jugglers see themselves as different from aerialists (and there are often additional differences in cultural preferences) but club jugglers will differentiate themselves from hat jugglers. Within these tiny centres, not dissimilar to the expert–acolyte relationship of Paul Wilmot and Bruno (pp. 101–3), the hierarchy is based on levels of expertise so that there is a clearly defined goal to be attained. The almost obsessive dedication required may be at the expense of a wider variety of activities and interests with a consequent reduction in multi-faceted perspectives, particularly because training spaces are often geographically isolated from the outside world and, with work and life inter-mingling, these dedicated individuals tend to socialise with those who can appreciate the difficulties and dedication involved. Combined with the personal 'flow' bubble of practice, these specialisation bubbles encourage an introspection so that the wider world is of no great concern. This often leads to a tendency to include within routines 'in' jokes and technical feats whose difficulty can only be appreciated by fellow specialists.

On a wider scale, the 'world' of circus performers is separate from 'outsiders'. Historically this division was clearly visible with the circus wagons drawn up in a circle around the back of the tent. The vulnerability of this group of outsiders to thieves, fans and the curious must have created an acute awareness of who was 'in', known and trusted and who was 'out'. This defensive strategy towards exterior threat at the large scale could be considered to be applicable to the smaller scales of specialist 'bubble' and individual 'flow bubble': they represent a withdrawal from interacting with wider concerns. As I have indicated in earlier chapters, this introversion creates suspicion of outside influences and an emergence of orthodoxy.

In modern times the perception of separation and difference continues, not only because of the extra-ordinary skills but because there is a perception that in order to become remarkable, circus artists will have had to have made sacrifices, such as relinquishing the positive sides of predictability. Anyone giving serious consideration to a circus career recognises that likely financial rewards bear little relation to the time invested as compared with mainstream society. It is common that circus performers spend years of practice in order to begin to achieve an income that is comparable with other industries and by then the longevity of their career may be restricted by physical demands on ageing bodies. Stability, security and continuity may have had to take second place to dedication. However, most performers do not think in conventional time–income parameters; for them their work is not distinguishable from their leisure. For many, earning through performance is merely a necessary means to enable them to 'work' (train) more.

This would seem to suggest that circus performers reject capitalist and other central norms, but this is only partly true. Certainly within the un-funded commercial sector, the comparative earning potential within and between specialist bubbles is a significant factor in establishing a position in hierarchies. Circus acts are of relatively short duration and maximising income is seen as efficient and allows time for more training. The goal-centred approach to income genera-tion means that work is often targeted on the expectations of the market and therefore challenge and experimentation have little value. Following and adapting to whatever is fashionable is necessary for survival, as was exemplified by Bassi's family's adaption to the introduction of roller-skates. More generally, because circuses are expected to present spectacle, they have always been on an edge between maximising scale and financial unpredictability. It is therefore not sur-prising that some within circus culture tend to be functional in their approach to performance. Typically, this will follow a principle of maximising fame and fortune with the minimum of necessary investment.

The circus proprietors who take financial risks successfully may gain a sense of self-confidence, independence and, as indicated by Robertson's 'Winner Effect',[30] this may become arrogance and entitlement. This may be compounded because it is common for those who lead circuses to have had a formative period as a performer before starting their own company and therefore to have spent many years in an environment in which physical risk-taking is validated. As I have shown with Bassi, Banksy and Baron Cohen, the controls necessitated by continual risk-taking lead to the formation of their own stridently inde-pendent organisations. In addition, the relatively brief careers of performers and rapid turnover of other workers means that the proprietor soon becomes the longest serving member of the company. From Astley's time until the begin-ning of new circus, companies were named after the entrepreneur–proprietor, almost as an extension of that person's identity. As 'self-made' men, these proprietors tended to have meritocratic values. A key signifier of this set of values was the hierarchical emphasis, with a star performer (usually male) rather than an ensemble. Another was the circus competition, with prizes, judged by a panel of experts, similar to the way sporting competitors such as ice-skaters or gymnasts are ranked. As independent minded, self-reliant individuals, used to being masters of a separate physical entity and hierarchy that they had created, these entrepreneurs relied on their own judgement of management controls and were resistant to restrictions imposed by the wider society, such as wage demands and animal regulations. With such a strong sense of their own centrality and independence, shifts in society would be regarded as either irrelevant or as a threat. Given all these factors it is unsurprising that circus proprietors are resistant to any imposition of outside controls. In the UK there have been public disputes about regulations concerning animal welfare and safety. In both these examples the new regulations were represented by circus proprietors as an unwanted extension of local, state or EU control, but they also reflected wider changes in society. Similarly, many of the practices and aims of those working in contemporary circus have been resisted by those in traditional circus.

So there appear to be several factors that encourage conservative tendencies. Firstly the linear, target-centred training, secondly the three layers of 'bubble' which reinforce borders, thirdly the requirement to meet the expectations of the market and, finally, the effects of risk-taking, which may lead to 'making safe', tight controls and the arrogance of the 'Winner Effect'. It is therefore not surprising that circus has a tendency to look inwards, reinforcing its own norms and scornful of those who do not share the same appreciation, leading to a fundamentalist attitude, resistant to changes in the cultural and political environment. Having established this context, the ambivalence inherent in the most iconic circus narrative can be considered.

Circus as a cultural threshold

As circus established itself as a discrete, ex-centric world in itself – a liminal centre – it naturally began to become associated with escape and fantasy. In an age of increasing industrialisation it was both accessible and exotic and therefore began to be associated with the iconic narrative: 'running away to join the circus'. Like Banksy's anonymity, this narrative was a result of marginalisation that has taken on a life of its own, defining its identity to the wider public. The narrative of escape has been implied since the beginnings of circus, escape from gravity being the most obvious. However, the expansion of imagination, by means of exotica, battle re-enactments and unconventional gender representations, was also a release from central norms. Moreover, the essence of all circus is the expansion of perception of human capabilities. This positive, potentially inspirational, communication was as relevant to a populace engaged in the repetitive physical drudge of mass-production lines as it is to the increasingly less physical working environment of modern sophisticated economies. In both cases the uplifting attraction is the remarkability of the individual in contrast to the anonymity conveyed by mass systems.

'Running away' is both a story about an individual and a bigger metaphor. It is a good example of a bifurcation which can be seen at different scales: as a human story, as company development and as a cultural sector in relationship to the surrounding context. Although the term suggests mere escapism it indicates a significant shift into new values and a new environment. Actual stories of individuals were hyped up by local press, as pre- or post-publicity for circus companies, but they were not fabricated.[31] For an individual the significant decision to abandon a known life for the unpredictability of circus life could not be taken without a critical imbalance in the individual's life prior to the decision. As such, it is comparable with the kind of bifurcation events observed throughout complexity theories as an entity splits apart due to internal imbalance. Davis cites examples of family pressures, romantic complications, the lack of fulfilment and the lack of prospective advancement in the work environment as causes for these decisions. A hundred years ago this might have meant conventional family life and the linear work systems of industrialisation. The circus offered other kinds of community: the camaraderie of a team within a geographically widely spread network. Even within the hierarchy and caste systems of the vast three-ring circuses there was a sense of 'family'. The military style organisation meant that everyone worked in clearly defined teams that would eat at the same table and share the same accommodation.[32] In smaller operations the team included all the members of the enterprise. For all circus workers there is a sense of shared achievement in the physical construction of large spatial structures, particularly if it becomes a site of wonder constructed on 'waste' land which is validated by the attention of large numbers of local people. In recent times 'running away' may represent a rejection of consumerist values in favour of validating bravery to take risks: physical, artistic or financial.

'Running away' also marks a shift of control; taking ownership of the decisions and discipline affecting one's future rather than having that future decided by others within normal structures of advancement. As indicated above, this ownership of control and responsibility for self-advancement can create a resistance to other perspectives. On the other hand it creates an attitude of aspiration; early new circuses conveyed the positive message: 'Live your dream; you can do it' both in performance narratives and through offering participation experiences. To run away to the circus was, and still is, something of a risky proposition. The itinerant nature of classic circus and its relatively marginal position meant that individuals could be exposed to horrors as well the wonders of foreign parts. There are risks of physical suffering, both on- and offstage (circuses in the early twentieth century were notorious as sites of brawling); there are risks of being duped or seduced in an unfamiliar world, risks of harming those left behind and the risk of having to abandon the decision and return home humiliated.[33] More significantly, the individual is likely to have been excited and anxious about being transformed in some unknown and unpredictable way, perhaps to become more exotic and flamboyant, even to become a performer themselves. Clearly they were placing themselves on an edge:

> By 'running away' with the circus's subterranean rovers, one directly experiences the world in the immediate present, on the edges of society. The circus's simultaneous contradictory impulses of nostalgic, normative representation and subversion of established social hierarchies made it an appropriate emblem of the age of transition.[34]

Through the experience of successfully taking such a major risk to 'run away' there would be personal empowerment.

'Running away' to join a discrete, separate world appears to be the opposite of provocation but derives from a similar dissatisfaction with the surrounding context. Petit, Bassi, Baron Cohen and Banksy can all be said to have 'run away' from the various backgrounds they were brought up in. The difference is that the provocateurs in question appear to have some sense of injustice that compelled them to re-engage, or that they felt their prowess needs to be asserted beyond the world of entertainment. 'Running away' has connotations of hiding, retreat and refuge.[35] Because they became associated with childhood, many circuses have traded on the romantic notions of a bygone era, as I shall discuss below. The release that is signified in the 'running away' narrative is not from controls per se but from those imposed by central institutions. The creation of separate centres with liminal norms provides a safe haven for those ex-centrics who have removed themselves from mainstream society. This suggests that it is hard to maintain a position on an edge and that the exposure to unusually high levels of risk in an initial phase may actually be a significant factor in the attraction of structure in a subsequent phase.

Modern conservatism

Observing students coming to train at Circomedia over many years, one is struck by the number who mark the transition by taking on the external trappings of circus performers: the tattoos, exotic hair and clothing styles as well as the activities. The students seek identification with those who are assumed to be extrovert, wild and unconventional people. The assumption of freedom often conflicts with the amount of discipline and commitment required. Moreover, the external signs of difference are not so much a lack of convention but an adherence to a marginal norm. The frequent rigidity of adherence to these signifiers suggests a liminal form of conservatism. From observation of circus students over decades it is apparent that the ability to take risks in one area of life does not necessarily mean that risks can easily be taken in other areas. A common example is the case of those aerialists who take substantial physical risks but who are very fearful of physical or verbal improvisation. This conclusion is backed up by my research into risk at the Circelation series of master-classes on the subject of risk (2005). This confirmed the differentiation between risks of competition (in Carse's terms: closed play) and risks of complex unpredictability (open play).

So it is not only the older traditionalists working in the commercial sector who display these conservative tendencies. They can also be seen in the contemporary circus schools, which may receive public subsidy and are notionally responsible for developing contemporary circus. The FEDEC organisation (European Federation of Professional Circus Schools) has embarked on an ambitious project to 'harmonise' the teaching methods of circus schools. As a way to raise standards of safe and efficient practice in the teaching of technique it has been effective in challenging the methods of independent-minded schools and teachers. However, as it moved into the less linear areas of artistic practice the harmonisation project has proved more complex and problematic, leading to suggestions of limited definitions on the *purpose* of circus techniques. Like those in the field of visual art who insist on the importance of the age-old skills of drawing and painting rather than pushing the boundaries of the artform, the term 'circus arts' is taken to mean carefully honed items of craft rather than the more open-ended sense of exploring and enlarging perception. Bassi was driven to split away from the circus life he had been brought up in because of this tendency towards tenaciously held orthodoxies that had become outdated. FEDEC appears to be applying a progressive Modernist approach, to define and refine rather than embracing the diversity of outcomes implied by the mixing of artforms that is characteristic of twenty-first century culture.

Similarly, there have been repeated attempts by the Arts Council and other bodies in the UK, over the last twenty-five years to bring together the circus industry in order that their shared aims can be considered for policy-making. However this has been highly problematic, partly as a result of differences of scale, income streams and cultural perspectives, and partly because of the suspicion of outside control by these independent centres. Even on a local level there is a similar resistance to assimilation. In Bristol, an organisation called CAST (Circus And Street Theatre) was formed (2002) to lobby for better facilities and greater support from funding bodies. After five years it became clear that with such diversity of perspectives, contexts and priorities there was little that was shared by its members except in the use of circus techniques. So, in the early twenty-first century, it is difficult to talk about *the* circus with such a diversity of cultural perspectives. There is political diversity from the left-leaning Clowns Without Borders, Circus2Iraq[36] and Archaos through to the more culturally conservative and capitalist enterprises in North America. There are those, such as the Gandini Company or Ockham's Razor, who are redefining the use of circus skills, and others who are deeply embedded in the past with a form and aesthetics derived from music hall, revue, retro, gothic, steampunk or 'classic circus'. These latter can be more easily associated with the escapist tendencies implied by the 'running away' narrative. For the former there is a sense of challenge because they must work within the expectations created by the use of the word 'circus'. Indeed, despite the continuous juggling throughout their performance, the Gandini company briefly dropped the use of the term 'circus' in their publicity because families and children's groups would arrive expecting clowns and light entertainment and were not prepared for their avant-garde dance and contemporary music.

New circus: emergence and atrophy

As outlined above, the values expressed by the old circus (pre-1975) were firstly about prowess, either denoted by technical skill level,[37] size or financial success, and, secondly, about the preservation of itself. Many early circus magazine reviews of new circus companies, Cirque du Soleil and Big Apple Circus, repeatedly ask the question 'but is it circus?'.[38] Established circuses insisted on the older model. Herb Clement in *Circus Report*, an industry magazine, typified this view when writing about Cirque du Soleil in 1988: 'Among the more cardinal of its sins against circus is the fact that the two-year-old edition offered in New York offers audiences not a single animal – not even a horse, upon which the very circus as we know it has been solidly based since its creation by Philip Astley in 1768'. The use of the word 'sins' implies the extent to which circus practice had become a dogmatic orthodoxy. Traditionalists dug their heels in and refused to adapt but have gradually been forced to give way under commercial pressures over the ensuing decades.

In contrast, a new circus ethic was less competitive. 'Everyone can be a winner' was a principle shared by many educationalists at the time.[39] The new notion of circus as a vehicle for personal transformation was reflected in the community circus movement whereby young novices were presented in public after a short course in basic circus skills. In the late 1970's some left-wing theatre groups in the UK, such as Interaction's Doggs Troupe and Theatre Workshop, used the empowering effects of learning circus skills to raise the confidence of inner-city youth. The seminal work of Reg Bolton in Edinburgh and Glasgow was disseminated by his book, *Circus in a Suitcase*[40] and influenced the work of all new circuses in the UK as well as its first circus school, Fool Time. His work in the UK and then in Australia, added to work already being done by the Pickle Family Circus in California, Cirque du Soleil in Montreal and Circus Oz in Australia. Later the Big Apple Circus began working in paediatric wards. The positive social effects of this work encouraged government funding and meant that these organisations were partially released from total dependence on income from ticket sales. No Fit State Circus, based in Cardiff, the longest surviving new circus in the UK, have used this avenue to build up their equipment and expertise over decades to become renowned for their artistic work as well as community work.

As a consequence of this democratising ethic, the traditional circus competitions, with prizes and a judging panel, seemed inappropriate. An oft-quoted marker of difference between traditional circus and new circus is the former's tendency to be guarded about its techniques whereas in new circus sharing skills is ubiquitous. The juggling convention (from 1978 in Europe) was a new model, in which the vast majority of participants were not intending to become performers but were interested in the shared activity, partly as means of making new social connections. As well as these conventions, the other meeting ground in Europe is the outdoor festival circuit, where circus performers will also see and interact with street theatre, music and dance and thus have a wider range of influences than at the traditional circus competitions that are exclusively of the same genre. By extension, new circus tends to favour ensemble practices to a greater or lesser extent. This may be in simple performance terms, using a chorus onstage or, more fundamentally, collaborative devising practices as used by the Pickle Family Circus, Archaos and others.

However, the key factor in the emergence of new circus was the adherence to the use of animals by the traditionalists. It was not particularly that new circuses were strictly evangelist about the non-use of animals (both Archaos and Cirque du Soleil used domesticated birds in their early shows), but, perhaps because of being at an early stage in their development, they could be more flexible about whether to include animals or not. This gave them a boost in audience numbers from the growing section of the public that found performing animals problematic and also provided greater opportunity in the places they were able to perform. Municipal authorities had been tightening animal welfare regulations since the late nineteenth century but during the 1980s this transferred into local bans on circuses that used animals. In the UK, Gerry Cottle saw the commercial potential of an 'all human circus'. In the London area, animal acts were banned and so he had no significant competition there for a few years. Using a government funded training scheme he invited eighteen young people to train and perform in a project which ran for two years from early 1984. The issue of animal rights marked a fundamental shift in attitudes to nature as environmental threats came to the fore in the latter half of the twentieth century. A wider understanding of the inter-dependence of species and the value of biological diversity led to a greater appreciation of 'nature' and there was less fear of 'wildness' and less desire to prove man's (and it usually was male) domination over it. In such a cultural climate the image of animal trainers, such as Gunther Gebel Williams with his performing tigers, seemed out of touch.

In much the same way, it is possible to perceive the shift from hierarchical structures in circus to more cooperative systems as part of this shift. Even the lowest paid workers usually had the benefit of legal contracts rather than being at the mercy of casual and un-proveable agreements that had traditionally been sealed with a simple handshake. As a result of less hierarchical relationships, decisions over such issues as artistic control, financial deals and travel arrangements were made on a case-by-case basis rather than being prescribed by the require- ments of a larger system that necessarily cannot operate with such variability. In this way a contract was seen more in the equal terms of a collaborative exchange rather than the unequal relationship between employer and employee. Pay differentials within companies reduced or disappeared altogether. Pretensions of high status by 'stars' were frowned upon. In Archaos the lines between per- former and backstage crew were continually blurred as the crew were invited to participate onstage and encouraged to contribute ideas. Similarly the level- ling of gender status was a feature of new circus, either by presenting powerful images of women, as in Archaos, or by de-gendering into the androgynous creatures often featured by Cirque du Soleil. Often these creatures were animal-like or alien-like humans, thus diminishing further the distance between human, animal and 'otherness'. Another sign of this levelling of status was the increasing use by aerialists of safety lines in public performance, a practice scorned by traditionalists who viewed real risk as another issue of dogma. 'Real risk is the coin of authentic circus. And without risk, our big tops are being emasculated one by one' states Hammarstrom,[41] who seems very clear as to which gender circus belongs to. New circus shifted emphasis from the danger to the elegance of the movement or significance of the action.

Another key difference was that the early new circuses had a more conscious and overt ideological dimension. Many early pioneers viewed circus principally as a popular form that could be used as vehicle for disseminating ideology rather than as a display of physical skill. In common with Bassi, Banksy and Baron Cohen, the formative period was in the 1970s, influenced not only by the protest events of 1968 but also the interest in pre-industrial folk culture and declining popular forms, such as music hall. So new circus tended to use democratising themes; the first Cirque du Soleil show to be presented in the USA in 1987 began with a masked chorus of 'ordinary' people who are invited to live out their dreams and perform. This became a central narrative for many new circuses: Cirque du Soleil used it again with the child's voyage of fantasy through a circus world (*Quidam* 1996 ongoing). A much smaller circus in the UK, Snapdragon, used a hapless 'council official' as the everyman to be transformed into a transgressive performer. The theme of empowerment is not only a generalised, universal one but also implies support for the under-dog or outsider. Cirque du Soleil provided support for the Pickles at a time of financial crisis and, as mentioned, Archaos elevated backstage labourers into performers.

The founders of the Pickle Family Circus, Larry Pisoni and Hovey Burgess, had both been involved with the San Francisco Mime Troupe (1972–5), which combined a Commedia del Arte style with agit-prop. Pisoni staged two circus pieces for them using juggling or club passing as a metaphor. One, entitled *Frozen Wages*, demonstrated the terrors of having to keep up with an assembly-line speeding up.[42] The Pickles were less overtly political and, in common with other new circus artists at the time, including myself, hoped that the implicit form would convey the political message.

> The Mime Troupe had been very explicit [in its messages]. So we didn't want to go down that route. What I wanted to do instead was, by example, show people that you can do wonderful things together. If we had tried to be didactic it would have failed miserably.
>
> (Pisoni interview[43])

The 'example' was demonstrated by the Pickles in their use of gender, the absence of performing animals, the cooperative organisation and their trademark finale, 'the big juggle', which involved all the company, including backstage workers, passing clubs in a manifestation of interactive synchronisation. Influenced by McLuhan's dictum ('The medium is the message'), there were general concerns within the new circus movement, including my Mummer&Dada company, about appearing didactic and thus limiting appeal to solely those within the counter-culture. This led to a process whereby political/ideological standpoints gradually became less overt and less related to current events. Themes became more 'poetic' and generalised, such as dealing with attitudes to the natural world or wider concerns of the human condition. Some companies celebrated the power of the imagination and fantasy, distancing themselves from the contemporary context. In so doing they created a bubble that encouraged an inward focus, allowing the specialisms to develop as a hierarchy of mini-centres with increasingly delineated borders. As a result there was less mixing of techniques than in visual arts, for example, where artists seek out the techniques and materials that are most appropriate to the concerns they are working with.

Cirque

At this stage it is necessary to differentiate between two different tendencies or attractors within new circus. The first is more radically different from the traditional circus, appealing to the adult counter-culture, and may be exemplified by the practice of Archaos, and the other, which I refer to as 'cirque', seeks to appeal to a wider audience. The prime exemplar of this tendency is Cirque du Soleil. Their history provides a useful example of a gradual softening of radicalism towards a complete rejection of any hint of ideology, in order to suit the demands of the market. This company's work was initially received in the USA (1987) as a radical alternative to the American model because of its lack of performing animals, its use of one ring rather than three and its theatricalisation, appealing as much to adults as to children. Since then it has come to exert such a strong influence worldwide that it has attracted imitation in various ways and has therefore set up a new norm. In 2011 they had twenty-two companies performing at different sites across fourteen countries. The ability to have so many different companies operating simultaneously is unprecedented and has resulted in their wide influence and staggering financial success. This success has been enhanced by marketing that is carefully targeted towards adult professionals, permitting higher ticket prices, comparable to those in ballet and opera, which in turn enables higher production values. Their use of high-quality sound systems and theatrical effects, such as smoke machines, was seen as innovative in 1987. Later shows made use of CGI (*Totem* 2010) or drones (*Sparked* 2014).

In spite of their controversial beginnings they gradually abandoned an ideological stance. Their early advocacy of not using animals was renounced in favour of a more neutral stance.[44] When collaborating with the Swiss Circus Knie, they went as far as incorporating animal acts into their show: 'Our philosophy is when in Rome you have to be like the Romans, so for the Swiss it was something natural to use the animals' (Jean David[45]). A source of resentment and suspicion by traditionalists in the USA was Soleil's state funding but the proportion of their income from that source has gradually diminished or been channelled into the non-profit making offshoots such as their community circus programmes, so that they appear less challenging to the US model of free entrepreneurship. It is unusual for the USA to have a 'foreign' company exerting such a strong cultural influence over a popular entertainment form that is as iconic to Americans as baseball and apple pie.[46] It appears that Cirque du Soleil has sought to avoid controversy and appear as acceptable as possible in whatever culture they perform in. This attempt at a universally acceptable product is inevitably problematic. Themes such as that of *Totem*, which attempted to blend creation myths from around the globe, require identity difference to be glossed over. As well as diminishing gender difference in their early shows, their androgynous, semi-human choruses further diminished individuality with their tightly synchronised choreography of similar body shapes. Similarly, the technical acts, that comprise the majority of the performance, do not display real individual personality traits or significant emotional engagement in relationship with the feats, the performance situation or the audience. This task is left to the clowns who must struggle to overcome the separation of distance imposed by the vast spaces in which the company performs. Whether these clowns succeed or not, their individual personalities are obscured under a generic clown persona, which, although not as tightly codified as the red-nose norm of traditional circus, is nevertheless an artificiality masking the individual.

In attempting to find common ground in cultures across the world they inevitably have to negotiate difference. When making a feature of gender difference they tend to follow a conservative agenda. For example, a roller-skate act performed by two Native American characters in *Totem* involved the erotic undressing of the female by the male, prior to being whirled around by the man. Similarly the portrayal of Native American culture is stereotypical to make it more recognisable and thus 'safe'. So the idealistic suggestion of global harmony is attempted both through simplification and obscuring difference. However bland the result may seem to some viewers, it must be acknowledged that the notion of referencing different creation myths rather than a single one may appear to be unacceptably radical to those of a more fundamentalist religious perspective.

Their ideological standpoint in the early years motivated their support for various community programmes and these continue around the world. However, their prime aims have become providing well-paid employment for their staff and a good return for their shareholders. Albrecht describes how this shift in ideology occurred.

> Artistic director, Guy Caron ... insisted that art must predominate over business. For him business was merely art's handmaiden. Guy Laliberte, on the other hand, felt that business and art should work together as equal partners. His vision prevailed then and continues today.[47]

Since this statement was made, commercial considerations appear to have taken precedence and this is manifested in the tension between initial artistic intentions and the final product. In the version of *Varekai*, performed in London in 2010, an environment of forest creatures was established and a theme of ecological interdependence began to unfold. The cohesive theme was interrupted by a comedy act by two performers dressed in costumes from glitzy show business. This surprising intervention can only be explained by the over-riding concern to make the performance more acceptable to more people by lightening its tone. The product, therefore, appeared to privilege market demands over artistic intention.

I have suggested that the more that centres are inward looking, relying solely on internal feedback and defined borders, the more they are vulnerable to atrophy. In business terms the company is highly attuned to feedback from its customers. Their website invites comments on all shows at all venues and it is clear that these include the whole 'customer experience': issues such as parking, ticket collection, front-of-house staff and refreshments, as well as comments about the show itself. The immediacy of the responses allows the company to make rapid adjustments to their operation if not the show itself. There are two consequences of the quality of this feedback; one is that the centre of the organisation is well connected to the interface with the environment and therefore the whole entity can respond and adapt to changes on that edge. The other consequence is that, because the company prioritises the concerns of the customer over that of the artist, it will inevitably move towards the centre of mainstream culture. For example, the shows for the Las Vegas hotels are designed to provide a pleasant experience for a clientele who enjoy lavish, conspicuous consumption and who have the financial means to risk gambling. As such, they may not welcome artistic challenge. Although novelty is attractive, entertainment in this context is required to be reasonably predictable as well as of high quality. All Las Vegas entertainers, therefore, tend to be at a stage of their development, usually towards the end of careers, when what they offer is well-established and consistent rather than in the process of development. The context discourages deviation from known formats and thus there is less artistic development. With seven shows performing in the same city simultaneously (2011) Cirque du Soleil must offer diversity whilst also guaranteeing consistency of quality. They succeed in avoiding challenging their audiences but provide novelty, such as in their aquatic show, *O*, which features high diving and synchronised swimming.

In artistic terms the company enables its borders to be porous by seeking out new ideas. They invite leading theatre directors (e.g. Robert Le Page for *Totem*), popular musicians (e.g. George Martin and the Beatles for *Love*) and well-established performers such as Slava Polunin to bring in their ideas and practices. Soleil can scour the planet for new ideas through its audition process. Held in every continent, these auditions search the world for talent. All audition pieces are video-recorded so that the company possesses a catalogue of many thousands of, not only performers, but ideas for acts. If the company engages the performer they gain the rights to the act, which may remain in the repertoire after the performer has left the company. Despite this openness it is inevitable that the success and dominance of the company means that some of its assumptions will not be challenged. These are reinforced through its close connections with the Ecole Nationale de Cirque in Montreal. Christine Barette stated in 1992: 'It is important to us to leave them [the students] free to express their individual creativity and emotion. They are not bound to a particular style. If there is a style here, it is that everyone is unique'.[48] Despite these professions of stylistic freedom it is inevitable that any school defines styles by setting parameters, priorities and methods. The existence of a long-standing and well-travelled entry route into the world's biggest circus company is bound to affect the style of the students. Although the school is not an exclusive source of performers, the ex-students reinforce the precepts of the company's identity.

In the context of the USA, Soleil demonstrates a move towards the centre from a controversial position on the edge, adapting to the cultural and business environment in which they operate. Other companies have adopted the style of Cirque du Soleil. Some of these are large-scale ventures, such as the Big Apple Circus and Cirque Eloize. By contrast in Europe they were never considered far from mainstream tastes because their arrival in London in 1988 coincided with the more radical Archaos. The Soleil style has become the norm for bespoke events for the corporate market and dinner shows across Europe. By means of this imitation, the public has moved towards regarding their style as the new norm, distinct from both traditional circus and other forms of new circus.

Other examples of new circus

Because of the current dominance of Soleil, the rest of the new circus movement tends to be perceived in relationship to it. For many companies in Europe, the main difference from the Soleil model is that the primary purpose is not to produce a profit. If there is potential for state funding, the companies are released from the priority of simply pleasing the audience by confirming their ideological and cultural norms. In return, the state may expect exploration of boundaries, developing the artform. Therefore, there is a different relationship with the public, with popular expectations secondary to the concerns of the artist. Unlike in more commercially driven work, the artist can afford to appeal to a 'niche' section of the public rather than attempting to please a wide-ranging audience. As such, work can be more diverse and hence there is more variation. The sector is comprised of a plethora of small companies appealing to different audiences, using a wide variety of scale, types of presentation and locations. It is an open-ended experimental culture rather than one with a fixed target or central model. The circus techniques may be allied to aspects from other genres such as Live Art, text-based theatre, stand-up comedy, Burlesque, visual art and the grotesque. Formats from outdoor performance practice, such as promenade performance and site-specific work, may be incorporated: examples of this in the UK include Ockham's Razor, No Fit State and The Invisible Circus.

Although Ockham's Razor became one of the most well-funded creators of new circus in England to date, their work does not look like circus. The expertise in aerial disciplines of the small company (two to six performers) enables them to manoeuvre their bodies on ropes and bars, but there are no trapezes or other recognisable circus equipment. Their 2009 show, *The Mill*, used a large, suspended, wooden 'mouse wheel', which could be rotated by performers walking on top or inside. This action motored a system of ropes and pulleys, connecting to a floor-based cable spool. Speech was limited to a few repeated phrases. Characterisation was defined but understated, costumes were neutral and in muted colours. There was a slight hint of comedy, but none of the more exaggerated traits of circus clowning. The piece had a simple cohesive narrative, but came across more as a play with space and materials rather than theatre. It lasted an unusual forty-five minutes, too long for a conventional circus act but too short for a conventional theatre piece. The work cannot be easily categorised as dance, kinetic sculpture or theatre, let alone circus. By contrast, No Fit State Circus declare their genre in their name and, although their equipment and techniques are recognisable as circus, the format of their performances is unconventional, in that there is usually no seating and the audience are expected to select their own viewing position as the focus of the performance changes location within the tent in which they usually perform. This promenade format is by no means new, but is nevertheless a surprise to the family audiences that are attracted by the term 'circus'. The audience are required to alter their normal spectating habits and are challenged to become active participants in the event. One of the benefits of this approach is the intimacy possible as performers may be within physical reach. The nuances of breathing and eye movement can be observed as they engage with the physical tasks so that they are experienced as real people more than as artificial characters. Therefore, there is a necessity for any characterisation to be based closely on the identity of the performers themselves. For the show *Immortal* (2005–7) the characters appeared to be variations of southern European circus folk from the mid-twentieth century. Similarly, the group choreography for the finale, although based on simultaneous identical actions allowed for a diversity of movement from the individual identities rather than striving to achieve the tight replication of a Cirque du Soleil chorus.

The Invisible Circus also use promenade style performance but combine it with a site-specific approach. Their *Carneyville* (2008–10) was presented at the old Police and Fire Service buildings in the centre of Bristol. The outdoor central courtyard was surrounded by performance stages; swinging trapeze and tightrope were used over the heads of the contained spectators. Inside the buildings were installations, sideshows, one-to-one performances as well as a more conventional cabaret. The vast majority of the audience were in themed fancy dress, interacting with walkabout performers, so that it was difficult to distinguish between performer and spectators. These elements derived as much from such events as the Lost Vagueness area within the Glastonbury Festival as from street theatre and contemporary theatre performance. The strangeness of this world and the hazing of conventional parameters place the spectator in a state of alertness and a potential suspension of normal behaviour. In their formal performances, the Invisibles tend to play with the conventions of traditional circus, using irony or carnivalesque inversions, for example by presenting the traditional clown as a sinister figure. The Invisibles did not receive funding for this show and, although this was not a free performance, it relied on over one hundred unpaid volunteers to mount the spectacle. Like the Pickle Family Circus, thirty years previously, but on a larger scale, decisions are taken collectively so that the volunteers experience some ownership of the event. The ticket income was used to pay overheads and for equipment. Although some performers may receive benefits, such as free practice space, the majority participate for the sake of sharing the creation of an exciting and popular event. Such bartering practices are clearly far from the model of Cirque du Soleil.

Other examples of new circus include those combining techniques with other genres, such as Sean Gandini, who combines contemporary dance, Live Art and chance with complex juggling patterns, or those that combine narrative theatre with circus such as the French Cirque Baroque under the direction of Christian Taguet (1987 onwards) or my own Mummer&Dada (1985–91).

Other experiments simplify rather than adding new elements; Cirque Nu, in a small-scale intimate performance (1992), stripped back circus to its essence of (near naked) human bodies accomplishing arduous tasks, such as the excruciating display of walking across the tops of a line of vertical wine bottles. The Circus of Horrors was created by the well-known UK circus entrepreneur, Gerry Cottle and inspired by the grotesqueries of Archaos. Cottle invited Pierrot Bidon to direct, hoping to recapture the spirit and the audience of the French company. The result was much closer to traditional circus than the original, losing much of the carnivalesque layers of paradoxical ambivalence that had characterised Archaos and focussed more on the blood and gore aspects. This can be seen as a good example of incorporation of an edgy model into a wider (traditional circus) system and losing its integrity. It is one of many examples of how the commercial world looks to the edge for new ideas, often cherry-picking the results of experimentation done by others.

So, to summarise the range of contemporary circus work, there are two main centres: the traditional norm of circus, which may be referenced either nostalgically or ironically, and, secondly, the cirque model, often simplified to a simple presentation of elegant circus feats with a loose poetic theme and high production values. In addition to these centres there is hybrid work, mixing circus with existing genres, such as narrative theatre, dance, Burlesque, as well as experimental work that looks unlike anything gone before. If we consider the whole development of modern circus (from 1768) as a single entity it demonstrates, on a large scale, the process of development of an entity and the benefits of operating on the edge. It can be summarised thus: the first phase was marked by fluidity, elements were gradually added, some of which were discarded after only a few decades (Harlequinades and Pantomimes). Once the initial aggregation of elements had settled, the form ossified, turning inwards, becoming increasingly separate from the wider culture, reinforcing its own norms through family traditions and competitions of circus performance, increasingly hermetic in its separate reality. The third phase sees a major break, creating a separate movement with new values, materials and methods. This is comprised of a diversity of experiments, some falling away, others settling into a distinct new entity (cirque), others generating an ongoing process of experimentation and regeneration. Despite initial resistance from the traditionalists, the new edge has reinvigorated the entity of circus, allowing it to discard values, materials and methods that had become redundant as wider culture had moved on.

The 'life' of Archaos

In the previous two sections I have outlined how circus companies tend to conform to current ideology and to conform to its own established norms. The outstanding exception to these tendencies is Archaos who explicitly attempted to challenge dominant ideology and circus norms. Given the tendencies towards conservatism with circus culture, the breakaway of Archaos and their inability to be incorporated seem the more remarkable. Their history provides a good example of an entity going through the process of splitting away from a larger one, thriving by being on the edge, becoming a centre of attraction and facing the consequences of establishing a centre. The history can be considered in three phases; the first (1975–86) was a period of decline followed by a rebirth, the second phase (1987–92) was the time of widespread notoriety, and the third (1992–5) was marked by attempts to recover their former success. The sequence will help us to consider the problems of remaining on the edge as well as the advantages.

Archaos evolved out of Cirque Bidon:

> a group of twenty-strong youth who all took the surname of Bidon and were united by a desire for adventure and life on the road … There was no boss, no producer, no contract, no box office, no tickets. Outdoor shows have been given away free, a hat was passed round at the end and the public was encouraged to give whatever they could.[49]

This format not only reflected the romantic utopianism of rural hippies but, in its communal egalitarianism, reflected influences of the 1968 political defiance. They travelled with horse-drawn wagons, nostalgic for a vanishing circus tradition with its animal acts. Adrian Evans, later UK producer for their work, described the early incarnation that he saw in 1986: 'It was a bit of a disaster of a show, if I'm being honest. There were chickens, a couple of horses, a dog in the juggling act and a pig wandering around, all in this scuzzy marquee'.[50] However, pitching up amongst the industrial estates and social housing at the margins of urban centres, they became aware of the disjuncture between their culture and their context. So they replaced the horses with motor-bikes and adopted the industrial aesthetic, materials and heavy rock music of the urban environment.[51] As Pierrot Bidon expressed it:

> We live in an industrial world, which is just as wild and just as glamorous as all the nostalgic tinsel and tatty tigers. So we decided not to reject but to embrace it.[52]
>
> Our project was to make circus more like life – violent and cruel, but with love and tendresse as well.[53]

This radical shift of style seems to have been born as much out of a desire to escape a gruelling schedule of one-night stands as it was out of a growing awareness of their lack of relevance to the urban youth. Either way, the change was relatively rapid: by 1988 the newly named Archaos was headlining the London Circus Festival with a fully developed new style. This rapid evolution can be compared with bifurcations seen in complexity theories – changes to the environment (rural to urban) causing an internal imbalance that leads to a splitting away from a central model (traditional circus).

To credit entirely the subsequent success of Archaos to the impetus for change provided by Bidon and his wife is too simplistic. The contribution from figures such as Franco Dragone and Michel Dallaire (who had worked with the emerging Cirque du Soleil) was significant, as was that of the other performers who, at this stage in the company's development (1986–8), operated as a collective. Meetings were protracted and difficult as the strong independent personalities found it hard to compromise. However, an informal hierarchy began to emerge and there was a sense of solidarity in a shared mission. After their breakthrough onto the international circuit, the decision-making mechanisms began to change. By 1989 the group was larger and key figures from the early years had left and were replaced by others, including ex-students of the new French National Circus School. Guy Carrara and Bidon were elected as joint managers. The collective creative process gradually shifted into one in which Bidon selected material from improvisations but there remained a sense of team. 'The teamwork of Archaos was staggering. The imaginations and technical abilities knew no bounds. Pierrot was a persuader, a man who knew how to talk to us and finally have his way'.[54]

By 1990 there were two companies, one touring Australia with *The Last Show on Earth* and a second touring *Bouinax* around Europe. Inevitably, the size of the operation led to a more hierarchical structure; the complexity of logistics led to a division of responsibilities. The company was attracting not only greater numbers of audience but also all kinds of people wanting to join. As well as professional circus performers these also included many who just turned up off the streets. These were referred to as 'bouinax' and they helped to inject new enthusiasm and inventiveness as well as maintaining connections with street culture as the company grew. These newcomers were attracted by sharing in the meteoric rise of this cultural phenomenon rather than the earlier mission of a reinvented circus aesthetic. Success, measured in notoriety, became the attractor. The obvious danger with this position is that, if success falters or novel forms become familiar, the attraction can rapidly fall away and there may not be enough to hold the entity together.

As well as notoriety, the other indicator of success was the invitation into the mainstream; in 1990 *Bouinax* ran for several weeks at the home of French traditional circus, the Cirque d'Hiver. A film of *Compilation* (a combination of work from the two shows) was shown on television in the UK, during the traditional Christmas Day slot. The invitation to tour North America in 1991 seemed to promise further horizons of success and expansion. In Toronto, en route to bookings in New York, the accommodation of performers in identical mobile homes, the isolated out-of-town location and the huge, uninspiring, traditional tent were physical signs of the company being forced to adapt to a different cultural environment. Ticket prices were high because of other costs, excluding the kind of people that would have identified with the Archaos aesthetic. Because of travel costs the bouinax were not present in such critical numbers. Without the raw integrity they provided and the counter-culture in and around the tent, the company seemed more like other circuses and Bidon struggled to give the incoming circus artistes, many from Eastern Europe, some 'attitude'. As Adrian Evans says: 'Archaos' radical chutzpah chimed with the times in recession-hit Britain. The vibe just didn't translate to Toronto'.[55] The lukewarm reception in Toronto led to cancellation of the New York leg of the tour. In the same period strong gales in Ireland destroyed the tent of a second company and, despite heroic efforts to replace it within a matter of days, the subsequent costs and financial confusion led to a disgruntled public and the company refusing to perform to invited sponsors. Finally, after a run of *Metal Clown* in Paris failed to fill the vast 2500 seater tent, serious questions were asked about the company's ability to deliver and, as a result, the bookings for 1992 were also cancelled. The party was over. Although there were subsequent Archaos shows (*DJ 92, DY 93, DJ 94* and *Game Over* in 1995) which managed to deliver 'slick' productions, they did not have the 'spirit' of the successful shows and Bidon and Carrara worked separately on other projects.

From this brief history there appear to be several factors involved in the rise and fall of the entity that was Archaos. The main factor in their rise was that there was a difference from other comparable companies; this was manifested by their attitude to the audience (which I will discuss in the next section) and wider society as well as their materials and aesthetic. This difference was a result of their responsiveness and adaptability whilst on a cultural edge. Arguably this adaptability was aided by the multi-voiced dynamic and fluidity of their structure (described as 'a tribe without a leader'[56]). The difference had a novelty value that attracted energy in its initial stages but could not be sustained as the company became better known. Not only was wider society acknowledging this attraction but the company was forced to adapt to norms of behaviour, becoming more hierarchical and less fluid in order to adapt to the increasing demands of sustaining bigger budgets. As with the contemporaneous Cirque du Soleil, the company adapted to dominant surrounding environments. The difference between the two companies is that Soleil adapted to the more conservative culture and business models of the USA whereas Archaos had a longer ideological distance to cover in order to do so and were more artist-centred. Despite these provocateurs being challenged they prevented themselves becoming entirely incorporated into the wider capitalist economy. Maintenance of their cultural identity and the pressures of the environment conflicted.

> Ordinary circus has become incorporated. It's dull. People are in it for the money and the spirit suffers. What we have tried to do is recapture the spirit and the passion for performing. No-one here was born in the circus; we all grew up on the street.[57]

The main factor in their fall appears to be a bravado in expansion that was not matched by internal controls. Although the company had already operated two tours simultaneously in the critical year of 1991 the scale envisaged for 1992 was more ambitious. The early shows had a smaller audience capacity (850 in 1988, 1200 in 1990). By 1991 they were aiming to fill 2500-seat tents for runs of up to six weeks in one location. 'The only way to improve is to go big; that was the Archaos mentality'.[58] Their fearlessness in taking on this scale was part of their carnivalesque attitude of laughing in the face of danger but this collided with the demands of sustaining an upward curve of success. Although the 'folly' of the company culture was balanced by their thorough practicality, it can be argued that it contributed to their inability to survive. If the company is reliant on ever-increasing expansion and competitive success to maintain its celebratory spirit, which, in turn, is the engine for its expansion then the company is in a feedback loop that will become increasingly vulnerable to collapse, unless the internal structure is robust and internal communication is extremely efficient. The fact that their tent was uninsured when it was destroyed in Dublin, that their box-office system was un-computerised, which led to confusion, and that the unpaid company refused to perform in front of the sponsors suggests that the company culture was not meeting the demands imposed on it. The concentration of control in a relatively small number of people may have left the majority of the company less engaged in the project. Unlike in the early years, the performers themselves were not on such an edge, with precedents already established and responsibilities delegated upwards.

However, the management was certainly remaining on an edge, financially and organisationally, as well as dealing with the ongoing safety risks, all while exploring new markets. Adrian Evans defined the qualities of Pierrot Bidon, Archaos' leader, thus: 'his personal courage, willingness to take risks, his openness and his ability to adapt'.[59] Although their preference for fluid informal structures was problematic it did aid them in trying to meet the expectations of new environments; the use of a more standard tent and a more cohesive narrative in Toronto (about the overthrow of a Brazilian dictator) were evidence of this. However, this compromised the identity that was the source of their attraction. In Cologne, in the same year, the show was sold on its sex and violence but the chic spectators expected something closer to the slick (if risqué) cabaret, more common in Germany. The rough-edged, raw qualities of the bouinax did not meet their expectations; as Evans put it, 'there was no connection'. Two conclusions can be drawn from this; firstly, that they were being forced to market themselves in a way that could be understood by the local environment and, secondly, that there needed to be some pre-existing cultural familiarity. These conclusions suggest that the company would have needed to compromise their identity in order to connect to their audience. The following section goes into greater detail about this identity in order to give a clearer impression of how they were provocative, both to some of their audiences and also to the wider societies in which they operated.

Archaos performatives

When considering the work of Archaos most commentators (*The Guardian, The Times*, etc.) focussed on the use of chainsaws and motorbikes or on the presentation of different attitudes to gender.[60] While these are important, the most outstanding feature of their work, in the context of traditional circus that came before and, indeed in the context of contemporary circus, is their radically different relationship with the audience. This is best illustrated by an incident just prior to the beginning of one of their first performances at the London Circus Festival in 1988. There was much curiosity about this large unknown company and therefore there was a slight crush to get ringside seats. It was not clear whether this crush was caused by a problem with one of the chairs or because the company were getting impatient with delays in starting or even because what occurred had been prepared to set the right tone. However, there was a rapid escalation of the hubbub which led to shouting and wild gesturing by members of the company who then began to evict a section of the audience from their chairs and began to throw the chairs around, smashing some in the process. Rows of spectators nearby cowered, not knowing whether to laugh or run. The irate members of the company were then berated by others who arrived on stage and an argument ensued with much French cursing and Gallic gestures. Meanwhile, the bewildered and slightly frightened spectators, with no guidance on where to watch the show from, tentatively returned to the pile of overturned chairs and began to sort themselves out. The effect of this occurrence was that the rest of the audience became alert for danger to themselves as motorbike engines roared behind and below the seating. Performers climbed up into the web of ropes that hung on the inside of the tent, above the audience, watching like spiders waiting to strike. The ensuing show contained many examples of the kind of misdirection that conjurors use; while attention is pulled into one area, another action is launched, swinging into view as if from nowhere, increasing the audience's sense of its own vulnerability. This multi-directional focus created a sense of chaos and became a consistent feature of their work.

The prime aim of circus performance in the twentieth century up to this point had been entertainment: to simply please the audience, providing them with a culturally reassuring experience, even while providing a vicarious thrill. The performers served the expectations of the public as far as possible, from a status position lower than that of the spectators. Archaos demonstrated with their first actions that this status relationship was reversed; the audience were seemingly of no great importance to the performers whose primary aim appeared to be having fun onstage. In part this glaring difference between Archaos and con- temporary new circus companies in North America was due to the differences between a culture where 'the customer is king' and French culture where artists generally enjoyed a superior status. This apparent lack of concern for the public was manifested in many different ways, not only by an apparent carelessness for safety, such as running into the audience with an active chainsaw, but also with a disregard for transgressing normative cultural boundaries such as displaying almost total nudity or simulated masturbation. Some images would have shocked more conservative spectators, such as the laughing, crucified Jesus figure of the 1988 show, others would have shocked more politically correct audiences, such as the swaggering macho figure of Pasualito, striding into the front row and forcing a kiss onto the seized face of an unsuspecting woman. As Guy Carrara bluntly put it: 'It's our mission to shock society. I'm here to shoot society in the head'.[61]

The overriding message of the work of Archaos is that, as both individuals and as a company, they did not 'care' for the accepted precepts of mainstream society. The company privileged what Bakhtin termed 'gaiety' over seriousness and laughter over fear. This profession of disdain for norms, of a 'devil-may-care' attitude towards risks of danger or causing offence appears to be part bravado and partly a manifestation of the new style of *bouffon*[62] and the perspective of Bakhtin.

> Laughter liberates not only from external censorship but first of all the great interior censor; it liberates from the fear that developed in man during thousands of years; fear of the sacred, of prohibitions, of the past, of power.[63]

Out of this importance given to laughter emerges a general spirit of playfulness and a more profound validation of folly. Because the laughter is aimed in all different directions it destabilises 'a tendency toward the stability and completion of being, toward one single meaning, one single tone of seriousness'.[64] This is reflected in their presentation of the double-sided nature of the grotesque.

> The essence of the grotesque is precisely to present a contradictory and double-faced fullness of life. Negation and destruction (death of the old) are included as an essential phase, inseparable from affirmation, from the birth of something new and better.[65]
> ... the conception of the world as eternally unfinished: a world being born and dying at the same time, possessing as it were two bodies ... Such an image crowns and uncrowns at the same moment.[66]

This double-sided aspect manifested itself as the reversals, inversions and cross-dressing, described below. The multi-perspective, fractured assemblage of disparate elements was an extension of this double-sided nature, both in terms of objects (the reconstructed vehicles) and in terms of show structure.

Archaos inverted hierarchies, lowering what is normally elevated and raising up what is normally abject. As well as the more obvious iconoclasm, it was also directed at social fetish objects such as television sets, which were smashed or blown up, or cars, which were burnt, sawn in half, exploded, rammed, disfigured or even transformed into a mobile aquarium. Their almost obsessive interest in large mechanical objects was paradoxical, revelling in the brute power and mechanical complexity but also playfully abusive. Apparently influenced by the *Mad Max 2* film (1981), the company was endlessly creative with its welding surgery, amputating parts and attaching others. The application of unique, original creativity to an object that is normally fixed, finished and therefore 'dead' was an affirmation of the power of humans to regenerate. The deep roar of a powerful engine, the blast and smell of exhaust fumes, the hard rock of the live band, all gave the same kind of visceral effect as had been received by audiences watching battle re-enactments or the large animals in previous eras of circus.

Thus, following on from the punk phenomenon ten years previously, notions of beauty were redefined, contrasting with the slow-paced, rural hippy culture of the previous decade.

Similarly, their attitudes to gender were paradoxical; both revelling in macho stances and images of female sensuality but also undermining them. They drew attention to the male gaze on the near-naked female acrobats and contortionists. The inherent sexuality of acrobatic or aerial actions is often unacknowledged by many performers in a circus culture which perceives itself as un-erotic as sport, or contemporary dance, and in which the close contact and positions have become normalised through the many hours of practice. However, to observers from outside circus culture, the close-fitting costumes, the opening of arms and legs, and the straddling of equipment or other bodies, can have an erotic interest. Archaos exposed and foregrounded this unspoken actuality, for example by introducing the middle-aged male figure of Jean-Pierre Venet into a contortion act by the young female, Manu. With her hips raised and legs open, he approached and examined her with a magnifying glass. During the same show (*Bouinax* 1990) a chorus of ringboys simulated masturbation during the near-naked acrobatic balance act of Peter van Valkenhoe and Gelbrich Bierme. This act was presented on a platform, their statuesque body shapes suggested high art, their actions were erotically innocent. The masturbation, therefore, not only subverted the circus act but also subverted established notions of beauty. It also challenged the notion that 'artistic' nudity and 'pure love' can somehow be completely separated from the erotic gaze.

The frisson of voyeurism was also present in the shocking scene in which ringboys queue to copulate with a woman in the back of a car, whilst BMX bikers perform stunts on the top. The male dominance is reversed when she subsequently pushes an innocent third man in for another session. The gender play is further confused when Venet appears again, dressed grotesquely as a lollipop-sucking little girl, and grabs a fourth man for another round. Whether he represents another woman or a cross-dressed homosexual is left deliberately ambiguous. Spectators were caught between voyeuristic interest, laughter at the absurdity and shock at the representation of sexual abandon. This scene is an example of a direct challenge at the interface between performance and spectators. By contrast, many of the other performance features, such as music and costuming, reassuringly confirmed the culture of much of the audience.

Gender was subverted in other ways, particularly in presentation of female muscularity but also with elegant, sensuous male performers such as Ramon Fernandez, who sinuously performed on the corde-lisse[67] as well as ballet-dancing with a man pretending to be a dog. Women used assertive body actions; what Tait terms *aggro femme* exposed cultural beliefs that aggression only happens in masculine physical interactions and reversed the way gender identity is also constituted through the body's action.[68] Women were shown to not only rebuff macho advances with a strike into male genitals, but went as far as a simulated beheading of a man with a chainsaw followed by the female executioner using the severed head to masturbate with. This combination of violence, eroticism and female domination was also reflected in sado-masochistic images such as a female dominatrix leading a crawling man on a leash. Care of the young and old was also subverted in *Bouinax*. A man was dressed in a nappy/diaper (another degradation of the male); after anarchically throwing food into the audience the 'baby' is then abused, for example by having its doll exploded. Similarly an old lady is seen at intervals surrounded and bewildered by fire, vehicles and chaos. In the final moment of the show she is toppled by a radio-controlled model car.

Attitudes to the body were expanded by the inclusion of Jean-Claude Grenier, who was a small person who suffered from brittle bone disease and was without legs. His body shape would have qualified him as a circus freak in the early twentieth century but, instead of merely presenting him as a monstrous oddity, his presence was used to reveal attitudes to physical abnormality. His onstage entrance was from the belly of the work coat of Jean-Pierre Venet. After this 'birth' he was carried and cuddled by this mother-man who protected his very real vulnerability in the midst of a mayhem of fire blasts, chainsaws and massive trucks. The paradoxical combination of the male lewdness of Venet, mentioned above, and this tender maternal image was carnivalesque in its embodiment, connecting and inverting opposites. Similarly this caring attitude was juxtaposed with shocking disregard when Grenier was unceremoniously bundled into a dustbin by a woman and the lid closed over the top. Thus, the paradoxical relationship of mainstream society towards physical abnormality was juxtaposed; it parentally cares for the 'victims' but also hides them from public gaze, placing them in the 'dustbins' of sealed hospital wards; thus reinforcing public ignorance and lack of awareness about the edges of human physicality. The position of Grenier's role was further complicated by his involvement with the Valkenhoe–Bierme acrobatic act, mentioned above. His close presence watching these 'perfect' bodies not only juxtaposed contrasts but prompted questions about his gaze upon them. When he presented Bierme with an apple he transformed the naked pair into Adam and Eve and himself into the Devil, not only confounding current perceptions of 'victim' but also much older associations between deformity and diabolic monsters.

Central to the work of Archaos was the foregrounding of one of the essential features of new circus; the privileging of the underdog or outsider. As well as elevating the artist in respect of the audience and women in respect of men, Archaos more generally validated the imperfect, battered and scarred. Early publicity images included the image of the broken-toothed grin of Patou, one their original clowns, who wore crash helmets and a corrugated iron sheet on their backs so that they could be bashed, dragged and burned, in a grotesque amplification of slapstick comedy, all whilst laughing gleefully.

> Thrashing is ambivalent as abuse changed into praise … The one who is thrashed or slaughtered is decorated. The beating itself has a gay character; it is introduced and concluded with laughter.[69]

Bloodshed, dismemberment, burning, death, beatings, blows, curses and abuses all these elements are steeped in merry time, time which kills and gives birth, which allows nothing old to be perpetuated and never ceases to generate the new and the youthful.[70]

The aesthetic of the company was rough; the trucks surrounding the tent, a key signifier of the identity of a circus, were decorated in a diversity of styles and colours, including work by graffiti artists, rather than in a homogenized style common to most circuses. The validation of the underdog or outsider was also manifested in the openings given to anyone who was capable of something clever, such as the BMX bike stunt riders, or who could demonstrate something eccentric, such as the reporter who could physicalise a barking dog.

At each location local political activists ran the bar and were able to promote their cause. The company also had a high-profile presence at demonstrations about unemployment and racism, unafraid to strike a clear political stance, unlike Cirque du Soleil, who try to avoid being controversial. Of course all performances reflect the ideology of its creators but in Archaos this link was conscious and overt. Archaos members referred to 'the life',[71] implying that it was more than a profession. Their ideology and the manifestation of 'the life' 'performed' to the outside world beyond their tent shows. The 'folly' they manifested onstage was integral to their way of life demonstrating the lack of differentiation between life and art, and between actors and spectators. One press story about the company claimed that female Archaos members had been banned from a ferry because of displaying under-arm hair. This story, like others spun about the company by their creative publicist, Mark Borkowski, may or may not have had a basis in fact but, nevertheless, reflected an image and a cultural stance that the company proposed. Although the performatives were overtly counter-cultural, the avoidance of linear 'meaning' avoided the didactic invective of some contemporaneous messages in punk culture, for example. This attitude might explain why Pierrot Bidon was 'an amazing negotiator',[72] whether he was dealing with the commercial promoters, the local authorities or with the misfits that he welcomed into 'the life'.

Their levity enabled them to display both sides of gender politics without seeming contradictory. All rules were able to be disregarded including those of political correctness. Like other shows before, *Bouinax* finished with an invitation to the spectators to enter the performing area and dance with the company, hazing divisions between spectators and performers, the more so because the 'bouinax' were untrained as performers and behaved and dressed in a manner similar to that of many of the spectators. The culture associated with the company, partly emanating from rumours about their legendary after-show parties, was one of celebratory excess: alcohol, drugs, sex, dancing and madcap antics. The latter was typified by the image of Colin, the human pyrotechnic, who rigged his tightly fitting costume with firecrackers and ignited himself, dancing while appearing to destroy himself, a 'victory of laughter over fear'.[73] The apparent disdain for personal safety can be seen as simple bravado, another example of the macho and aggro femme culture, but it can also be seen to more widely signify contempt for childhood warnings about the danger of playing with fire as well as the actual regulations governing safety. Although taking physical risks does not necessarily mean that the individuals concerned are willing to take other sorts of risks, it does nevertheless suggest to an audience a freedom from prohibitions. It was this sense of liberation that made Archaos attractive and inspiring. By demonstrating that a particular kind of transgression did not necessarily result in serious consequences they refuted the legitimacy of those rules, placing them in a position of relativity rather than of absolutism. By taking responsibility for the consequences of their choices rather than accepting received wisdom they questioned the top-down (or centre-outwards) direction of established precepts. In other words, an individual who is prepared to face the consequences of personal pyrotechnics is less likely to accept the assumptions of trickle-down capitalism.

Confirm or challenge

In interview, Adrian Evans made the point that in the UK in the late 1980s there was a substantial section of young people who embraced the values espoused by the company although, in London, their audiences were comprised of more young professionals than the counter-cultural community. It may have been that the emergence of punk in the London of the late 1970s meant that ten years later the aesthetic, the music and the iconoclasm had been familiarised and, to some extent absorbed into wider youth culture. Therefore the Archaos success in London may have been due to endorsement of the values of the audience rather than challenging them, confirming rather than provoking. If this is the case then Archaos appear as comforting to the sub-culture as mainstream entertainers do in the wider culture. There was certainly a very positive feedback loop operating: with the increasing attention given to the company, the 'hotter' the remaining tickets became and the more excitement was generated by attending and consequently the company rose to meet the level of endorsement. Those within counter-cultures, because they are under threat, derive great pleasure from the sharing of cultural references. The oppositional stance to the mainstream unites its isolated, heterogeneous parts, gaining a sense of strength in solidarity. This pleasure in conspiracy against a dominant other can be observed in the development of alternative stand-up comedy. The anti-Thatcher, anti-sexism, anti-racist messages from Alexei Sayle, Ben Elton *et al.* developed a new audience for comedy by reflecting the views of an angry politicised generation. It articulated and reinforced the views of the audience just as much as the older generation of stand-up comedians did in the working-men's clubs. Although the new comedians could make bold comments about wider society they were rarely in conflict with the majority of their own audience.

Three conclusions follow from this supposition. Firstly, that in considering provocative practice we should be wary of confusing this excitement of identification with the frisson of encountering the unfamiliar. Secondly, that, in order to be attracted to a particular edge, there must be some prior knowledge of its nature and that, as with other risks, the location of the edge is particular to each individual. What is boring to one person may be impossibly unapproachable for another person. Thirdly, the outward signs of counter-culturalism send a message of difference that may attract or repel, but conveys expectations based on established premises; there will be no surprises. By contrast, if there are no overt signs of difference and the provocateur(s) appear normal, their behaviour may appear the more surprising and confusing, thus taking the spectators into a greater sense of alert exploration. It is for this reason that Bassi and Baron Cohen are so effective in their work.

In terms of the analogies of edges, that I have proposed, the work of Archaos displays all three. The blade analogy is apparent in the stripping away of many of the traditional trappings of circus to reveal aspects of its inherent nature, for example in the acknowledgement of the erotic gaze or attitudes to disability vis-à-vis 'perfect' bodies. The border analogy is apparent in their clear identification with the counter-culture and their play with the acceptable limits of behaviour. The fulcrum analogy is apparent in the tensions between the unstructured consensual arrangements of their origins and the requirements for structure that were demanded by the larger scale and complexities of their years of prominence. This latter issue is pertinent to the question of whether it is appropriate to maintain an ideological position if the conditions change. Ideological consistency in the face of changed circumstances may be regarded as a virtue or, conversely, as 'burying your head in sand'. As such, the reluctance of Archaos to compromise and adapt can be viewed as an entity that resisted challenge: the provocateurs were provoked. A more benign interpretation is that Archaos resisted the pressures of incorporation, of adapting their work to suit the market expectations of different contexts. Their failure to play by the rules meant that they had to be returned to the margins. By implication, their contribution to the development of culture could be seen as brief and insubstantial, particularly in comparison with Cirque du Soleil. However, the latter's lack of overt ideology or engagement with the experience of living in the post-modern world means that, beyond the establishment of a distinct style, their work may have little long-term effect. Archaos, on the other hand, left a long-term resonance by confirming and empowering the ideological positions of many who saw them or who followed the controversies in the media. In particular, their elevation of women, disability, non-professionals and 'low art' can be seen to have played a part in solidifying attitudes that are common currency in early twenty-first century Britain.

Archaos and Cirque du Soleil both began their existence in the mid-1980s. The different nature of the centres that were formed produced very different outcomes. In their early years, both companies had a culture of exploration as they tried to crystallise the shared values of their members and establish an identity. In both cases this process was done by a small group (between ten and twenty) who operated without a formal hierarchy and through a process of trial, error and reflection. Both companies encountered an edge of antagonism in the environment and were forced to adapt to prevailing conditions. The ability of a small, nascent enterprise to explore and adapt with fluidity gave them an advantage over competitors, who were fixed in their identity and practice. However, as the two companies found fame they became more locked into the public image they had created; a new norm was formed. In both cases, but in very different ways, the companies mirrored the culture of their core audience and thus were tied into the expectations of that audience. This newly established norm had to be repeated in order to build their audience, following the logic of the commercial entertainment industry to achieve greater financial success. This repetition was more of a problem for Archaos whose image and practice were haphazard, exemplified by the intuitive but unmethodical way that worker–performers were hired. Arguably, the atmosphere of carnivalesque spontaneity and chaos that they tried to create was in direct conflict with the controls that were necessary for safe repetition. This was particularly the case because Archaos performances were a direct reflection of what company members called 'the life' rather than having the normal separation between onstage and offstage realities. Although the internal structures of both companies became more hierarchical and less fluid as a result of increasing scale, the internal feedback controls within Archaos were much looser than those existing in Cirque du Soleil. Soleil maintains tight control over its performers[74] and a strict hierarchy. It can also control by influencing the pedagogy of the Montreal circus school, a source of many of its performers. Its efficient system of online feedback from spectators suggests a highly developed internal communication system, which enables the centre of the company to control its peripheries.

Provocateurs provoked

What the circus examples provide is an ambivalence between conservative tendencies (caused by both the inherent nature of circus practice and also its need to respond to market forces) and its tendency to set itself apart from the cultural mainstream (by exploring the unknown and manifesting the unconventional). These polarities can be seen as manifestations of the two sides of the fulcrum analogy – structure and release – exemplified by Archaos and Cirque du Soleil. The 'we don't care' folly of Archaos was so open and unstructured that the entity fell apart. The playful appearance of Cirque du Soleil masks its targets and controls, epitomising the benign aspect of strategically engineered consumerism, of which it is so much a part. Arguably it is because of Cirque du Soleil's emphasis on structure that its products can be so escapist and playful. By extension, on a wider scale, the cultural vibrancy (play) within Western democracies can be seen as only being possible because of laws being respected and the management of popular aspirations through advertising (structural control). Conversely, in the same way that I have argued applies to other artists, Archaos were enabled to present serious, ideological messages (e.g. the anti-macho) because they were so playful with their form.

In terms of the question of popularity and challenge the two companies reflect the two senses of the popular that I have suggested (p. 25). Cirque du

Soleil is a good example of the popular mainstream and Archaos displays all three aspects of popular in the sense that Bakhtin used it. They provided the thrill of danger and transgression, they provided a sense of communitas by endorsing the values of the counter-culture, which made up a large part of their audience, and they provided many empowering images. In terms of challenge, Archaos used both kinds: provoking directly those that were present at the performances and challenging distant powers by means of the controversies they stirred in the press and media. They cleverly exploited the marketability of challenge. In terms of power negotiations, it is clear that Archaos created a 'splash' that gained power through the popularity of their work and that, for a short period in Thatcherite Britain, they became the visible representative of the counter-culture and wider opposition. Although, like Banksy, there was no attempt to take on a leadership role or support a structured opposition they did make a visible presence at anti-racism demonstrations in France. In comparison with other new circus companies, they remained relatively consistent in their expressions of ideology. Indeed the very last actions of Bidon on his deathbed are reported to have been the hippy peace-and-love 'V' sign from one hand and a punk gesture (the upraised middle-finger) from the other.[75]

In terms of the nature of centre formations the interrelation of small scale and large (fractals) is apparent. I have argued that, as well as the more obvious top-down influence, the small scales of individual practice and specialisations can affect the large scale of a sector's socio-political outlook. Whilst this interaction has been observed in the generation of conservative tendencies it is nevertheless empowering to perceive that forms of organisation on a small scale *may* have wider impact in the long term, if conditions are favourable. Layers of 'bubbles' at various scales, as well as threats from outsiders, encourage creation of borders. The ensuing solidification can be seen to have led to a splitting away phenomenon which can be observed at various scales: of individuals 'running away', of Cirque Bidon/Archaos adopting and then rejecting romantic notions of circus, of the whole new circus movement breaking away from the traditional. In turn, these reflect the fantasy, escapism and physical separation of the whole circus phenomenon in relationship to mainstream society.

The difficulties of maintaining a position on the edge can be observed as new circus companies were keen to widen audience appeal out of their original counter-cultural niche, both for reasons of accessibility (avoiding marginalisation) and increased income (opening the door to incorporation). The differing fates of Archaos and Cirque du Soleil illustrate the two most likely outcomes of an initial position on an edge – marginalisation (and extinction) of one and incorporation of the other. However, the early controversy around both companies moved circus culture forward. The retreat from ideological statements within circus reflects the wider advance of capitalist values into prevailing attitudes. The narrowing of concerns towards those of consumerism creates a reduction of potential challenges to wider injustice. Apathy towards politics creates a vacuum that enables established power to encroach. All the provocateurs I have discussed have expressed concern about widespread apathy. Sacha Baron Cohen referred to Ian Kershaw's thesis that it was apathy that allowed Fascism in Germany to dominate (p. 91). In the boom years of the early twenty-first century the apathy appeared to have been caused by excess of consumerist opportunity. Since then it appears to be caused by despondency about altering the direction of the global capitalist juggernaut. I have attempted to demonstrate how certain provocative actions have activated large numbers of people, however fleetingly, and whatever the consequences to the provocateur. While we remain within nominally democratic systems the attempt to counter the apathy of despondency must have some value.

Conclusion

This book has focussed on those artists that work within popular forms and use the power it provides to provoke various forms of centre. They must constantly maintain a balance between being too provocative, thus losing many of their audience, and being too popular, thus removing any challenge. Archaos and the three individual artists, but especially Baron Cohen, demonstrate the effectiveness of combining mainstream popularity and universal popularity, because together the opposition to the dominant is disguised as mere cheekiness or at least appears less confrontational and therefore more widely acceptable.

There are two sorts of challenge: one is directed towards dominant powers or their representatives; this may be popular because it is empowering and also because it engenders feelings of shared conspiracy. Even Baron Cohen, who does not 'support' a particular community creates a transitory sense of 'us', implicit in the act of sharing a joke about 'them'. It may also be popular because of the thrill of transgression. The other sort of challenge is directed at immediate observers and this has the potential to be uncomfortable. It includes many forms, from the sense of threat and stylistic shifts of Bassi and Archaos, to Baron Cohen's nudity and disregard for political correctness, to Banksy's impositions on public space and 'violent' poster image. All the artists appear to share an acute awareness of the limits of public acceptability – the edge-as-border.

Provocation can be designed as a progressive 'nudge' (Bassi at the oil lake, Archaos performatives), or an act of resistance (Banksy's poster), or may be simply a 'splash', making trouble without serious regard for the consequences (Borat at the rodeo). It may result in a slight alteration in the behaviour of the target or a major 'landslide' if either the target is already unstable or it sets off an escalating series of conflicting feedback (*Revelación* and the Catholic Church). Risk-taking involves placing oneself in a vulnerable situation but, if successful, this has the double effect of personal empowerment and attracting admiration. With admiration comes popularity and thus power, which may be used to provide the resources necessary to mount more ambitious challenges. Although hard to prove in all cases (with the exception of Banksy), it appears that the provocateurs have stimulated some level of cultural transformation. However, this is not because they work at a precise, context-specific point on the play continuum, but because they use ambivalent combinations simultaneously; for example, by holding to consistent serious ideology in their aims but being inconsistent and playful in their forms and norms. The cross-currents of structure and fluidity are both a strength and a weakness. Game-changing is effective to confuse and undermine larger and more consistent modes of operation but fluidity can dissipate the effectiveness of destabilisation because inconsistency removes the potential of following up an initiating action. Despite this weakness, destabilisation at a macro level can cause activation at a micro level. The spectacle of contest tends to create a feeling of partisanship that provides an important condition for activating a wide range of people, distant from the events.

I have examined centres at three different scales: large formations (including 'the circus'), the smaller 'communities' with whom the provocateurs identify (including circus companies and specialisations) and thirdly, individuals, including the provocateurs themselves. From the changes to individuals' practice, it has been possible to observe the development of structure out of spontaneous communitas, either because higher risks require controls to be applied (e.g. the FEDEC harmonisation project) or because norms of operation are not shared (e.g. Bassi in the *Radical Hits* project). During this process the provocateur shifts their role from one of cooperative spokesperson to an instructor.[76] They may become more autocratic within the centre they have created if their power is unchallengeable within the small marginal centre, especially if its clandestine nature means controls have to be rigorously enforced. The gradual shift from provocative outsider to established centre may lead to bifurcations (e.g. new circus) or to becoming a target of provocation (Forced Entertainment). At the large scale, it is possible to see four defensive reactions to provocation: suppression, reinforcement, marginalisation and incorporation. Ironically the popularity of risk, transgression and challenges to dominant powers has commercial value and the resulting fame and fortune may lead to incorporation of the work if not the provocateur. A fourth reaction is that of the centre accepting and adapting to the challenge as a result of public pressure. Provocateurs, such as Bassi, Banksy and Archaos, provide a focus for disparate communities and confirm their ideology, partly by placing them in a contest with a dominant centre and thus stimulating the defensive reaction of reinforcement, even if that reaction is unformed and inarticulate, as in the Tesco riots.

Finally, I have looked at how provocateurs maintain an existence on different kinds of edges. Placing oneself in a vulnerable position risks loss of power in various forms, whether it is a matter of personal danger or loss of credibility, status or career prospects. Placing oneself at risk repeatedly has a number of consequences. Firstly, there is the defensive reaction of evasion – hiding behind characters (Baron Cohen) or maintaining anonymity (Banksy). Evading suppression may lead to marginalisation but in both these cases a way has been found to create a mystique out of the evasion which has increased popularity and prevented marginalisation (Pussy Riot). Secondly, the threat of suppression creates an acute sense of 'us' against 'them' and a somewhat exclusive organisation. However, combined with the outsider status that marked their formative years, it leads them to identify with other outsiders/marginals. Their isolation, therefore leads to some configuration, even if that is loose and distant. Thirdly, successful risk-taking leads to augmenting empowerment and sense of independence (the 'Winner Effect'). This leads to an insistence on retaining independence of action, even whilst maintaining a shared ideological perspective with other outsiders or outsider communities. The confidence derived from successful risk-taking may lead to a release and expression of suppressed norms and ideology, which may even include the freedom to revel in the fame-and-fortune benefits of incorporation, in return for an abandonment of ideology or at least a cessation of provocative actions. Finally there is some evidence that the practice of risk-taking can lead to an 'aptitude to evolve' both in the sense of a sudden revelation of new ways of working and also an intense and rapid creative development over a period of many years.

I have used three analogies in order to arrive at a more precise definition of Edge but what, if any, is the relationship between them? The border analogy refers to provocations that heighten awareness of cultural difference. The effect of it is to create or strengthen order. As seen in the Exeter incident and Banksy's anonymity there are elements of aversion and retreat. The blade analogy, by contrast, refers to release, 'letting go' or falling away. It uses risk and play as a tool to reveal what is hidden. As glimpsed in moments such as Bassi's dance in the transparent tube or the confused faces of Baron Cohen's drill sergeants, risky play and careful planning lead to uncertainty. The fulcrum analogy is the tipping point between stasis and chaos. As such it is the balance point between the other two analogies, between risk and control, release and aversion, expansion and contraction; which is why, in Bassi's work, there is such ambivalence between, for example, incitement and structure or playing at politician and being a politician, splashy sensationalism and serious intention. Using the notion of fractals, this conclusion is confirmed by almost insignificant experiences in walkabout performance, where the balance between aversion and release is an ever-present concern.

This book has woven its way through a complexity of complicated practice, in order to perceive the patterns within a rather chaotic fluidity. I have also attempted to give some structure to these patterns by providing a theory of an Edge that is more than a collection of practices and their effects. I have aimed to make a correlation between the patterns observed in complexity theories and transformative processes in specific cases of human societies. It is clearly impossible to prove such a correlation and yet as Feyerabend says:

> It is often assumed that general views do not mean much unless the relevant evidence can be fully specific ... [but they may] become a nucleus, a crystallisation point for the aggregation of often inadequate views which gradually increase in articulation and finally fuse into a new cosmology including new kinds of evidence.[77]

In species evolution, developments build on advantages and mitigate deficiencies. When challenged, there may be rapid development using loopholes and other opportunities, perhaps by means of extreme adaptation, or by developing a specialist 'niche' that is highly dependent on the environment being consistent. In both the political and evolutionary models the challenge from within signifies a disjuncture (bifurcation), either as a result of changes to the external environment or because of augmenting internal imbalances or both. If so, the challenger is separated and pushed to the margins. The challenge may also come from outside the entity. There may be major challenges that have little long-term effect (such as many terrorist incidents, forest fires) or minor challenges that cause major avalanches (the 'Butterfly Effect' in the downfall of Ceausescu, cited by Banksy). It may be ignored if it is minor and remains marginal. If more threatening, the challenge may be blocked (censorship) or the challenger suppressed, but these reactions may only defer a resolution. Resolution will happen either as a result of adaptation by the dominant entity (acceptance) or by the marginal entity (incorporation). In extreme situations one or the other is destroyed. A final possibility is the establishment of a relationship of symbiotic co-existence, such as those instances of small birds or fishes being tolerated by much larger beings because they clean them. This relationship is only possible if the larger entity recognises the necessity and importance of the intrusion. It is this recognition that I have aimed to facilitate.

Notes

1 Csikszentmihalyi, M. (1975) *Beyond Boredom and Anxiety*. San Francisco: Jossey-Bass.
2 Etchells, Tim (1999) *Certain Fragments*. London and New York: Routledge: 18
3 Quick, Andrew, Bloody play. Games of childhood and death. In: Malzacher, Florian and Helmer, Judith (eds) (2004) *Not Even a Game Anymore: The Theatre of Forced Entertainment*. Berlin: Alexander Verlag: 146.
4 Etchells, Tim, A text on 20 years with 66 footnotes. In: Malzacher and Helmer (2004): 287.
5 Etchells. In: Malzacher and Helmer (2004): 124.
6 www.spoonfed.co.uk/index.html. Accessed 20/10/2010
7 Moher, Miran, 'A Letter in Defence of Alexander Brener' (14/02/1997). www.ljudmila.org/nettime/zkp4/69.html. Accessed 01/08/2010.
8 Ibid.
9 Quick. In: Malzacher and Helmer (2004): 148.
10 Heathfield, Adrian, As if things got more real. A conversation with Tim Etchells, In: Malzacher and Helmer (2004): 83.
11 For example: Davis, Janet M. (2002) *The Circus Age, Culture and Society under the American Big Top*. Chapel Hill, NC: University of North Carolina Press. Hammarstrom, David Lewis (2008) *Fall of the Big Top*. Jefferson, NC: McFarland.
12 Phillip Astley (1742–1814), the 'father of the modern circus' (*The Book of Days*. W. & R. Chambers, 1864: 474).
13 Bassi, Leo (2005) Lecture at Circomedia (28/10/2005).
14 Ibid.
15 Davis (2002): 193.
16 Tait, Peta (2002) *Circus Bodies*. London and New York: Routledge: 21.
17 Ibid.: 38
18 Davis (2002): 168

19 Assael, Brenda (2005) *The Circus and Victorian Society*. Charlottesville, VA: University of Virginia Press: 15–16.
20 Davis (2002): 62–3.
21 Tait (2005): 126.
22 Bassi (2005).
23 Hammarstrom (2008): 9.
24 Tait (2005): 139.
25 Ibid.: 90
26 In the large spaces, commonly used for circus, the performer may be faced with the problem of conveying the various tension levels at a distance from the spectators that is too far to read facial expression, let alone expressions of the eyes.
27 This 'making safe' can be taken to such extremes that it can cause suspicion; for example, in the way that some children's clowns can be suspected of concealing motive or identity behind the painted smile.
28 Carse, James P. (1987) *Finite and Infinite Games*. New York: Ballantine Books.
29 Circus activities transform perception; simply by hanging upside down the world is inverted. Aerial work has visceral thrill, working on the edges of fear of falling, partner acrobatics requires tactile, close cooperation in the shifts of weight and synchronised effort. Manipulation uses the body as a partner; the juggler must 'tell' the body to adjust the precise angle and force of the throw; the instant feedback loop (to succeed or drop) ensures rapid learning and a consequent pleasure in self-achievement.
30 Robertson, Ian (2012) *The Winner Effect, How Power Affects Your Brain*. London, Berlin, New York, Sydney: Bloomsbury.
31 Davis (2002): 74.
32 Ibid.: 62–5
33 Davis (2002) cites a few examples of unsuccessful runners-away but less is heard about them.
34 Ibid.: 228.
35 Kevin Brooking related to me that traditional circuses in the mid-West USA (c. 1980) became a refuge for gay men who were freer to enjoy flamboyance and transgressive behaviour as clowns than would have been possible in their home towns.
36 See Jo Wilding's account in *Don't Shoot the Clowns* (2006) Oxford: New Internationalist Publications.
37 'The real benchmarks of a circus act are the number of revolutions turned in flight, the number of clubs sent into orbit, the manner in which a pair of aerialists perilously interact' (Hammarstrom, 2008: 176).
38 Albrecht, Ernest (1995) *The New American Circus*. Gainesville, FL: University Press of Florida (2006): 2.
39 Although this principle provides encouragement for novice performers, it, arguably, hampered the development of new circus because it discouraged rigorous artistic feedback. This was further compounded by the lack of adequate reviewing of new circus, certainly in the UK, until the early twenty-first century.
40 Bolton, Reg (1985) *Circus in a Suitcase*. Bristol: Butterfingers.
41 Hammarstrom (2008): 181.
42 Albrecht (1995): 22.
43 Ibid.: 27.
44 Ibid.: 219–21.
45 Quoted in Albrecht (1995): 221. This fluid approach to ideology is comparable with that of Sacha Baron Cohen (p. 89).
46 Ibid.: 224
47 Ibid.: 144.
48 Ibid.: 192.
49 www.archaos.info. Accessed 21/09/2013.
50 Ibid.

51 This encounter may have had similarities to those I experienced, at a similar time, when first performing as part of the Kaboodle clown company in 1978. We were engaged to perform at summer playschemes, around central London, usually located in areas of social housing. One of the prevailing influences on clowning at this time was that of the naif and sensitive Pierrot, influenced by Gelsomina in Fellini's *La Strada* (1954) and exemplified in the 1970s by Marcel Marceau's Bip and Nola Rae's clown personas. Combined with the peace-and-love smiliness of simpler interpretations of hippy idealism, the clown could be associated with non-violence and utopianism. However, entering environments that interpreted signs of failure and weakness as an opportunity to demonstrate superior power, the vulnerability and naivety of such clowns attracted abusive heckling, spitting and stone throwing. On this edge between cultures we quickly learned that demonstrations of bravado, such as walking on broken glass, lying on beds of nails and fire blowing, were an effective means of winning over the streetwise kids. This is an example of an entity undergoing radical and rapid adaption in order to survive in a hostile environment. The resulting change made us 'fitter' and, building on what we had learned, the new combination of clowning with acts of bravado (the failing macho) gave us a competitive advantage for several years.

52 *The Independent* (01/05/2010).

53 www.theartsdesk.com. Accessed 19/09/2013.

54 Sankey (undated) www.archaos.info.

55 www.archaos.info.

56 Ibid.

57 www.archaos.info; *The Independent* (2010).

58 Evans (2011) www.archaos.info/pages/?id=14.

59 Ibid.

60 Tait (2005): 121–4.

61 www.archaos.info.

62 Michel Dallaire refutes any conscious connection with *bouffon* at that time and describes the result as a combination of post-punk and the 'humanity of the clown'. In an interview (2014) he described the performer–creators as 'having a lot of anger' and, as director, he simply tried to bring this out and combine it with a clownesque naïveté.

63 Bakhtin, Mikhail (1969) *Rabelais and His World*. Bloomington: Indiana University Press (1984): 94.

64 Ibid: 101.

65 Ibid.: 62

66 Ibid.: 166

67 A single soft rope hanging vertically.

68 Tait (2005): 137.

69 Bakhtin (1969): 203.

70 Ibid.: 211.

71 www.archaos.info.

72 Evans (2011).

73 Bakhtin (1969): 90

74 As was made very clear from an interview I did with the clown Rumplestiltskin in 2011 who worked in *Love*.

75 www.archaos.info/pages/?id=3.

76 The enthusiasm for Forced Entertainment's work in academic circles meant that they became instructors beyond their physical reach.

77 Feyerabend, Paul (1975) *Against Method*. London and New York: Verso: 124.

Index